# Inside European Identities

BERG

## Ethnic Identities

SERIES

*General Editors*:

Shirley Ardener, *Director, Centre for Cross-Cultural Research on Women, University of Oxford*

Tamara Dragadze, *School of Slavonic and East European Studies, University of London*

Jonathan Webber, *Institute of Social and Cultural Anthropology, University of Oxford*

**Forthcoming**:

**Contemporary Christian Identities**
Edited by Soterios A. Mousalimas

**Dress and Ethnicity**
Edited by Joanne Eicher

*Music and Identity*
Edited by Martin Stokes and Sharon Macdonald

**Transmission of Culture in Diaspora and Exile**
Edited by Victor Lal and Tamara Dragadze

# Inside European Identities

## Ethnography in Western Europe

EDITED BY

*Sharon Macdonald*

# BERG

*Providence / Oxford*

**Berg Publishers Limited**

Editorial offices:

221 Waterman Street, Providence, RI 02906, USA

150 Cowley Road, Oxford, OX4 1JJ, UK

## Library of Congress Cataloging-in-Publication Data

Inside European Identities: ethnography in Western Europe/
edited by Sharon Macdonald.
    p. cm. – (Ethnicity and identity)
    Includes bibliographical references and index.
    ISBN 0–85496–723–0
       0–85496–888–1
    1. Europe–Ethnic relations. 2 Minorities–Europe.
I. Macdonald. Sharon. II. Series.
D1056.I49 1993
305.8' 0094–dc20                                 92–14740
                                                  CIP

## British Library Cataloguing in Publication Data

A CIP catalogue record for this book is available from the British Library.

ISBN 0-85496-723-0 (hb)
0-85496-888-1 (pb)

Printed in the United States by Edwards Brothers, Ann Arbor, MI.

# Contents

**Contents**

# Preface

This volume brings together some recent ethnographic studies of West European cultures. Although these studies pre-date the single European Market and the recent dramatic social and political upheavals in Eastern Europe, these events demonstrate vividly that it is vital that we understand the nature of people's allegiance to their nation, state, locality and ethnicity. As the face of Europe is being redrawn, we need, perhaps more crucially than ever, to be able to get inside the identities of its peoples.

The original reasons for deciding to collate a volume on West European identities were less momentous, though the motives always included an awareness that the subject was of direct social importance as well as being of ethnographic interest. In January 1988 a workshop entitled 'Ethnographic Approaches to Ethnicity' was organised by myself and Tamara Kohn with the assistance of Shirley Ardener at the Pauling Centre for Human Sciences in Oxford, and the chapters here are largely based on presentations made at that workshop. The workshop was inspired in part by the 'History and Ethnicity' seminar run by the late Edwin Ardener. Financial support for the workshop came from the Institute of Social Anthropology, Oxford, and I thank, on behalf of myself and the others involved in the workshop, the Institute, and particularly Dr Wendy James, for the assistance. In the event we were inundated with offers of fascinating papers on many dimensions of ethnicity from many parts of the world. In the face of what were simply too many papers to be accommodated in one easily manageable event we decided to focus on Western Europe on that particular occasion, and follow up the widespread interest which had been revealed in a series of weekly seminars on various aspects of identity. These seminars are organised by Jonathan Webber, Tamara Dragadze and Shirley Ardener, and are held at the Institute of Social Anthropology, Oxford. The first theme of these seminars was East European identities. Following up this theme a complementary volume to the present one will be published in this new Berg series on ethnicity and identity.

I would like to thank all of those who participated in the 'Ethnographic Approaches to Ethnicity' workshop, and particularly Tamara Kohn for her enthusiasm and support for the original project.

Shirley Ardener, who was also involved in the workshop, has been a constant and invaluable source of wisdom and help both with regard to this project and to me personally over many years now. I extend special thanks to all of the contributors to this volume, and to Dr Marion Berghahn, Alison Duncan, Margaret Hardwidge and Nigel Hope of Berg Publishers, for their work and for putting up with my various requests and changes of address.

SHARON MACDONALD
Keele University

# Identity Complexes in Western Europe: Social Anthropological Perspectives

## *Sharon Macdonald*

**T**oday, as many of the old political barriers between Western and Eastern Europe are collapsing, and as increased economic and political union within the European community becomes a fact of life, the question of what 'Europe' means – and could come to mean – to its diverse peoples takes on even greater significance. The events of the 1990s would seem to have the potential for radically reshaping people's identities. But will they? Any attempt even to begin to answer questions such as this must address the multiple issues raised by the national, ethnic, regional and local identities within Europe. Where do people's allegiances lie? How deep do identities run? How far does a local identification preclude a supra-local one? And how are such large-scale categories as 'Europe' – or even 'Britain', 'France' or 'Spain' – actually experienced in everyday life?

Questions of identity come to the fore at times of social and political change. While on the one hand it might seem that as borders become weaker – as people and goods traverse them more easily – there will be a consequent relaxing of the sense of allegiance to place and people, very often the reverse is actually the case. Notions of 'us' and 'them' become stronger still; immigrants are perceived as a threat. Witness the revival of aggressive and racist neo-nationalisms in many parts of Europe at this present time. Clearly, the way in which social identities are manifest needs to be understood in terms of the changing social, economic and political contexts of the many social groups within Europe's diverse countries, as well as in terms of the various social and cultural frameworks for thinking about the question 'who

1

are we?'. Who will perceive the present and future changes as a threat, and who will perceive them as an opportunity, depends crucially on the nature of the identity which they hold.

These are all issues which require detailed study and understanding of the peoples and cultures of Europe. In this book we bring together recently completed or ongoing ethnographic research on various regions of Western Europe. This research is based on detailed studies of particular groups and peoples and involves, at least in part, long-term and first-hand study (i.e. ethnography). The theoretical arguments which we bring to bear are for the most part drawn from social anthropology, the discipline which has particularly developed the ethnographic method, and that in which the contributors to this volume were trained. A single narrowly defined theoretical perspective, which would be uncharacteristic of social anthropology, is not reflected in the contributions here. The intention of the book is not to map out a comprehensive picture of West European identities – research is still far too patchily distributed and thin on the ground even to begin to do so. Although the territory covered here is large, and there are some lacunae and imbalances arising from the contingencies of research funding, current ethnographic and individual predilections, and the specific history of this particular collection, we hope to show what can be illuminated by an ethnographic study of identity. In particular, we hope to highlight some of the issues involved in identity formation, maintenance and change 'on the ground' within Western Europe – issues which are often overlooked in the recourse to rhetoric and generalisations at a time of social and political change.

## What is Western Europe?

Given the changes taking place in Europe, and their ramifications for the whole concept of Europe, it is impossible to introduce a collection such as this without being acutely aware of the historically contingent nature of the categories within which we are working. Perhaps 'Western Europe' might already be said to be a category from the past. What is more, it is, of course, far from being an unequivocally defined and unanimously agreed upon geographical or political entity today, never mind one which can be read back unproblematically into the past. Countries such as Britain and Greece, to take but two examples, have a rather ambiguous and ambivalent allegiance to Europe (though both are members of the European Community). The various European – and it is notable that this term is so often used to refer exclusively to

West European – economic and defence organisations, established since the Second World War, have involved discontinuous sets of countries, though a core has remained fairly consistent. Historically, the picture is complicated further by central Europe, a middle region which has dropped out of many conceptual maps of Europe after the Second World War and the East-West polarisation. Nevertheless, 'Western Europe' is a category much used in political discourse, and there has been general agreement, until the re-unification of Germany in 1990, that geographically the line dividing the West from the East stretched from the boundary between Italy and Yugoslavia in the South to that between the two Germanies in the North. More significantly for our purposes here, however, is that Western Europe is typically credited with a number of historical developments of massive global relevance which make it important to consider as a frame of reference, particularly for the study of identities.[1]

In addition to, and inextricably linked with, the gestation of industrialisation and capitalism, Western Europe is generally accepted as the birthplace of the nation-state and the rise of nationalism. These, like the ethnonationalism which has followed in their wake, have, of course, been widely exported and are major forces in world politics today. Detailed understanding of the ways in which national, regional and local identities are created and experienced within Western Europe is clearly of importance to any wider understanding of these movements in general.[2] Colonialism too is part of the shared history, and its consequences part of the contemporary social and political complexion, of many of the West European countries. Like nationalism and ethnonationalism, colonialism and its consequences raise questions about identity – about cultural sameness and difference and the boundaries between peoples. What is more, the social and political fallout of colonialism – in particular, immigration from formerly colonised regions – has been, and continues to be, a major factor involved in shaping contemporary European identities.

---

1. I should emphasise that in focusing on Western Europe the aim here is not to reify this as an ethnographic category to the exclusion of all other possibilities. Ethnographers working in the area have used various frames of reference – e.g. the Mediterranean, the British Isles – and our intention is not to deny any validity these may have. For some recent commentaries on the anthropology of Europe, see: *American Ethnologist* (1991); Ulin (1991).

2. Cf. Llobera (1987a: 113). There is a substantial literature now on the development of nationalism, some of it by social anthropologists. See, for example, B. Anderson (1983), Gellner (1983), Llobera (1987b).

Shared historical currents (though felt to greater or lesser degrees in different countries within Western Europe) and common contemporary social and political characteristics and concerns provide a rationale for discussing identity formation within the context of Western Europe. Nationalism, ethnonationalism and colonialism – all deeply rooted, one way or another, in Europe – are, then, among the wider movements which shape the Europe within which more localised identities are realised.

## Social Anthropology and European Identities

Shared historical currents within Europe have also shaped anthropology and the social sciences in general. In other words, they have also shaped the ways in which we look at questions of identity and the like. Although various histories of the social sciences can be written, it is generally accepted that the social sciences 'crystallised' in Western Europe in the late eighteenth century (Restivo 1991). That is, they came into being at around the same time as the nation-state, and with growing European expansion. Attempting to understand the social changes brought in the wake of industrialisation – and those associated with the rise of the nation-state and the encounter with 'other' peoples – was the intellectual motivation for the development of the new disciplines.

Right from the beginning a concern with social identity lay at the heart of the social disciplines. A key question was that of the nature of social relationships and social bonds as the industrialised countries apparently became caught up in a wave which shifted the majority of the population's lives from a community-based existence (*Gemeinschaft* in Tönnies' famous formulation), in which the units of organisation of social life could be readily apprehended through face-to-face contacts, to an association or society (*Gesellschaft*) based social organisation, whose boundaries and leaders might be various and distant (see Tönnies 1955). Social theorists concerned themselves with questions of what kinds of allegiance to social group, and what kinds of sense of belonging or of alienation, would develop as people moved out of networks of kinship and community and into larger, apparently less personalised, organisations.

At another level too, sociology and anthropology could be seen from their very beginnings to be deeply implicated in questions of identities in Europe. For the attempts to understand social change, and different types of society, were simultaneously attempts to characterise the nature of 'rational', 'developed', urban society. Anthropology – despite (or indeed because of) being apparently about 'exotic' or 'other' cultures – played a significant role in the self-definition in which Europe's intellectuals were involved. These 'others', who unwittingly acted as a kind of *alter ego*, were not, however, found only in geographically distant lands, but also in the margins of Europe itself (see Chapman 1978; Herzfeld 1987). One consequence of this has been that the study of Europe by social scientists has been marked not only by the political and cultural boundaries erected by Europe's peoples themselves, but also by an overarching binary divide created and sustained partly by social scientists, between the declining Europe of small rural communities with quaint customs and 'folk-life', and the rapidly expanding Europe of rationality and rationalisation, social problems, urban life, and change. This division into two Europes is not, of course, held only by social scientists – and the interweaving, and feedback, between popular and academic categories is a feature of the study of Europe – but the problem is that it is a division which is often assumed rather than thoroughly investigated and critically assessed.

In the second half of the 1970s a number of anthropologists attempted overviews of the social anthropological study of Europe up to that point (see especially Boissevain 1975; Cole 1977; Davis 1977; Grillo 1980). They were particularly critical of anthropologists' concentration on small rural communities of Europe – and especially of assumptions that these communities somehow existed outside of, and untouched by, the forces of state, nation and capitalism. European anthropologists, the majority of whom conducted detailed studies of individual communities, were accused of engaging in 'an analytically restricting village fetish' (Gilmore 1980: 3) and of ignoring in the process much of that which was characteristic of European life. Europe, it was suggested, had been 'tribalised' (Boissevain 1975: 11) by social anthropology itself.

Ralph Grillo complained that 'Anthropological research ... in Europe has often turned its back on precisely those issues on which a "European" anthropology might be constructed' (1980: 4). Important among these issues were: 'the emergence of supra-local identities and cultures (the "nation"); the rise of powerful and authoritative institutions within the public domain (the "state"), and the development of particular ways of organizing production and consumption (the "economy")' (ibid.: 1). Literacy and the existence of documented history, racism and immigration, were also issues which were singled out as not having been adequately taken on board by those working within Europe (see especially Davis 1977: ch. 6; Grillo 1985). In brief, the 'big' issues of Europe, those features which, if not wholly unique to Europe, were surely present in a rather major and even original form (Europe as the cradle of nationalism, for example), had – by and large – been ignored. These big issues, of themselves, raised questions about identity. Centralised government and institutions, economy, communications, immigration and national cultures raised the problem of the autonomy of groups across space, and documented history and change raised the problem of the persistence of social groups over time.

It is at least partly in response to this critique, and in an attempt to move beyond it, that most of the studies in this volume were formulated. While we do not necessarily put a taboo on villages or rural locations, the critique of community studies (much of which was actually begun in those studies themselves: see Frankenberg 1966, 1989; Bell and Newby 1971) has implications for the ways in which identities are analysed here.

## Inside Identities

I have not in this introduction attempted to set out a technical definition of 'identity', and have not done so because such an attempt would run counter to the guiding spirit of this book, which is to explore the ways in which identities are defined and experienced by various peoples themselves. The contributors to this book are, however, in broad agreement about the ways in which questions of social identity – allegiance to people, group and, often, place and past – should be tackled. We begin from the premise that 'the "people" themselves play the part of theoreticians in this field' (Ardener 1989: 67). Our concern is with the ways and circumstances in which peoples define themselves and are defined by others; and with the social relations and consequences of identity formation 'on the ground' within Western Europe.

While the rhetoric of ethnic identity in particular often alludes to its 'real' or 'essential' nature, we do not maintain that identity exists apart from – or beneath – its social representation. Identities do not exist outside their making. Rather, they are socially created in specific historical circumstances, though they may be reified and perpetuated through all kinds of essentialist models. Intangible as identities may be, however, they are clearly not intangible in their effects and should not be regarded as epiphenomenal to more readily grasped economic and social phenomena. Identities can act as motive forces of history. As we have seen so often in European history, and as we see in this volume, individuals may lay down their lives for their people or country; and boundaries may be mapped out with bullets and bombs.

In this book we are concerned with '*inside* identities' in two senses: firstly, with identities as they are perceived and experienced within the lives of some of Western Europe's peoples, and secondly, with our own identities as ethnographers working within Western Europe; though these can never, of course, fully be separated. The aim here is not, however, to focus on the personal experience of carrying out fieldwork *per se*, but to examine issues raised by doing fieldwork in the kinds of places encapsulated by the label 'Western Europe' (without assuming that the area is homogeneous). The argument is that the experience both of doing the fieldwork and of analysing it constitute part of the data. They act as more windows on to the concerns and cultural complexes that may arise in Western Europe. The fact that social anthropology has its own roots in those particularly (though not exclusively) European experiences of colonialism, nationalism and industrialisation – that it has developed within the same cultural framework as the subjects which we are investigating – gives us the opportunity (and creates the necessity even) to examine our own discipline critically as we set about investigating the cultural patterns of European identity formation.

## Identities, Communities, Minorities, Ethnicities

Although I have suggested that a concern with issues of identity can be seen as a key founding feature of the social sciences, as a specific, named subject of study it is much more recent. Interestingly, though unsurprisingly perhaps given the interweaving of academic and popular discourses within the European context, academic interest in identity as a subject runs concurrently with a more widespread popular interest.

The conception of 'identity' not simply as a neutral synonym for sameness or equivalence, as it is used in mathematics and logic for example, but as a positively valued socio-psychological construct became widespread during the 1960s, though it was by no means a wholly new development. Identities became not merely relations which were present or absent, but actual phenomena which could be relatively strong, weak, confused, disordered or in crisis. Popular psychological writings, such as those of Erikson (e.g. 1968), promoted this identity-health model; and popular sociological writings came to extend the model to that of groups or populations. Indeed, popular books and pamphlets using this kind of discourse have been noted during fieldwork by many of us writing in the present volume. Ethnicity – the sense of belonging to an ethnic group – in particular came to be regarded as of especial importance for an individual's sense of identity.[3] And just as the lack of a personal identity was defined as a malady, so too became the lack of an ethnic identity. Parallels were drawn: just as individuals might find their identities lost or confused through amnesia or not having come to terms with their childhood, so too might societies or peoples suffer identity crises if they lost hold of their history or roots. This health model was ethically inflected, identities being conceptualised as both necessary and good. What was more, what it meant to have an identity – in particular an ethnic or local identity – became, at least as seen from outside, increasingly culturally formalised, as I discuss below.

These particular understandings of what it means to have an ethnic or local identity have, I suggest, been widely influential – though far from unequivocally dominant – both on the ground in Western Europe and within the study of it. The ethnic resurgence beginning in the 1960s – mentioned in a number of the studies in this book – was part and parcel of a social movement and rhetoric against centralisation, against the alienation of Society, and for local ethnic and cultural heritage and identity. It was during this period that many ethnic minorities – their language, customs and cultures – came to be accorded political and national significance.

There has been a good deal of argument about the extent, bases and causes of this revival or awakening; and in particular over the extent to which the movement emanates from the 'grass roots'. John Edwards, for example, has argued that the 'revival' has been largely one of 'ethnic symbols', making already existing ethnic groups more visible (Edwards 1985: 115). Others see the movement as having more extensive formative power, involving the actual construction of ethnic groups – the creation of a sense of groupness, shared history and so forth where little or none existed before. It has been suggested that the

---

3. For an account of the etymology of the terms 'ethnic' and 'ethnicity', and their use in social anthropology, see Chapman, McDonald and Tonkin (1989: 11–17). The growth of emphasis on ethnicity in Western Europe since the late 1960s is discussed in Smith (1981), Edwards (1985: ch. 4), Tiryakian and Rogowski (1985), and Roosens (1989), among others.

ethnic revival may have been largely a middle-class phenomenon (see ibid.: 9–10), an idea supported by some of the ethnographic research on the subject (see especially McDonald 1989).

The research in this volume suggests that the relationships between different social groups in identity formation and expression is often complex and inflected by the specificities of the case involved. On the one hand, there certainly is much evidence for an educated middle-class involvement in the construction of politicised ethnicities. In such identity-construction (something not necessarily as conscious as the building metaphor might imply) the intellectuals, if we may use the term loosely, generally have recourse to some kind of existing group identification – be it of a linguistic, territorial or cultural nature – and it may well be one that does map on to the self-identification of a particular group. In such cases there may even be a sense in the ethnic group more widely of intellectuals giving voice to sentiments long felt but unexpressed. In other cases – and it is really only through detailed ethnographic fieldwork that this can be determined – either the ethnic group identified by the intellectuals may be one that bears little relation to any *at present* identified with by those so designated, or (and perhaps more commonly) the structural and cultural criteria of ethnic identification may be significantly different from those of the group being represented. In other words, a self-identifying ethnic group might not see itself as part of a set of oppressed minorities, defined in opposition to the majority; or the shared cultural markers of ethnic identity might not include, say, folk dance. It is crucial to point out, however, that although ethnic groups frequently legitimate themselves through a discourse of origins and continuity with a distant past, their definition may change significantly over the course of time. Edwin Ardener has pointed out that being identified by others, being 'named', may effect a self-identification (1989: chs 3, 7 and 14); a point which is developed by Maryon McDonald in her discussion of stereotypes below. In addition to the process of identifying or naming groups or identities in general, there may also be change in the structural identification of groups over time – that is, whom they are defined relative to may shift; and they may also change culturally, a point long recognised within social anthropology (see Barth 1969) but which, as I suggest below, often occurs according to a recurrent pattern within contemporary Europe.

Much of the subtlety of these processes of according and defining identities is overlooked within popular and political and economic discourse about ethnic and local groups within Europe. Overlooking these processes is also something risked by ethnographers working within the community studies paradigm.

By the very nature of the way in which these pioneering European ethnographers chose to define the subjects of their studies – both geographically and by topic – they were in danger of reifying rather than critically examining a set of popular assumptions about the nature of cultural distinctiveness and identity and where these were to be found (cf. Herzfeld 1987: 1–4). In other words – and this is a hazard which is still not always addressed by ethnographers – ethnography risked finding itself in the position of simply illuminating the rich cultural heterogeneity located in the peripheries of European society, rather than asking whether assumptions of rich cultural heterogeneity themselves drew on, say, common notions of what it means to be a rural European.[4] By focusing on the traditional, the local and the ethnically distinctive, anthropologists were adding micro-scale colour to the macro-scale picture already sketched out in a set of neat oppositions. Working with the implicit assumption that local, ethnic and minority identities were necessarily good and healthy phenomena, and that larger majority ones were somehow suspect, privileged one set of statements *a priori*, tempting ethnographers to describe any local claims of the values of modern society as symptoms of false consciousness and the decline of community.

The problem for people living within the much studied and romanticised peripheries was that they could find themselves 'museumised', turned into quaint exemplars of outsiders' visions. Although in abstract terms being the subject of somebody else's fantasies might seem harmless enough, it can in practice have all sorts of very real social and economic implications, as we see in some of the case studies here. Paradoxically, it also risks imposing a singular notion of what it means to have an ethnic identity – and very often a standard package of 'ethnic culture' (folk dances, music, art and community museums) – onto diverse groups.

It should be emphasised that in talking of identities we are not necessarily referring only to minorities, though it is significant that, as with the term 'ethnicity', there has been a tendency for identity to be

---

4. Cf. Strathern's comments on British rural communities (1987: 32). Though it begins from the opposite concern, the following point on the ethnographic study of Europe by Michael Herzfeld is also pertinent here: 'It may be that similarities will emerge as generously as differences. But this is a question to be asked repeatedly, not begged once and for all. Otherwise, taxonomic form ("they"/"we") suppresses reflection on what difference and similarity *mean*' (1987: 4).

equated with minority.[5] The slippage towards this equation is itself a symptom of the classificatory structures highlighted above. Nor in talking of identities are we necessarily talking only of ethnic identities. As Ardener, noting the shift from using the term 'ethnicity' to using 'identity' in social anthropological research, has pointed out: 'The resort to "identity" as a term, was an attempt to restore the self-definitional element that seemed to be inherent in the idea of "ethnicity", but which was shared by entities other than ethnicities as normally conceived – many kinds of entities have identities' (1989: 211–12). Majorities may have identities too – though perhaps they are less likely to be expressed in a form which is regarded as 'an identity'. We should not assume either that majority identities are necessarily secure, unambiguous or morally dominant, for, as Forsythe has shown us of German identity, this may not be the case (Forsythe 1989). These are all subjects for further research, and ones on which we need to understand the folk models involved. Clearly, however, majority identities need discussion, and indeed, such discussion is imperative for a proper understanding of minorities (Ardener 1989: 212).

## The New European Anthropology: Directions of Research

Following the flurry of critiques of European anthropology in the late 1970s, there has been little attempt to bring together research emerging from them. Although the contributors to the present book were not asked specifically to respond to those critiques, the research projects of the majority were conceived within such a framework, and this is reflected in the various ways in which identity is tackled here.

For most of us here, carrying out our fieldwork during the 1980s, this critique – with various different emphases – was important in shaping the way in which we went about our research: we were, by a variety of tactics, trying to move beyond the community, and beyond the sometimes crude assertions of the community-studies critique. Speaking subjectively and impressionistically about this, it was something about which we felt both exhilarated and rather nervous (after all, the problems of just *how* to do it had not really been

---

5. These points have been particularly well made by Chapman, McDonald and Tonkin (1989); Ardener (1989: ch. 14); Forsythe (1989); McDonald (1989); and McDonald, ch.10 below

resolved); sometimes self-righteous and often fearful; pioneering yet doubtful about whether we really would acquire the right sort of anthropological credentials from this foreign yet familiar domain. And the closer to home we worked, the more we experienced doubts over our academic identities. After all, we were often surrounded by indigenous or self-appointed experts. Our statements on, say, the Welsh or the Scots might easily be challenged at seminars not just by those who had done fieldwork in the region but by colleagues who had themselves lived, worked, or descended from 'our' areas. No doubt this – this ever-present challenge to boundaries of all types – influenced the rise of identity as a key topic for ethnographers of Europe.[6]

So how have social anthropologists attempted to go beyond the community? In particular, how have they dealt with the big issues identified by the critiques? The key feature of these is, after all, the fact that they exist beyond the community and so are not *prima facie* open to study by participant-observation fieldwork. There have been, I suggest, three main types of response to this problem: to alter the scope of the study – and in particular to incorporate analyses of history and text; to shift the focus within the study – especially towards groups such as bureaucrats and intellectuals; and to be reflexive. These are not, of course, mutually exclusive. In all of them, though especially the first, there is a danger of throwing out what is generally seen as ethnography's specific contribution to social and cultural studies – namely, sensitivity to locality and distinctiveness – along with the community model. However, as we see below, in tackling the supra-local, anthropologists need not necessarily abandon their traditional strengths.

### The Scope of the Study

An obvious response to the critique of community is to avoid studying entities which look like communities; in other words, to work in urban and industrial locations. Although there are increasing numbers of social anthropologists working within such areas in Europe, there has been little attempt to co-ordinate or theoretically develop issues arising from this research (though see Kenny and Kertzer 1983). What is more,

---

6. It is notable in this context that some of the most important collections on the social anthropological study of identity – notably those edited by Anthony Cohen (1982, 1986b) – have been directly concerned with the British Isles. These studies have for the most part been concerned with illustrating the cultural heterogeneity, and the variety of ways in which identities are symbolised, within the British Isles, and not so much with issues of reflexivity.

working within urban localities does not seem of itself to have necessarily tackled the European big issues, and the majority of urban-based studies seem to take a narrower focus (a specific institution, say) and to pay even less attention to synchronic and diachronic interrelationships extending beyond this, than have many community studies.

Another important domain of study within European anthropology is that of migrant and immigrant communities; communities whose presence in Europe is often bound up with colonialism. This is a field which was to some extent already established as 'race relations'. It is, however, vulnerable to many of the community model criticisms. In particular, models of assimilation and integration often cast the nature of the relationship between ethnic groups – between the minority and majority culture – in over-simplistic terms, either overestimating or underestimating the autonomy of the ethnic group (cf. Mason 1986: 8–9). Much of the work on migrant and immigrant communities is concerned with questions of the maintenance of ethnic identity, especially across generations,[7] and most focuses on the internal dynamics of 'ethnic communities' and often provides valuable indigenous perspectives on majority society. Other studies, such as Grillo's study of immigrants in urban France (1985), consider the ways in which immigrants are represented within majority society, so providing insight into the workings of dominant ideologies and structures. This work is to be welcomed too for illuminating how immigrant groups – and strangers and outsiders of various sorts – may unwittingly play definitional roles in the construction of majority ethnic identities (c.f. Okely 1983; Ardener 1989: ch. 14), a point made too by Rosemary McKechnie in her discussion of Corsican identity (chapter 6 below). This work, in highlighting the structures in which immigrants are incorporated, also has clear implications for understanding responses to immigration which are likely to arise as a consequence of present political and social changes.

The other main strategy employed in the social anthropology of Western Europe to deal with the big issues is to turn to history. This is an expansion of scope in that ethnographic studies traditionally focus on a very shallow time-frame – generally the one to two years spent in the field. Historical studies have been undertaken either as a prelude to

---

7. For examples of work in this field, which we do not focus on in the present collection, see, for example, Castles et al. (1984); Boissevain and Vermeulen (1984); Boissevain and Verrips (1989).

fieldwork, the intention being fully to situate the fieldwork-based aspect of the ethnographic account historically and in terms of the wider social, political and economic movements; or to stand by themselves.[8] The approach to history has become increasingly sophisticated. No longer adequate is the type of historical background often provided by earlier studies which, as John Davis has noted, typically took the form of 'historical information [being] included in the Introduction along with a hundred years of population growth, a little rainfall and some notes on schists' (1977: 244). Nor is it enough simply to provide more history without taking an adequately critical look at its construction, or at the distinction between history known to the subjects of the ethnographic study and that not known (Davis 1980: 534).

Historical research has been used in the social anthropological study of Western Europe to explore the big issues, though there is undoubtedly still much to be done. Historical sources have been used to chart the emergence of supra-local identities – especially national and ethnic, and in a number of cases to draw on anthropological theorising to show the structuring processes by which different identities are defined relative to each other over time. Such accounts situate contemporary study rather than allowing it to hover somehow outside time, space and politics. The economy has been similarly tackled, often drawing on Marxist or political-economy theorising (e.g. Schneider and Schneider 1976). Some of this work has illustrated very starkly the dangers of assuming local economic practices to be relics left over from a previous era simply because they happen to be located within a 'community' and have a form which we associate with the traditional. As has been well shown by work on the Scottish Hebrides, for example, 'traditional' economic practices – weaving Harris tweed, crofting – may well be products of capitalism, and of the specific role of these regions

8. Some of the particularly successful examples of anthropological treatments of history emerging from or during the late 1970s critiques are Chapman (1978); Frykman and Löfgren (1987) and, for a geographically tangential case, Hastrup (1982, 1985, 1990) (though the publication of a contemporary ethnography is to follow). Of those studies which make substantial use of history as well as ethnography particular attention should be drawn to McDonald (1989). Earlier studies which show innovative and sensitive use of history include Lison-Tolosana (1966), Blok (1975) and Schneider and Schneider (1976). The issue of the use of history in European anthropological studies has been the subject of debate – see for example Llobera (1986, 1987a) and *Critique of Anthropology* (1987). This particular debate, however, is somewhat limited in its scope in that it does not include reference to some of the interesting newer approaches to history which fall beyond its geographical scope (the Mediterranean), or have been published subsequently (e.g. Tonkin, McDonald and Chapman 1989). Most contributions to the debate are of limited theoretical importance too in their implicit acceptance of the idea of 'real' history.

within a modern capitalist economy (Condry 1980; Ennew 1980).

Although Europe provides us with much documented history, rather than this allowing for the writing of necessarily reliable histories, it raises particularly acutely the problem of different histories. One of the directions which anthropological work on Europe has begun to take is to investigate the construction of histories, and in particular to do so through analyses which emphasise the structuring processes involved in history creation, various forms of historicising and different relationships which groups may have with the past.[9] Forms of knowledge about, and relationship to, the past are not only embodied in formal academic histories, of course, but also in texts of many other kinds – fiction, faction, popular, high-brow; and in other forms of recollection and cultural connection with the past – e.g. oral histories, genealogies, traditions and customs, family photograph albums, and, increasingly, local history societies and community museums. How are these different histories regarded and experienced? What are the social relations of their production and consumption (cf. Davis 1989)? How formative can they in turn be of social relations? What role does the past – or rather, various visions of the past – play in the present? There is clearly much to be done in this direction, and as yet there have been few attempts to explore these issues fully, though there is important West European ethnographic research which provides a start (see n. 9).

The studies in this book reflect the growth of this attention to the past, history and text. Cris Shore, in looking at Italian Communist identity, shows how the Italian Communist Party has articulated itself in relation to wider movements of European history – Fascism in particular (see also Shore 1990); and how the strategy which it has employed to do so is analogous to that of ethnic group formation. Texts play a crucially important role in this, a line of intellectual descent through Marxist theorists acting as blood ties might do in conventionally accepted ethnic groups. Shore looks too at the writings of Gramsci – and the concept of hegemony in particular – as part of the ethnographic field, and considers how these ideas play a part in defining the nature of Italian Communist identity.

The development of ethnic identities in historical context, and in particular the structural aspects of this development, is sketched out in most of the case studies in this book. Ethnic identities, in the West

9. Some particularly interesting and innovative anthropological analyses using history in this way in the West European field are: Chapman (1978); Emmett (1982); McDonald (1986, 1989); Cohen (1987, especially ch. 4); Collard (1989); and Llobera (1989).

European case at least, are unlikely to stretch back to time immemorial in an unchanged and unchanging form, even if their advocates may make such claims. The politicisation of ethnic identities – ethnonationalism – frequently brings with it new cultural markers of ethnic identity, and sometimes, as in the case of the Basques, a rather frenzied reading of ethnic connotations into the most everyday of activities (MacClancy). What is more, paralleling the rise of ethnonationalism as a function of the development of the nation-state, there is in some parts of Europe increasing fragmentation as sub-ethnonationalisms, or regionalisms, develop (as in the case of Navarre; see MacClancy), an issue itself worth comparative historical analysis.

The contemporary role of texts as vehicles for articulating and legitimating identities is evident in all of the studies here. Rosanne Cecil pays attention to the religious tracts which play a part in the rhetoric of Protestant and Catholic dissent in Northern Ireland – texts which appear to leave little room for equivocation about identity. By contrast, Fiona Bowie, in her discussion of Wales, points to texts with such titles as *When was Wales?* and *Wales: The Imagined Nation*, indicating uncertainty over the nature of Welsh identity. The production of histories, and identification of texts which may act as legitimations of particular groups, seems to be a key feature of ethnic identity formation in Western Europe. The reinterpretation of a local tax revolt as an act of assertion of Catalan identity, and the inscribing of this into text, is noted by Oonagh O'Brien; and the fact that Navarre was mentioned by Shakespeare and Dante, and was temporarily home to Chaucer, is used in claims for the emerging Navarran regionalism.

The relationship between texts and identities is not only one of texts as voice for existing and emerging identities: texts can also play a part in shaping and even creating identities, often over a long time period. Rosemary McKechnie discusses the history of literary interest in Corsica, an interest through which Corsica has been constituted as romantic and peripheral. The processes involved here, she suggests, are the same as those involved in the construction of other European peripheries – in particular the Celtic fringes – and so it is not surprising that we may find common features across them. This point is extended by Maryon McDonald who finds similar structuring processes at work in the definition of blacks and various other minorities and majorities in Western Europe. Romantic literary interest, and its power to define, is a subject too of Malcolm Chapman's study of Copeland, a region hidden behind that heartland of English Romanticism, the Lake District. The contrast of Copeland, or more specifically its most famous landmark, Sellafield, with the romanticised Lakes has more than purely literary implications, however. Rather, it sets up a moral divide, and this has very real effects on the lives of the people of West Cumbria and their ability to be heard on the national stage. The same can be said too of many other groups within Western Europe.

Of particular interest for the subject of identities is the local production of texts which self-consciously reflect upon the subject of identity, something which brings us to the issue of reflexivity discussed further below. Both Fiona Bowie and Ronald Frankenberg discuss plays, produced and performed during their fieldwork, which illustrate particularly subtle, multi-layered commentary on the complexities of identity. Frankenberg points to the continuous and prolific production of texts in his own fieldwork area in Tuscany, and considers the implications of this for identities: '[does] the continual creation of texts … necessarily … crystallise and unify local identities in such a way as to make them disappear through over-identification'? (p. 58). This question, as Frankenberg observes, is one that can be asked too of texts produced by outsiders – by strangers – a category that includes, of course, ethnographers; a point to which we return below.

### The Focus Within The Study

While some studies have been expanded outwards, as it were, through the use of documentary sources and through using history to deconstruct the ethnographic present, others have attempted to disrupt the assumptions of the community model by shifting the focus within studies, in particular by considering bureaucracy and intellectuals.

The study of bureaucracies as a way of studying the state is argued for by Grillo and is illustrated by a number of the studies in his volume (1980) and that of Boissevain and Friedl (1975). The specific problems of identity for those who occupy bureaucratic positions have not, however, been substantially addressed. Oonagh O'Brien sets out to tackle this problem in her case study by focusing on state officials, *fonctionnaires*, in Northern Catalonia. She shows how this particular occupational association with the state is generally regarded as synonymous with a French identity. However, because Frenchness is regarded ambivalently within Northern Catalonia, many *fonctionnaires* emphasise their Catalan identities even more strongly than do the majority of their Catalan peers. This raises a more general question for the study of identities too: that of differing and multiple interpretations and experiences of ethnic identities within ethnic groups. That we cannot assume ethnic identities to be necessarily homogeneous is a point made – and theorised to varying extents – by most contributors to this book (see also, Cohen 1986a; 1987).

Intellectuals – or those who might more usually classify themselves as observers – have not been much studied within social anthropology generally, though their insights upon their societies often constitute vital 'information' for ethnographers. A number of European ethnographers have begun, however, to treat this information as data, a move not infrequently regarded with suspicion by those intellectuals (see especially McDonald 1986, 1987). In this book, intellectuals of various sorts are a central focus of a number of the chapters – those by Shore, McKechnie, Chapman and McDonald in particular, and those by the other contributors to various extents. The category, of course, is a problematic one. The criteria we use to identify and define 'intellectuals' may be far from unequivocal. Frankenberg, for example, points out that the writers of the play at the centre of his analysis might equally be regarded as young intellectuals or Tuscan peasants; and we might even want to conclude that with the rise of literacy, and with what appear to be increasingly sophisticated levels of self-commentary in West European everyday life, the study of intellectuals is inevitable as they are, quite simply, ubiquitous. As with history and text, of course, this points inexorably towards reflexivity.

### *Reflexivity*

Reflexivity has become a decidedly fashionable subject in social anthropology since the mid-1980s, though it is still quite common for reflexivity to be thought of as either involving any autobiographical comments whatsoever or as omphalopsychic irrelevance (or both). The former leads to token introductory sections in ethnographies about finding accommodation and experiencing self-doubts which are about as searching and pertinent as the comments on rainfall and local history noted by Davis. The latter dismissive perspective, however, ignores the important theoretical issues which can be raised by attention to ethnographic practice and theorising.

At the level of ethnographic practice there has in recent years been an increased interest in the ethnographer's own identity and the effect that this may have upon fieldwork.[10] While this is clearly an issue for all fieldwork, it takes on a number of specific dimensions when

---

10. This is not in itself a new interest, of course (see, for example, Ellen 1984 for an overview). It has, however, been accorded a more central position in social anthropology, and tied up with questions of anthropological theorising and the status of the discipline as a whole (see below).

anthropology is carried out in familiar settings. Questions of difference, of whether European anthropologists exoticise the familiar or fail to perceive the familiarly-glossed unfamiliar, have bedevilled anthropologists working in many parts of Europe, particularly the North. Significantly, some areas – notably the Mediterranean and the Celtic fringes – have received extra ethnographic attention because of their perceived 'remoteness'; and have become perceivedly more exotic through ethnographic attention.[11] Those old questions of studying up, studying down and studying across all arise with increased frequency and often increased complexity in fieldwork regions to which the subjects themselves belong. These are not simply matters of academic credentials or reflexive posturing, however, for as Just (1973) has pointed out, following Ardener, the issue is one of anthropological methodology being based on a 'critical lack of fit', a mismatch of categories (or 'otherness') without which interpretation is, it would seem, superfluous.

One of the major problems raised for anthropological analysis in Western Europe is that identified by Marilyn Strathern in her discussion of anthropology at home.[12] Problems of a particular order arise, she suggests, when anthropological study is conducted within the context which produced anthropology, an enterprise she terms 'auto-anthropology' (1987). In such a case, what is shared is not simply a matter of language or overt aspects of culture, but 'premises about social life' itself (ibid.: 16). In other words, concepts we employ for analysis ('class', say, in the British context, or 'patronage' in the Mediterranean) are not thrown into relief – are not highlighted as 'contrivance' – by their application as they might be in a more unfamiliar context. Whether all parts of Western Europe are 'home' as implied by 'auto-anthropology' is a matter for debate – and, importantly, for empirical investigation. However, the long history of interrelationship between academic and literary ideas – often through embodiment in social policies of multiple kinds – and the peoples of

11. Malcolm Chapman (1982: 142) gives a particularly graphic description of this. See also Ardener (1989: ch. 14); Davis (1977); Herzfeld (1987).

12. Strathern is not herself talking of Western Europe, but focusing more specifically on work within Britain. The geographical extent of 'home' is not specified in her article, and is probably not easily mapped in this way in any case. It seems likely too that 'home' in Strathern's sense is expanding. Certainly, tales of academic terminology being used in the most apparently foreign and distant lands are common among anthropologists. How far what is expressed by this terminology is that which an anthropologist might expect is still, of course, a question for investigation.

Western Europe, makes such an overlap one to which the ethnographer should at least be alerted. Certainly, ethnographers writing in this book have found themselves faced with this kind of 'conceptual reflexivity' (Strathern 1987: 18) in their fieldwork. Rosemary McKechnie, for example, writing of her quest for identities in Corsica, describes her disquiet at finding 'how neatly...the terminology people used to describe their own life fitted with academic constructions of identity' (p. 141).

However, although on the one hand we may well be offered textbook categories in our fieldwork, it would probably be surprising to find them contextualised and interpreted quite as they might be by academics. Let me take an example from my own fieldwork in the Scottish Hebrides to illustrate the point (Macdonald 1987). I found myself working in what was locally identified as an exceptionally good example of a community. Already sensitised to some of the analytical dangers of community, I was determined to avoid it as far as possible.[13] However, what turned out to be particularly interesting was the ways in which a discourse about community was variously constituted, ignored, negotiated and put to work (e.g. to acquire money for a community hall). While this discourse was largely drawn from outside, there were various, more longstanding, local classifications of people onto which it could at times be mapped. In looking at this concept, and its very recent emergence in the area, I was drawn in to more detailed consideration of the term and its connotations within social studies in general.

My suggestion, then, is that Western Europe is likely to provide a particularly, though certainly not the only, fertile ground for a fine-grained conceptual reflexivity (cf. Macdonald 1990). We will be drawn in to more sensitive and detailed empirical studies which try to tease apart various cultural understandings of shared terms and symbols; and to further reflection on our own discipline, and the structuring processes by which it has been shaped.[14] This is a reflexivity which is about Us (be that Us 'anthropologists', 'intellectuals' or 'the West')

13. Just as the community paradigm tended to discount local statements about the worth of Society, there has been a tendency in some of the work emerging from the Community critique to discount local statements about the value of community, heritage and so forth. This is, however, to make the same order of analytical error. The interesting questions concern the ways in which supra-local discourses are appropriated and what is said through them (see Macdonald 1987).

14. This is, of course, a process already under way, though at a broader level than that of West European ethnography. There is, needless to say, a good deal of debate about the directions such disciplinary reflection should best take. See, for a limited number of examples – though ones which reflect some of the different positions: Parkin (1982), Clifford and Marcus (1986), Marcus and Fischer (1986), Geertz (1988), Fardon (1990) and Kuper (1991).

and Them. It promises too to ultimately undermine any easy acceptance of such a dualism by highlighting its making and its various and varied recontextualisations, internal divisions and interpretations. It is decidedly not a luxury or cosily self-centred, it is simply a matter of being both theoretically and empirically sensitive. Let me conclude, then, with some thoughts on such issues as they arise in the study of identities in Western Europe.

## Ways of Identifying

While many of us carrying out our fieldwork in Western Europe experienced doubts over quite how to look at identity – or, indeed, quite what identity was – we were faced very often with people who had extremely well-articulated ideas about it. They could tell us where to look for identity (see especially McKechnie), which aspects of social and cultural life were manifestations of 'real' identity, which were pathological intrusions, the value of asserting ethnic or local identity for the vitality of the people, the importance of recovering cultural heritage, and so forth. There was also a fairly standardised set of cultural symbols with which an ethnic or regional identity was associated: in particular, language, local history, ethnic dances and music. Sometimes these ideas were articulated by activists, or individuals otherwise at the forefront of cultural change, but increasingly it seems, as these models become those through which more numerous peoples are imagined into new ethnic and local communities, this discourse is becoming that of a great majority of the populace. What is more, it seems that this ethnic or regional identity increasingly forms a framework within which other social identities – for example, occupational, political, generational – are played out. At the very least it is there at the ready for presentation to anthropologists or others who express an interest.

None of this is to say either that there was a lack of any sense of place, past, people or culture previous to this, or that the identity-health model is somehow a sham. There can be no doubt that the model is one which serves to articulate experiences and concerns which are widespread in Western Europe at the present time. However, there may be other models of identity too, and these alternative models, and those who live them, may be relatively muted by such persuasive and well articulated expressions of what it means to be, say, a Scot, an Italian, a Corsican. Identity, groupness, belonging, the classification of peoples – call it what you will – can be defined in many other ways than through those more obviously presented as identity. Take the example of smoking on the bus described by Fiona Bowie, the political affiliation read into the colour of the ethnographer's braces in the case of Jeremy MacClancy, or the desire for designer clothes in Corsica. Identities do not necessarily have to be expressed by looking backwards to the past, by holding on to tradition, by the standardised markers of ethnicity. They may lie in ideas about family structure, about gender relations, about politics, about how to treat animals, about house design, or even underclothes. They may lie in notions of place and past – but these may be configured in unfamiliar or unexpected ways. They will inevitably also lie in ideas about outsiders, strangers or 'others' of some sort or another. And in these classifications of ethnicity, of course, there may well be things with which a liberal democratic observer might be uneasy. There is at least in the identity-health model, and its generally innocuous realisation in legends, landscapes, music and the like, a kind of moral and political safety.

Which models we, as observers, read – and which we ignore – is itself significant. The fact that ethnicity and locality are the order of the day among academics, and that notions of national character and stereotypes are dismissed as crude or false, is a matter to be looked at in its social and historical context.[15] Certainly, as Maryon McDonald argues below, we cannot assume that stereotypes do not have real and even formative life within West European, and other, cultures. The task for ethnographers, by detailed empirical studies that are both  socially and historically aware, is to map the creation and appropriation of models of identity, and their generalities, intricacies and specificities as they are realised in everyday life. It is to this task, then, that the present book is intended as a contribution.

### Acknowledgements

I would like to thank Mike Beaney and Tamara Dragadze for valuable comments on a draft of this chapter. I also thank the contributors to the present book and the 'Ethnographic Approaches to Ethnicity' workshop, and colleagues at Brunel and Keele Universities, for some stimulating and sustaining discussions along the way.

---

15. For some relevant related commentary see P. Anderson (1991) and Duncan and Savage (1991).

# References

*American Ethnologist* (1991), *Representations of Europe: Transforming State, Society, and Identity* vol. 18, no.3

Anderson, Benedict (1983), *Imagined Communities: Reflections on the Origin and Spread of Nationalism*. London: Verso

Anderson, Perry (1991), 'Nation-States and National Identity', *London Review of Books*, 9 May, pp. 3–8

Ardener, Edwin (1989), *The Voice of Prophecy and Other Essays*, ed. Malcolm Chapman. Oxford: Blackwell

Barth, Frederik (1969), 'Introduction', in F. Barth (ed.), *Ethnic Groups and Boundaries. The Social Organization of Culture Difference*. London: George Allen and Unwin

Bell, C. and H. Newby (1971), *Community Studies*. London: George Allen and Unwin

Blok, Anton (1975), *The Mafia of a Sicilian Village, 1860–1960*. New York: Harper and Row

Boissevain, Jeremy (1975), 'Introduction', in J. Boissevain and J. Friedl (eds), *Beyond the Community: Social Process in Europe*. The Hague: Department of Education Science of the Netherlands

\_\_\_\_\_ and J. Friedl (eds) (1975), *Beyond the Community: Social Process in Europe*. The Hague: Department of Education Science of the Netherlands

\_\_\_\_\_ and H. Vermeulen (eds) (1984), *Ethnic Challenge – The Politics of Ethnicity Ethnicity in Europe*. Gottingen: Herodot

\_\_\_\_\_ and J. Verrips (eds) (1989), *Dutch Dilemmas: Anthropologists Look at the Netherlands*. Assen: Van Gorcum

Castles, S., with H. Booth and T. Wallace (1984), *Here for Good: Western Europe's New Ethnic Minorities*. London: Pluto Press

Chapman, Malcolm (1978), *The Gaelic Vision in Scottish Culture*. London: Croom Helm

\_\_\_\_\_ (1982), '"Semantics" and the "Celt"', in D. Parkin (ed.), *Semantic Anthropology* pp. 123–44. London: Academic Press

\_\_\_\_\_ M. McDonald and E. Tonkin (1989), 'Introduction', in E. Tonkin, M. McDonald and M. Chapman (eds), *History and Ethnicity*, pp. 1–10. London: Routledge

Clifford, J. and G. Marcus (1986), *Writing Culture. The Poetics and Politics of Ethnography*. Berkeley and Los Angeles: University of California Press

Cohen, Anthony P. (ed.) (1982), *Belonging: Identity and Social Organisation in British Rural Cultures*. Manchester: Manchester University Press

\_\_\_\_\_ (1986a), 'Of Symbols and Boundaries, or, Does Ertie's Greatcoat Hold the Key?', in A. P. Cohen (ed.), *Symbolising Boundaries: Identity and Diversity in British Cultures*, pp. 1–19. Manchester: Manchester University Press

\_\_\_\_\_ (ed.) (1986b), *Symbolising Boundaries: Identity and Diversity in*

*British Cultures*. Manchester: Manchester University Press

_____(1987), *Whalsay, Symbol, Segment and Boundary in a Shetland Island Community*. Manchester: Manchester University Press (1977)

Cole, John, (1977), 'Anthropology Comes Part Way Home: Community Studies in Europe', *Annual Reviews of Anthropology*, vol. 6, pp. 349–78

Collard, Anna (1989), 'Investigating "Social Memory" in a Greek Context', in E. Tonkin, M. McDonald and M. Chapman (eds), *History and Ethnicity*, pp. 89–104. London: Routledge

Condry, Edward (1980), 'Culture and Identity in the Scottish Highlands'. Unpublished D.Phil. thesis, Oxford University

(1983) *Scottish Ethnology*. Edinburgh: Association for Scottish Ethnography

*Critique of Anthropology* (1987), 'Anthropology and Fieldwork: Responses to Llobera' (Parts I and II), vol. 7, no. 1, pp. 83–99; vol. 7, no. 2, pp. 79–99

Davis, John (1977), *People of the Mediterranean. An Essay in Comparative Social Anthropology*. London: Routledge and Kegan Paul

_____(1980), 'Social Anthropology and the Consumption of History', *Theory and Society*, vol. 9, pp. 519–37

_____(1989), 'The Social Relations of the Production of History', in E. Tonkin, M. McDonald and M. Chapman (eds), *History and Ethnicity*, pp. 104–20. London: Routledge

Duncan, S. and M. Savage (1991), 'Commentary: New Perspectives on the Locality Debate', *Environment and Planning A*, vol. 23, no. 2, pp. 155–64

Edwards, John (1985), *Language, Society and Identity*. Oxford: Blackwell in association with André Deutsch

Ellen, Roy (ed.) (1984), *Ethnographic Research*. London: Academic Press

Emmett, Isabel (1982), '*Fe godwin ni eto*: Stasis and Change in a Welsh Industrial Town', in A. P. Cohen (ed). *Belonging: Identity and Social Organisation in British Rural Cultures* pp. 165–97.

Ennew, Judith (1980), *The Western Isles Today*. Cambridge: Cambridge University Press

Erikson, Erik (1968), *Identity, Youth and Crisis*. London: Faber and Faber

Fardon, Richard (1990), 'Localizing Strategies: The Regionalization of Ethnographic Accounts', in R. Fardon (ed.), *Localizing Strategies, Regional Traditions of Ethnographic Writing*. Edinburgh and Washington: Scottish Academic Press and Smithsonian Institution Press

Forsythe, Diana (1989), 'German Identity and the Problems of History', in E. Tonkin, M. McDonald and M. Chapman (eds), *History and Ethnicity*, London: Routledge pp. 137–56.

Frankenberg, Ronald (1966), *Communities in Britain. Social Life in Town and Country*. Harmondsworth: Penguin

_____(1989, 1st edn 1957), *Village on the Border*. Prospect Heights, Illinois: Waveland Press

Frykman, J. and O. Löfgren (1987), *The Culture Builders. A Historical Anthropology of Middle-Class Life*, trans. A. Crozier. New Brunswick and London: Rutgers University Press

Geertz, Clifford (1988), *Works and Lives. The Anthropologist as Author*.
   Oxford: Polity Press
Gellner, Ernest (1983), *Nations and Nationalism*. Oxford: Blackwell
Gilmore, David (1980), *The People of the Plain: Class and Community in
   Lower Andalusia*. New York: Columbia University Press
_____(1982), 'Anthropology of the Mediteranean Area', *Annual Review
   of Anthropology*, vol. 11, pp. 175–205
Grillo, Ralph (ed.) (1980), *'Nation' and 'State' in Europe. Anthropological
   Perspectives*. London: Academic Press
_____(1985), *Ideologies and Institutions in Urban France. The
   Representation of Immigrants*. Cambridge: Cambridge University Press
Hastrup, Kirsten (1982), 'Establishing an Ethnicity. The Emergence of the
   "Icelanders" in the Early Middle Ages', in D. Parkin (ed.), *Semantic
   Anthropology* pp. 145–60. London: Academic Press
_____(1985), *Culture and History in Medieval Iceland. An Anthropological
   Analysis of Structure and Change*. Oxford: Oxford University Press
_____(1990), *Nature and Policy in Iceland, 1440–1800. An
   Anthropological Analysis of History and Mentality*. Oxford:
   Clarendon Press
Herzfeld, Michael (1987), *Anthropology through the Looking Glass. Critical Ethno-
   graphy in the Margins of Europe*. Cambridge: Cambridge University Press
Jackson, Anthony (ed.) (1987), *Anthropology at Home*. London: Tavistock
Just, Roger (1973), 'Some Problems for Mediterranean Anthropology', *Journal
   of the Anthropological Society of Oxford*, vol. ix, no. 2, pp. 81–97
Kenny, M. and D. I. Kertzer (eds) (1983), *Urban Life in Mediterranean
   Europe. Anthroplogical Perspectives*. Urbana: University of Illinois Press
Kuper, Adam (1991), 'Anthopologists and the History of Anthropology',
   *Critique of Anthropology*, vol. 11, no. 2, pp. 125–42
Lison-Tolosana, C. (1966), *Belmonte de los Caballeros. A Sociological Study
   of a Spanish Town*. Oxford: Clarendon Press
Llobera, Joseph (1986), 'Fieldwork in Southwestern Europe: Anthropological
   Panacea or Epistemological Straitjacket?', *Critique of Anthropology*, vol. 6,
   no. 2, pp. 25–33
_____(1987a), 'Reply to Critics. The Anthropology of Southwestern
   Europe: The Way Forward', *Critique of Anthropology*, vol. 7, no. 2,
   pp. 101–18
_____(1987b), 'Nationalism: Some Methodological Issues', *Journal of
   the Anthropological Society of Oxford*. vol. XVIII, no. 1, pp. 13–25
_____(1989), 'Catalan National Identity: The Dialectics of Past and
   Present', in E. Tonkin, M. McDonald and M. Chapman (eds),
   *History and Ethnicity* pp. 247–61. London: Routledge
McDonald, Maryon (1986), 'Celtic Ethnic Kinship and the Problem of Being
   English', *Current Anthropology*, vol. 27, no. 4, pp. 333–41
_____(1987), 'The Politics of Fieldwork in Brittany', in A. Jackson
   (ed.), *Anthropology at Home* pp. 120–38. London: Tavistock

_____(1989), *'We Are Not French!' Language. Culture and Identity in Brittany*. London: Routledge

Macdonald, Sharon (1987), 'Social and Linguistic Identity in the Scottish Gaidhealtachd'. Unpublished D.Phil. thesis, Oxford University

_____(1990), 'Anthropology Dangerously Close to Home: Reflections on Ethnography in a Parallel Context', unpublished MS

Marcus, G. and M. Fischer (1986), *Anthropology as Cultural Critique. An Experimental Moment in the Human Sciences*. Chicago: Chicago University Press

Mason, David (1986), 'Introduction. Controversies and Continuities in Race and Ethnic Relations Theory', in D. Mason and J. Rex (eds), *Theories of Race and Ethnic Relations*, pp. 1–19. Cambridge: Cambridge University Press

Okely, Judith (1983), *The Traveller-Gypsies*. Cambridge: Cambridge University Press

Parkin, David (ed.) (1982), *Semantic Anthropology*. London: Academic Press

Restivo, Sal (1991), *The Sociological Worldview*. Oxford: Blackwell

Roosens, Eugeen (1989), *Creating Ethnicity: The Process of Ethnogenesis*. London: Sage

Schneider, J. and P. Schneider (1976), *Culture and Political Economy in Western Sicily*. New York: Academic Press

Shore, Crispin (1990), *Italian Communism: The Escape from Leninism*. London: Pluto Press

Smith, Anthony D. (1981), *The Ethnic Revival*. Cambridge: Cambridge University Press

Strathern, Marilyn (1987), 'The Limits of Auto-Anthropology', in A. Jackson (ed.) *Anthropology at Home*. pp. 16–37 London: Tavistock

Tiryakian, E. A. and R. Rogowski (eds) (1985), *New Nationalisms of the Developed West*. Boston: Allen and Unwin

Tönnies, Ferdinand (1955, 1st edn 1887), *Community and Association (Gemeinschaft und Gesellschaft)*. London: Routledge and Kegan Paul

Tonkin, E., M. McDonald and M. Chapman (eds) (1989), *History and Ethnicity*. London: Routledge

Ulin, Robert C. (1991), 'The Current Tide in American Europeanist Anthropology: From Margin to Centre?' *Anthropology Today* vol. 7, no. 6, pp. 8–12

# 2

# Ethnicity as Revolutionary Strategy: Communist Identity Construction in Italy

## Cris Shore

## Foreword

This chapter was originally written for a conference on ethnicity in January 1988. Since then dramatic changes have occurred within both Italy and the communist world at large that have transformed the meaning of communism. The massacre in Tiananmen Square in June 1989 followed by the revolutions in Eastern Europe and the disintegration of the Soviet Union have had a profoundly destabilising effect on the communist parties of Western Europe. To attempt to analyse this, or even to document the changes that have occurred, is beyond the scope of this chapter.[1] Suffice to say that shortly after the breaching of the Berlin Wall in 1989 the Italian Communist Party began a process of revision that culminated a year later in a decision to dissolve the party and renounce the tainted 'communist' label. The result, however, has been further electoral decline and confusion among erstwhile communist supporters.

As with all ethnography, therefore, this chapter should be read as an account of processes and relations observed at the time of doing fieldwork – that is, in the 'ethnographic present' – rather than as a

---

1. For an analysis of different interpretations of the crisis of communism see Shore 1991.

commentary on current affairs. Despite being overtaken by events, that analysis of the way in which political identity is constructed, articulated and maintained, remains valid. The use of 'ethnicity' as a model for exploring identity formation in contexts other than those involving 'ethnic' groups in the strict sense of the term will, I hope, provide a useful framework for students seeking to interpret similar processes elsewhere. As Wallman has argued (1986: 230), differences between groups become ethnic boundaries 'only when heated into significance by the identity investments of either side'. For this reason, any understanding of ethnicity must necessarily be based on a wider understanding of identity formation.

## The Politics of Identity Construction

Italy, seat of the Vatican and centre of Roman Catholicism, is also the country with the largest communist party in the Western world. Founded in 1921, the Italian Communist Party (PCI) has grown from a small, clandestine group of conspirators before 1944 to a mass organisation that permeates Italian society in virtually all its public manifestations. In many communities it has come to rival, if not supplant, the traditional role of the Catholic Church as focus and sponsor of community events and symbol of local identity. Since the Second World War the forces of communism and Catholicism have become increasingly polarised as each has come to represent not merely an organisation antagonistic to the other, but frequently a rival and mutually exclusive cultural system. This conflict between communist and Catholic interests in Italy, which reflects older social and ideological cleavages, has become institutionalised in the Italian party system.

This chapter examines one aspect of this theme by focusing on communist identity. Our primary concern is not the history of Catholic-communist relations nor a comprehensive investigation into communist ideology and organisation (though brief consideration of both is necessary), but an analysis of some of the processes involved in the construction of communist identity and its impact on Italian society. The main questions addressed concern (1) the mechanisms involved in identity construction, (2) why the PCI has constructed its identity in the way that it has, and (3) what it means to be communist in Italy today – from the communist perspective and that of their opponents.

Three major arguments are developed. First, from the PCI's viewpoint identity construction is an integral part of a wider strategy for the conquest of power, central to which are the Gramscian ideas of 'hegemony' and a 'passive revolution'. Second, PCI identity has arisen from a process of continual conflict and struggle between communists and anti-communists, a struggle which, in the context of the democratic Italian Republic, has come to be waged increasingly on a symbolic and ideological terrain. The struggle for political power has become increasingly a struggle for popularity and electoral appeal, and much of the battleground upon which this conflict is fought out concerns the issue of 'communist identity'. In Italy communist identity has traditionally been defined by, and has defined itself against, its opponents – the Catholic Church and Christian Democrat Party (DC). It has evolved, therefore, through a dialectic of definition and counter-definition, a process which in turn has been shaped by historical and political events both within Italy and internationally (the Cold War and *détente*, for example). Third, 'ethnicity' (see below) provides an interesting model for understanding identity construction in the PCI for, though Italian communists do not constitute an 'ethnic group' in a strict sense, the mechanisms involved in ethnic group formation are strikingly similar.

In this chapter I combine ethnographic with theoretical insights into the structure and formation of communist identity. By analysing identity construction I also shed some light on a question of interest to political scientists as much as to anthropologists: namely, why Italian communism has been so successful when virtually all other European communist parties have splintered or declined.

## The Importance of Parties and Political Identity in Modern Italy

Few anthropologists in Italy fail to be struck by the profuse extent to which political affiliations have become institutionalised into major social cleavages. Party loyalties and political affiliations seem to cut deeply into the fabric of society and into Italian consciousness, which has important social ramifications (Barnes 1967). One aspect of this is that political patronage influences virtually every aspect of Italian social life, from the allocation of jobs and public funds to the composition of most major local and national government bodies. So pervasive is this phenomenon that Italians have invented a word for it: *partitocrazia* (literally, 'rule by parties').[2] This term is accurate: for reasons which are explained elsewhere,[3] political parties have come to dominate post-war Italian society and the state. This originated between 1943 and 1945. The collapse of the Fascist state had left a void in northern and central Italy and the only forces capable of assuming a leading role in post-war reconstruction were the Catholic Church and PCI, both having been important points of reference for Italians during the period of Fascist and then Nazi rule (Galli and Prandi 1970: 13–14).

It was Fascist one-party rule that set the precedent for the pervasive party organism present throughout different levels of society and enjoying an intensive relationship with the state apparatus (Pridham 1981: 4). This pattern was subsequently elaborated by other parties in the post-war period, most conspicuously in the organisation of the PCI and DC (Poggi 1968). Nowhere is party domination more evident than in the frequent use of government patronage by the ruling coalition parties to place their own favourites and supporters (*raccomandati*) in positions of power and authority. At almost every level of public administration the rewards and powers of office are divided out among party followers, usually on a basis of party strength at the polls. This division (*lottizzazione*) of jobs and appointments extends beyond government administration into other arenas of public life, from educational establishments to banks, state industries, television, public corporations and 'wherever the party apparatuses have managed to extend their tentacles'.[4]

Thus, according to Euginio Scalfari (1983), editor of the newspaper *La Repubblica*, the Italian political system has become a 'feudal pyramid ... which has swallowed public institutions and bodies in relationships of mortifying dependency and forced servility'. Similarly, Italians say that the parties 'have clientised millions of people and in so doing, involved them in a web of corruption and blackmail' (Ferrara 1983: 8). Party leaders are commonly portrayed as 'feudal barons' who have carved up amongst themselves half the Italian economy which is under the control of the state. Their 'vassals' have become the bankers, industrialists, and managers in the huge public sector, who owe their

2. For different views on this see Galli and Prandi (1970: 166-226); Nichols (1973: 113-27); Pridham (1981: 249-50); and Allum (1973: 22-3, 138).

3. See Shore 1990.

4. Cf. C. Page, 'When the Partitocrazia has to stop', *Guardian*, 21 May 1983, p.9; for an ethnographic study of clientelist politics within modern state bureaucracies see Shore (1989).

positions, and therefore their loyalty, to the individual politicians who have got them appointed. Far from declining in recent years this tendency has grown to the point where, according to the journal *L'Espresso* (1983: 6),

> nothing escapes from the logic of *lottizzazione*. Not only the hydrocarbon industry (ENI) and other State administrative bodies, but practically everything rests in the hands of administrators chosen by the parties: from the central milk agencies to the small and large banks, from television to hospitals. Some half a million people, placed at the heads of 40,000 public bodies, constitute the real ruling class of the country today.

Patron-clientelism in its various forms has thus become the *modus vivendi* of most state and para-state bureaucracies and is probably the single most important factor in determining recruitment to any public office.

To be called 'Christian Democrat', 'Socialist' or 'Communist' in Italy is not, therefore, an arbitrary label but a fundamental dimension of public identity; it means belonging to a clearly defined social and cultural group with clearly circumscribed rules and boundaries. These parties share much in common: each claims to be heir to a distinctive and unique ideology; each has a highly developed territorial organisation at all levels; each has become an instrument of propaganda, and each characteristically has a mass membership, a printing press, a theoretical journal, a weekly, often daily, party newspaper and a party machine employing hundreds if not thousands of full and part-time functionaries.[5]

In addition, the larger parties – through their control over appointments and allocating public money – also support a host of satellite bodies including trade unions, schools, women's and pensioners' groups, youth clubs and recreational circles, local bars, research institutions, radio stations, television networks, and publishing houses. The result, to echo Galli and Prandi, has been a peculiar politicisation as parties have penetrated all areas of social life.

## Communist and Catholic Worlds

So pervasive is this phenomenon that, as Barnes notes (1967: 27), 'some parties come close to encompassing the entire existence of many of their adherents'. The major parties are, in effect, cultural systems,

5. In 1984 the number of full-time functionaries was over 5,000. By the end of 1992 this had fallen to under 800.

and in a far more ambitious way than any comparable British party they compete with each other to win the hearts and minds of people and to dominate Italian society. This idea is epitomised in the Italian conception of the 'Two Worlds', '*il mondo cattolico*' and '*il mondo comunista*' (Riccamboni 1976). According to Kertzer (1980: 2), the Catholic Church and PCI 'try' to provide comprehensive and exclusive systems of belief and behaviour: they do not simply call for limited areas of allegiance but demand the individual's total support in a wide variety of roles and situations. In parts of Italy, notably the regions of Emilia-Romagna, Tuscany and Umbria, this Church-communist confrontation 'tends to divide people into two hostile and to an extent, socially autonomous worlds' (ibid.). According to this view, those people who are drawn into the web of organisations that constitute the Catholic or Communist World and who recognise the authority of the Vatican or Party are presumed to have 'an all-pervading allegiance to the social and political as well as to ritual and ideological edicts of the hierarchy' (ibid.: 2–3).

A second major element of the Italian political system is the powerful role played by Italy's leading party, the Christian Democrats. The rise and fall of fifty different governments since the founding of the Republic in 1948 gives the impression of profound political instability. In fact Italian politics are remarkably stable and the Italian state for over forty years has been dominated by the same party, the Christian Democrats, in coalition with the smaller Republican, Liberal, Social Democrat and Socialist parties. Moreover, the basis of that alliance and the cornerstone of its unity is its opposition to the PCI. Thus, anti-communism has provided the foundation of every Italian government since 1948 (Allum 1979: 135). It is against this political and historical context that communist identity has taken its shape and must therefore be understood.

### Fieldwork and the Problem of the Ethnographer's Identity

I researched Italian communism during two periods of fieldwork (1983-5 and 1986) conducted in an inner-city area of Perugia, a city of roughly 140,000 inhabitants. Perugia is an industrial and administrative centre, a university town and capital of the region of Umbria which is located in the heart of Central Italy. Traditionally this region has a special importance for Catholicism. It was part of the Papal States before Italian unification, but more importantly, it is the birthplace of several major Catholic saints and monastic orders, including saints Benedict and Clare, and the patron saint of Italy, Francis of Assisi. Yet Umbria is also characterised by the extraordinary strength of the Communist Party. With over 44 per cent of the vote the PCI is the largest party in the region and has dominated local government there since the Second World War. This makes Umbria the third region in Italy's so-called 'communist Red-belt' zone, after Emilia-Romagna and Tuscany. The initial research topic was the dialogue between communism and Catholicism in a city-wide context. This project, however, was eventually abandoned in favour of a detailed study of the PCI as it proved impossible to be in both 'camps' at once, not only for pragmatic reasons but also because it raised uncomfortable problems relating to the role and identity of the ethnographer.

While this chapter is not specifically concerned with the subjective experience of doing fieldwork, the implications of reconciling the researcher's identity with that of the subjects under study is perhaps a useful starting point for analysing communist identity construction. Amongst the communists of Umbria one of the first pieces of information sought about any newcomer is where they stand politically. Typically, this is one of the first questions asked of, or about, a stranger (see White 1980). Similarly, it is invariably communicated when introducing someone to fellow communists for the first time: 'this is so-and-so. He's a comrade.' The significance of this on behaviour and patterns of discourse is immediately apparent for it usually allows the speakers to adopt the personal 'you' (*tu*) and dispense with the more formal *Lei* that is usually appropriate among strangers.[6] Thus, in order to do fieldwork among Italian communists my political identity had to be established and accepted as proximity to party members and meetings was contingent upon that identity.

Being 'British' (*inglese*)[7] in Italy barely a year after the Falklands war was not helpful.[8] Even in Perugia there had been a wave of animosity directed against 'gli inglese' who were labelled aggressors

6. The precise rules of etiquette surrounding the use of *Lei/tu* are more complex than this (cf. Shore 1985).

7. In everyday discourse the term inglese includes all people from the British Isles - including the Scots and Irish who are not usually recognised as distinct nationals: 'it's just a trick to get four teams into the World Cup championship' was how one communist jokingly explained Italian scepticism

8. Similarly, 'being American' and Jewish had interesting ramifications for Kertzer who did fieldwork in communist Bologna. Kertzer reports (1980: 22) that local people at times suspected of him of being a CIA agent or an Israeli spy.

and imperialists by all shades of political opinion, and there were several incidents of British residents' shops, cars and windows being vandalised in spontaneous outbursts of anger. Where one stood on the question of Mrs Thatcher ('La Tatcher') was frequently used as a litmus test for political pigeon-holing.

Three other examples illustrate the pervasiveness of political and/or religious affiliation as a key factor in defining identity. One day over Sunday dinner in the Umbrian countryside the father of a close friend, a retired sharecropper and Catholic who had voted Christian Democrat all his life, asked whether I was Catholic. The answer 'no' was followed by further questions: Protestant? Jewish? Muslim? Answering 'no' to each of these I added that I had not been baptised into any faith. 'Just like an animal then!' ('Come una bestia!') was the reply this evoked.

On another occasion two members of the Catholic 'fundamentalist' group Comunione e Liberazione asked pointedly why I spent so much time in the company of 'those boring communists'. Asking in return why they so disliked communists the answer given was (sic) because communists were cold and impersonal automatons who, having crushed the individuality out of their members, went around calling each other 'comrade'. People from Comunione e Liberazione were different: 'we call each other by our Christian names'.

On yet another occasion during fieldwork in the company of Italian communists a PCI member in the act of divulging personal information about the local Party leadership stopped short when he realised that I was present, but was told 'don't worry, you can say what you like. He's a comrade' ('lui e' compagno').

Each of these examples illustrates the significance of this fundamental Catholic-communist cleavage in Italian society, the importance of political identity in defining boundaries of inclusion-exclusion (the classification of 'one of us' versus 'one of them') and the stereotypes and categories involved when these two cultural systems meet. Those communist and anti-communist stereotypes are extremely important in shaping communist identity, as we shall see later.

## What it 'Means' to be Communist in Italy

Italian communists have a very distinctive identity that is a clear source of pride and prestige for ordinary Party members. Indeed, the PCI's identity (understood in the sense of its national reputation) has become a valuable asset and treasured resource and the Party leadership has made strenuous efforts to cultivate this sense of distinctiveness. To be communist in Italy today means something very different from being communist in Britain or elsewhere. Italian communism enjoys far greater power and legitimacy than it does in Britain. It is a party with enormous prestige in Italy; it has over 9 million voters (or 27 per cent of the Italian electorate) and 1.5 million members. It also possesses probably the largest organisational machinery of any communist party in Western Europe.

The PCI has a diffuse and integrated social presence throughout Italy. Indeed, it is an accepted part of the fabric of community life. Thus in most Italian towns and villages a PCI section office now stands in the main piazza (the traditional centre of civic life), alongside the parish church and town hall (or *comune*). Throughout Italy there are monuments dedicated to communist partisans executed by the Fascists and Nazis, or piazzas named after PCI leaders - 'Gramsci' now being as common a street name as Cavour and Garibaldi.

Furthermore, the PCI has assumed the mantle as the major force of political opposition in Italy; it is the only major party excluding the neo-Fascist MSI which has remained outside government and therefore relatively free from association with government scandals and clientelism. Thus 'being communist', from the PCI viewpoint, means also being anti-Fascist, anti-government and anti-corruption. Finally, the PCI has gone farther than any other communist party in rethinking Marxism-Leninism: to its critics, perhaps even in its own words, it is the most 'revisionist' of Europe's communist parties and has become the pioneer of what, for lack of a better word, has been called 'Eurocommunism'.

From its sheer size the PCI has clearly succeeded in establishing itself as a social force with a highly popular identity among at least one quarter of the Italian population. The question is: how has it constructed this identity and what does that identity consist of? To answer this it is perhaps necessary to reflect briefly on the concept of 'identity' itself.

## The Concept of Identity: Some Theoretical Considerations

Identity or 'political identity' is an ambiguous term because it deals primarily with intangible phenomena such as perceptions and feelings. In short, it is based on sentiments, symbols and stereotypes, none of which can be measured or quantified according to any objective criteria. This has led some authors to argue that the term is so vague and over-used as to be rendered meaningless (McKenzie 1978). But whilst identity may lack precision and coherence as an analytical construct (like the concept of 'community' perhaps), this does not negate its validity either as a category for anthropological investigation or as a tool of anthropological enquiry.

Identity, as used in this paper, concerns both how a group sees itself in its collective self-definition and how it is portrayed by others: it therefore incorporates both image and self-image and draws simultaneously upon the classifications of insiders (the 'emic' view) and those of outsiders (the 'etic' view). These contrasting images and labels may also interact in a dialectical fashion. To give an example, the term 'Eurocommunist', which gained currency in the mid-1970s, was coined then elaborated initially by anti-communists as a derogatory label. As they conceived it, 'Eurocommunism' symbolised the fact that the 'new democratic face' of communism in Western Europe was an illusion or, worse still, a sinister disguise masking the old 'Stalinist wolf in sheep's clothing'. Initially, therefore, most communist parties rejected the label. The PCI, however, capitalised on this term, accepted it, then appropriated it for its own use and re-launched the concept as a vehicle for uniting those European communist parties like itself that were developing a democratic, national road to socialism and distancing themselves from the Soviet Union.

The 'Eurocommunist' label illustrates the fact that identity construction is essentially a process of social pigeon-holing which involves categorising and classifying 'others' according to given social/cultural markers. But it is precisely in the act of defining 'others' that people define themselves and their relationship to them. To put it simply, the classification of 'Us' presupposes a contrast with 'Them'. To be an 'insider' there must be a category of 'outsider'. The label 'friend' presupposes 'non-friend', 'relative'/'non-relative', 'Christian'/'heathen', 'national'/'foreigner' and so on. Hence, identity construction is always a two-way process.

The reason why defining identity is so problematic is that the 'identity' in question shifts according to context and relative to the position of the observer. In other words, the identity of a person or group is neither fixed nor stable, but infinitely fluid and changeable. In fact 'identity' proper does not exist in any *a priori* sense and cannot be spoken about save in relation to other identities. Identity may therefore be defined in theoretical terms as a classificatory device that is 'contextual' (in the sense of being specific to a given social and historical setting), 'oppositional' and 'relational'.

However, just as individuals play many roles in everyday life, so they have many identities each of which will shift according to the position of the actor in relation to others. The pattern that results from this is often a stratified structure of loyalties which correspond to different levels of perceived community. These tend to 'nest' one within the other (Epstein 1978: 113). For example, a man from Northern Ireland might define himself in different contexts as 'from Londonderry', an 'Orangeman', 'Protestant', 'Unionist', 'Loyalist' or 'Northern Irish', whereas a Catholic from roughly the same area would be defined alternatively as 'from Derry', a 'Republican', 'Fenian', 'Nationalist', 'Irish' or 'Northern Irish'. Each apparently minor shift from one label to another in fact conveys messages of considerable magnitude and political complexity. Similarly, in Northern Spain Christian (1972: xiii) notes the interesting correspondence between the organisation of Catholic shrines and the levels upon which people form images of identity and community: nation, region, province, vale, village barrada.

These levels of identity can be conceived as concentric rings analogous to the ripples formed from a pebble dropped into a pond. Each level defines a different identity. Each is also defined by specific boundary markers, which may be visible symbols (for example, shrines, football teams, style of dress), or largely non-visual (accent, dialect, attitudes and beliefs).

## The Construction of PCI Identity

Communist identity consists of a number of different, compounded and stratified sub-identities each corresponding either to different levels of Party involvement or to the Party's own territorial organisation and identity. The compounded identity is that of 'We Communists' (*noi comunisti*), a phrase used repeatedly in PCI discourse. Beyond this is the category of 'comrade' (*compagno*) which extends to include all people 'on the left' (*gente della sinistra*) or those allied and sympathetic to the PCI and the socialist movement. The identity of Socialist Party (PSI) members is significant here for there is disagreement on their status. For the PCI leadership, whose whole political strategy is predicated upon the PSI eventually abandoning the government coalition in favour of a left-wing alliance, they are 'comrades', even 'separated brethren' according to Enrico Berlinguer, former Secretary of the PCI. But much of the membership despise and deplore the PSI and privately would never define them as compagni (the common view is that 'they are even more corrupt than the Christian Democrats').

Beneath the identity of 'comrade' is a series of sub-categories: 'fellow section-members' (*compagni di sezione*), 'rank-and-file activists' (*militanti di base*), 'ex-partisans' (*partigiani*), 'party cadres' (*quadri*), leaders (*dirigente*). Other sub-identities correspond to territorial party organisation, for example *i comunisti della sezione di P. Togliatti, i comunisti perugini, i comunisti umbri* and so forth. This hierarchy of loyalties often blends with older identities concerned with attachment to place, particularly the pronounced local chauvinism called *campanilismo* that exists throughout Italy.[9] Identities also exist for the communist youth wing (the FGCI – *noi giovani comunisti*), the communist women's organisations (*le donne comuniste*), and occupational groups, for example communist local administrators, communist sharecroppers and communist steelworkers. Depending on the context, and what is politically expedient in the circumstances, the Party will emphasise different facets of its identity: hence it will appear as the 'party of the proletariat', 'the party of women', 'the pensioners' party' or 'the party of the environment'.

Thus the PCI has achieved mass support by being able to appeal to different social groups by exploiting different dimensions of its multifaceted identity. It has created in effect a vast collective identity built on a pyramid of smaller attachments to neighbourhood, section and community. Seen in this light party loyalty is comparable to nationalism; both are forms of collective identity and both are symbol systems based upon an idea of community, real or imagined (cf. Anderson 1983). Similarly, just as nationalism acted as a revolutionary force in nineteenth-century Europe, so communist identity, according to PCI strategists, has a revolutionary potential in Italy today (Bloomfield 1985).

## PCI Identity Construction in Historical Context

PCI identity is intimately bound up with Party organisation. Two factors are of primary importance in this respect: first, the PCI's shift after 1944 from the workplace cell towards the territorial section as its basic unit of organisation, and second, its abandonment of the Leninist party model.

---

9. For an ethnographic account of various aspects of *campanilismo* see Silverman (1975).

The history behind this can be stated briefly. After the war, PCI leaders, determined to prevent the rise of another Mussolini, and embarrassed by the way the institutions of the Left had so easily perished during the Fascist repression of the 1920s and 1930s, decided to rebuild their house on firmer foundations. With this goal in mind it abandoned the Leninist model of small, clandestine, sectarian party in favour of a mass party with deep roots in society; a party structure that could survive any amount of persecution and harassment. This necessitated a change in identity: the abandonment of the old vanguard, cadre-type of party and its replacement with a more open party that would win millions of Italians to the PCI cause of transforming Italy into a socialist society. Moreover, that identity needed to encourage a sense of unity and elicit feelings of belonging: to project outward a welcoming and all-embracing public image which, viewed from the inside, would fuel sentiments of exclusiveness and intensive party loyalty. Communist identity would thus be the instrument for attracting new recruits while at the same time resolving perennial problems of internal cohesion and control endemic to all mass organisations. The success of that attempt is witnessed in the rapid growth of the PCI from a meagre 6,000 in 1945 to over two million members in 1947 (Poggi 1968: 29, 311).

The model for the PCI's Partito Nuovo ('New Party'), launched following the liberation of Italy, was unique in the communist world. In fact, the model seemed to be a blend of structures taken from the Bolshevik Party and the Catholic Church. The mass, permanently mobilised party organisation with a visible presence in the heart of every working-class community was clearly inspired by the Bolshevik soviets. The territorial organisation based on hierarchically linked sections and federations, on the other hand, paralleled the Catholic Parish and Diocese. This debt to the Church's organisational model is evident in one of the 1945 PCI slogans: 'For Every Church Bell A Party Section' ('per ogni campanile una sezione comunista!'). Another was 'Every Party Section A Community Recreation Centre' ('ogni sezione un circolo!').

Like the parish church, sections pushed to become the focus and sponsor of all local public events. PCI sections housed the cheapest bars in town, card tables, bowling pitches, free newspapers, a TV room, and much more. The PCI initiated the *Feste dell'Unità*', local festivals that, in style and structure, were almost mirror-images of the traditional Catholic saint's day celebrations: only the symbols and political message differed. Instead of saints, rosaries, crucifixes and candles, the iconography is distinctly communist: red flags, hammers and sickles, clenched fists, banners denouncing imperialism, photographs of communist leaders and speeches paying homage to partisans martyred by Fascists. Twice during fieldwork I even attended 'communist funerals' where the service was carried out entirely by fellow trade union and party members. On the latter occasion the deceased, a former partisan in the Garibaldi brigades, was laid out before burial in full battle dress with a red handkerchief in hand and a tape recorder at the corpse's head playing 'The Internationale' as visitors came to pay their last respects.

In short, the PCI has consciously constructed a territorial network and symbol-system. But it has also constructed its identity through the successful projection of a PCI world-view and through the acquisition of political power. Thus the PCI in Umbria now commands jobs, grants and resources, and in PCI/PSI-controlled Perugia most of those employed in local government offices are, not surprisingly, either communists or socialists.

The conclusion to all this seems to be that since its foundation in 1921 the PCI has conscientiously striven to differentiate itself from the rest of society and, like successful minorities elsewhere, it has done so by creating a powerful 'we'/'they' dichotomy, a division that manifests itself morally, politically and socially. The social and symbolic boundaries that separate Italian communists from non-communists are now well defined. Like all communist parties it sees itself, somewhat ambiguously, as standing both 'outside' yet 'inside' society. It must place itself sufficiently 'outside' of society so as to influence macro-events and to avoid contamination by too much contact with bourgeois society and its ideological apparatus, but sufficiently 'inside' society in order to lead the working class and organise the revolution.

## Ethnicity: A Model for PCI Identity Construction

From the preceding discussion it becomes apparent that though Italian communists do not constitute an 'ethnic group' per se, they are nevertheless a socio-culturally distinct interest group that is as 'ethnic' as an ethnic group can be: as distinctive perhaps as Protestants and Catholics in Northern Ireland, or, to use Cohen's example, the Hausa within Yoruba society.

Though 'ethnicity' is sometimes used in a more restrictive sense to refer to ascriptive categories of people linked by biological ties (Barth 1969), the model of ethnic group formation provided by Barth, Cohen (1974 and 1976), Smooha (1985) and others is nonetheless extremely useful in exploring the way that social boundaries are created and identities are constructed and manipulated by groups that are not 'ethnic groups' but share many of the same features (see also the contributions to Anthony Cohen 1982). Indeed, according to the broader definition an ethnic group is 'any group of people who set themselves apart and are set apart from other groups with whom they interact or coexist in terms of some distinctive criterion or criteria which may be linguistic, racial or cultural' (Seymour-Smith 1986: 95). This echoes Barth's view that ethnic categories should be seen as 'organisational vessels that may be given varying amounts and forms of content' (Barth 1969: 14). As Cohen argues, the diacritics used may be physical appearance, name, language, history, religion, nationality, or any other object or behaviour to which people attach significance. Thus, there is no logical limit to the number or variety of markers that might provide common characteristics for group membership (R. Cohen 1978: 387). One is forced to conclude, echoing Grillo, that the concept of 'ethnic group' belongs more to systems of classification and ideology than to any objective racial difference (Grillo 1974: 124).

In this respect there is a close parallel between communist identity construction and ethnicity, for both are processes that involve a complex use of political and ideological strategies and the political exploitation of any number of items and objects drawn from their cultural situation. As in ethnicity where 'traditional customs are used only as idioms and as mechanisms for political alignments' (Abner Cohen 1976: 4), so, too, communist identity construction has entailed the conspicuous manipulation of 'values, myths and rituals and ceremonials to solve basic problems of group organisation' (ibid.: 15). Moreover, ethnicity, like identity construction, is built upon hierarchical levels of inclusiveness and exclusiveness (R. Cohen 1978: 387). But if creating a group identity is akin to the process of ethnicity, that process invariably concerns creating an identity. This point is echoed by Wallman: 'It is the identity element in ethnic boundaries which moves the boundary process. Differences between groups of people turn into ethnic boundaries only when heated into significance by the identity investments of either side' (1986: 230). In either case these boundaries are constructed 'only in situations where people of different backgrounds come into contact with each other or share the same institutional or political system' (Smooha 1985: 267).

What factors lead to the emergence of 'identity' and 'ethnicity'? According to Barth's pioneering work ethnicity crystallises in segments of a population when they share a combination of at least three factors: common descent (real or fictitious), shared and distinctive sociocultural characteristics and a common field of communication. In addition, for an ethnic group to become a group and not merely a collection of people it must identify itself, and be identified by others, as constituting a category different from other categories of the same type (Barth 1969; R. Cohen 1978: 385). In short, it must have a strongly developed consciousness of kind. When we examine the PCI we see that each and all of these ingredients are present.

### *Myth of Common Descent*

Like Irish Protestants, Basques, Jews and other ethnic groups, the PCI has evolved a shared myth of common descent. However, instead of 'family' or 'blood' or 'biological ties', ideology itself is the PCI's descent principle. The PCI claims direct intellectual descent from Marx, Engels, Lenin, the Russian Bolshevik Party, and then from an unbroken succession of Italian Marxists including Bordiga, Gramsci, Togliatti, Longo, Berlinguer and Natta. The PCI's concern with tracing and defending its Marxist ancestry is understandable. This is not only the essence of its self-image as a revolutionary party but also the key to its public identity and political credibility. Not surprisingly, PCI discourse makes frequent reference to the Party's 'patrimony of ideas' and 'intellectual heritage', and new policies are typically presented as 'organic' developments from previous ones (PCI *Statuto* 1983).

By tracing its ancestry to a body of ideas rather than biological ties the PCI can claim a symbolic link to all other 'sister' parties and 'fraternal' revolutionary movements in Europe and beyond. It can also claim to be part of a worldwide movement, linked by historic ties of comradeship and solidarity to fellow communists throughout the world. Indeed, at both a conceptual and a structural level these old ties are still evident. It is important to remember that, like all other communist parties from the Third International, the PCI was founded in 1921 following Lenin's instructions and having adopted his '21 Articles For Admission to the Comintern'. The PCI complied wholeheartedly with the Leninist party model. According to its own conception of itself then, it was to be a perfect replica and clone of the

Bolshevik Party; it did not even wish to be an independent organisation but merely a national section of the Communist International, whose headquarters and leadership were in Moscow. In fact, before 1933 the 'Italian' Communist Party (Partito Comunista Italiano) did not exist: it was called the 'Communist Party of Italy' (Partito Comunista d'Italia or PCI) – a title symbolic of its lack of any wish for an autonomous national identity.

### Shared Social and Cultural Forms

Though the PCI has no distinctive physical traits, dietary taboos or marital rules of a kind typical of many religious-based ethnic groups, PCI members – particularly activists – nevertheless share several socially relevant characteristics. The overwhelming majority in Perugia and nationally come from communist and left-wing families (Sebastiani 1983: 84–5). Nationally the PCI apparatus is also dominated by members from the 'communist "sub-culture" area' (ibid.) of Central Italy. Indeed, according to the PCI's figures 700,000 members (48.4 per cent) come from just four regions: Emilia-Romagna, Tuscany, Umbria and Liguria (PCI 1989). Many PCI activists therefore share the formative experience of growing up inside the political sub-culture of the communist Red Belt. Within this area, strongest support for communism still comes from areas which decades ago experienced peasant revolts, collective militancy, or rapid urbanisation. And where the PCI is strongly entrenched in local community life, the Catholic Church has usually been displaced from its traditional role as sponsor and focus of community events.

Moreover, among communists in Perugia social networks tend to centre around fellow 'comrades' and the Party. Often, friendships and loyalties are politically defined. Many members believe it difficult to have true friends who are not also 'comrades', or at least 'Left' and sympathetic.

### Field of Communication and Distinctive Behaviour

Without stretching the point too far it is fair to say that because of their distinctive ideology and Party organisation Italian communists also share a field of communication and certain characteristic behaviours arising out of these elements. This is particularly noticeable in the use of language among communists. In any formal Party occasion members adopt a special kind of 'PCI-Speak', a form of political discourse (or *linguaggio politico*) that is largely inaccessible to all but those conversant with that language. PCI-Speak is a jargon-ridden code full of subtle innuendos and veiled suggestions whose meaning is kept deliberately ambiguous. It involves both a distinctive style of oratory and a distinctive vocabulary drawn from the Marxist-Leninist-PCI lexicon.

Speeches by PCI leaders repeatedly use the terms 'hegemony', 'crisis', 'struggle' and 'the popular masses': other shibboleths include 'progressive democracy', 'historic compromise', 'democratic alternative', 'reform of the institutions', 'current historical phase' and, of course, 'class struggle'. There is also a standard PCI way of presenting arguments and opening meetings which regularly include hour-long introductions setting out the Party's 'perspectives' based on 'concrete' and 'dialectical' analysis of world events in 'the current phase of history'. Typical PCI behaviour – the *sine qua non* of 'being communist' from the PCI perspective – includes playing the role expected of a cadre or local-level militant (*militanti di base*). All members, according to Party rules laid out in the old Statutes, are encouraged and expected to be activists, to attend meetings, to defend the Party (against critics, enemies and Fascists), to promote the Party press and to give regular financial support to the Party coffers (through donations, fund-raising, regular debits and special subscriptions to party campaign funds).

Ostentatiously carrying a copy of *L'Unità*, the Party daily, is one example of a conspicuous identity marker as few people buy it apart from communists. Within the PCI there traditionally existed an ideal of what constitutes a model communist. This included the qualities of seriousness, prudence and self-discipline. The 'good communist' was someone guided by strong moral precepts, a sense of duty and political vision. She or he is dedicated, honest, and hard-working; someone who identifies with the working class, who has intellectual leanings, grasps the fundamentals of Marxism, and is conversant with the history of the Party and of other revolutionary movements.[10] Today members are not officially required to profess themselves Marxist-Leninists. Neither do they have to live up to the old Leninist conception of the true Party cadre. However, though the PCI is not the sectarian party it was prior to the 1960s or even 1970s, it still retains its sense of exclusiveness and still demands loyalty and obedience from its members.

---

10. This 'model communist type' is far more lax today than it was prior to the 1970s. Since the 1970s successive PCI statutes have explicitly stated that membership is open to all 'regardless of ideological conviction'. The only official criterion is that members accept the Party programme.

The 'good communist' also carries out a typical pattern of weekly, often daily activities in the life of the section or federation to which he or she belongs. These regular activities include debates, marches, rallies, demonstrations, canvassing, the Sunday paper round for *L'Unità* (*diffusione della stampa*), organising local public events such as festivals, sports tournaments, round-table discussions on local issues, running the local Party bar/community centre and an almost endless round of committee meetings.

There are also distinctive attitudes arising from a shared political socialisation, particularly evident in those who have received formal party schooling. In Perugia many older activists and Party cadres had attended courses at Party schools, either locally or at the PCI's national school outside Rome. Though these now encourage a more liberal approach to education this was not the case during the 1940s and 1950s when the Party was still extremely Stalinist, as PCI members themselves say. The official aim of these schools was traditionally that of 'ideological preparation' for Party cadres (*formazione dei quadri*). Inevitably, much of the older generation of PCI activists have retained many of the 'Stalinist' attitudes and qualities that the PCI considered necessary for the ideological formation of its leaders in former years.

### Consciousness of Kind

The most important aspect of communist identity is that Italian communists both perceive themselves, and are perceived by others, as distinctive and different from the rest of Italian society. PCI members share a similar world-view, one that sees society in terms of oppressors and oppressed, class and class conflict, forces of reaction versus forces of progress. It is a world-view that provides its members with a heroic image of themselves cast against the backcloth of the great movement of history. According to the traditional Leninist view communists are the 'protagonists of history', the 'political vanguard' whose historical role is to lead the class struggle, emancipate the working class and pioneer the revolutionary process that will eventually bring about a classless society at the 'end of history'. This is a powerful myth. Moreover, it need not necessarily be believed in wholeheartedly to be effective in mobilising sentiment and action. Indeed, when asked 'what does communism mean for you?' the most frequent response given by Perugian communists was, echoing Lenin, 'being a protagonist of history'.

This communist myth and larger world-view provides members with a powerful sense of purpose and belonging: 'purpose' in the communist cause (which in global terms means liberating mankind from capitalism and class oppression) and 'belonging' in the sense of comradeship that comes from sharing that historical mission. As noted earlier, 'belonging' is predicated upon a hierarchy of identities that nest one within the other. These combine in molecular fashion to form a chain of identification that extends from the local party section upwards to the national leadership and beyond to the international communist movement and the worldwide struggle against capitalism. Again there are close parallels with the organisation of the Catholic Church. Traditionally, the Church and the PCI have always represented much more than national groups; 'one inspired mainly by its universal religious mission and the other closely linked to the Soviet Union as the guiding power behind the socialist revolution' (Galli and Prandi 1970: 13).

| PCI Self-Definition | Anti-Communist Cold War Stereotype |
|---|---|
| Independent thinkers. Radicals. Political vanguard (raised social and political consciousness) | Doctrinaire ideologues. Deluded fanatics |
| Revolutionaries (protagonists in a project of social change) Dedicated, hard-working, honest | Social misfits. Amoral. Deviants. Perfidious and devious |
| Part of the Marxist intellectual heritage | Atheistic Marxists, enemies of Christianity |
| Agents engaged in a worldwide struggle against capitalism and imperialism | Puppets. Instruments of Soviet foreign policy |
| On the side of history/progress | On the side of Russian and the Eastern bloc dictatorships |
| Fighting for the emancipation of the working class | Enemies of freedom. On the side of evil |
| Comrades; united in solidarity | Barbarians. Destroyers of Catholic Civilisation (Church, family, private property) |
| Anti-Fascists Dangerous subversives Liberators of Italy Heroes of the Resistance | Not to be trusted with power |
| Anti-system (opposed to corruption and patronage) | Anti-democratic/anti-Western |
| Different from the rest of society (morally, politically, ideologically, historically) | Different from society (Aliens. Outsiders. Exponents of a foreign culture, i.e. Russian despotism) |

**Figure 1.** The construction of PCI identity after 1947

An 'ideal type' of communist identity as constructed by the PCI may thus be represented schematically (if somewhat simplistically) in Figure 1. The 'oppositional' and conflictual dimension of that identity emerges most clearly in the case of the 1948 general election in Italy and in the stark counter-image of communism mounted primarily by Catholic forces during the Cold War period. Confronted with the real possibility of a communist-socialist victory the DC and Catholic Church embarked upon a frenzied campaign of 'Red' scaremongering which transformed the electoral campaign into a manichaean struggle of apocalyptic proportions. The vote was depicted as a battle not simply between Catholicism and Marxism, but between good and evil, Christ and anti-Christ, Rome and Moscow (Kogan 1983: 39). Communists were depicted as exponents of an alien creed. They were atheistic Marxists, agents of Moscow who would destroy the very foundations of Catholic civilisation if elected into office. The result was a resounding defeat for the communist-socialist alliance.

## Ethnicity as Revolutionary Strategy

The defeat of 1948 led PCI leaders to reconsider both their strategy and their identity for, as Gramsci and others had argued, the creation of a collective identity, both as a nation and as a class, is a precondition of revolution. The aim behind the self-conscious aspect of PCI identity construction was to create not simply a revolutionary party but a revolutionary counter-culture. Whereas Lenin's vanguard party model stressed the idea of the capture of the bourgeois state by a highly trained group of professional subversives bound together by strict, almost military discipline, the PCI elaborated a different strategy, central to which was the idea of 'hegemony'.

This can be explained briefly as follows. PCI leaders had problems applying Bolshevik theory to the idea of revolution in the West. The reason was simply that these were far more developed and politically sophisticated nations with a more complex state and class structure. There was no Winter Palace to storm, no despotic Tsar to be toppled and no one single source of power and control centre waiting to be captured. Furthermore, Bolshevik-style seizure of power was not a very promising option in 1945 as Allied forces still occupied most of Italy. PCI partisans, though armed and experienced, were concentrated in northern and central Italy and the peasants in the south were unlikely to rally in support. Neither was the Red Army likely to cross the Rubicon and come to the rescue (as many PCI members had hoped).

Revolutionary action, therefore, required a more sophisticated revolutionary theory. Consequently, the PCI leadership decided to postpone the insurrection until a later date: the immediate priority was securing political stability and eradicating the last vestiges of Fascism. Hence, the PCI took the unprecedented step of becoming a constitutional party committed to the new ('bourgeois') democratic Republic.

But even before all this, Gramsci, writing from prison in the 1930s, had begun to elaborate a new kind of Marxism. Gramsci's main contribution to Marxist thought was a shift of emphasis from dogmatic economic determinism – which held that change in the relations of production would precipitate an inevitable change of consciousness – to a stress on ideology, 'hegemony' and the relative autonomy of 'superstructure'.

## The PCI's Concept of 'Hegemony'

In simple terms hegemony means the predominance of one social class over others. However, 'hegemony' is achieved not simply via economic and political control by a dominant class, but by its success in projecting its own particular world-view, so that this then is accepted as 'common sense' and part of the 'natural order'.

Gramsci's argument was that class struggle had to be waged on two fronts: a 'war of manoeuvre' and a 'war of Position'. In other words, while preparing for a possible moment of armed insurrection the Party must also instigate a 'passive revolution' through the slow conquest or overthrow of strategic institutions – schools, clubs, churches, trade unions, pressure groups, newspapers, journals, recreational associations, radio – all of which he saw as agents of socialisation.

This strategy envisaged a slow domination of society in all its institutional manifestations through the creation of a ramified network of organisations either controlled by, or allied to, the Party and always under its intellectual tutelage. Through an umbrella of satellite bodies the PCI would create a powerful communications network, a bloc of social forces through which it could diffuse a proletarian and Marxist world-view to challenge the hegemony of the bourgeoisie.

The anthropological significance of this is that revolution is seen not only as the transfer of political and economic power but as the spread of new forms of consciousness and experience. It is in effect 'the culmination of the Marxist process as a total cultural reintegration of society' (Williams 1960: 586).

What is envisaged here is not only a new social order, but the instrument for its achievement: the Party itself. The PCI is conceived as the 'New Society' in embryo 'growing up inside the womb of the old society', to use Marx and Engels' metaphor. Membership of the PCI means membership of this embryonic culture or, as one PCI theoretician put it, '[it] means entering into a life community, sharing a special sort of 'citizenship' and participating with other members in a common existential experience. To militate in such a party means not only assuming organisational duties, but the attempt to spread the proper conception of an associate life, its proper values and styles of life' (Baldassare 1983: 42).

In practical terms, this strategy was incorporated into the aforementioned 'Partito Nuovo' model of 1944 (discussed earlier) whose presence was to be felt in every community. The idea was to create a 'mass Bolshevik party' that would draw the masses into the web of communist influence (displacing the Catholic Church in the process) wherein its hegemonic forces could carry out their socialising function.

For years the PCI was able to follow a two-track strategy: the message to the membership was to accept the rules of bourgeois parliamentary democracy, but be prepared to take up arms. Meanwhile, the idea of insurrection, which was neither realistic nor a vote winner, was gradually allowed to recede whilst the PCI leadership constructed its new 'democratic' and 'Eurocommunist' identity. However, many older members still cling to their Bolshevik identity and the view that the Party should 'do what they did in Russia'. This resulted in the early 1980s in a serious generational and ideological clash between Eurocommunists and hardliners. Similar conflicts occurred in all Western communist parties, most of which were split and devastated as a result, but this did not happen to the PCI, which is perhaps testimony to the strength of its collective identity.

## Conclusion: Problems with the PCI'S Revolutionary Identity

Communist hegemony, executed through the process of identity construction, helps to explain the rise of the so-called 'communist sub-culture' throughout Central Italy. The construction of that identity has always been a two-way process; in part the result of a conscious PCI revolutionary strategy, in part a consequence and reaction to the forces of anti-communism. Thus, as stated at the outset, identity, like ethnicity, is relational and oppositional and crystallises in situations of political adversity. In Italy the major forces of social and political opposition are the DC and its allies and the PCI. This conflict, which has become institutionalised, reflects a far deeper polarisation between two cultural systems, one Catholic, the other Communist, which continues to divide Italian society.

A more comprehensive analysis of PCI identity should study the changing nature of communist hegemony and identity, which is beyond the scope of this chapter. What can be said, however, is that PCI hegemony has been progressively eroded by changes in Italian society. The PCI no longer exercises the same degree of control over the channels of popular communication as it did in the past. The growth of the mass media and television in particular (which the PCI cannot control) has undermined its influence, and the section and neighbourhood have declined in importance as loci of power and influence. In short, the Communist World and Catholic World are no longer containable micro-societies and both are conspicuously failing to recruit young people and socialise new members into their respective cultural systems.

Furthermore, PCI identity has not been immune to changes taking place elsewhere in the Communist World outside Italy. With the decline of 'Eurocommunism' and the increasing rift between the PCI and Moscow that was brought to a head with the Soviet invasion of Afghanistan in 1979 and the suppression of the Solidarity trade union in Poland in 1981, the PCI has been forced to re-evaluate not only its own path to socialism, but the meaning of communism itself. The conclusion reached by its former leader, Enrico Berlinguer, writing in 1982, was that the historical phase initiated by the Bolshevik revolution was over and that Moscow-style communism was now a degenerate and spent force. From the PCI's perspective, this judgement was vindicated by the popular upheavals in Eastern Europe towards the end of 1989, and the collapse in turn of each of the old Stalinist bureaucracies and communist party regimes, beginning with Poland and East Germany and continuing with Czechoslovakia and Romania. While the PCI enthusiastically welcomed these changes and has pioneered the critique of orthodox communism, the 'communist' label has nevertheless continued to pose problems for it, particularly in its quest for political credibility and electoral success. With these considerations in mind, Acchile Occhetto, the PCI's leader, seized upon the crisis of communism in Eastern Europe to announce on 14 November 1989 that the Party was considering dropping the word 'communist' from its name. The effect of this announcement on the

Party leadership generally, and the rank and file in particular, was highly contentious and deeply divisive (see Shore 1990: 192-95). While some PCI members see this as evidence of a profound identity crisis and the Party's loss of direction and purpose, others see it as a positive step and the only real chance the Party has of forging a new identity that will eventually lead it out of the political ghetto of permanent opposition into which it has been cast for over forty years. How, or in what form, the PCI will emerge from this process is uncertain. What is certain, however, is that the PCI's extraordinary influence on Italian culture and society will remain for a long time to come. But in a similar vein, the dominant or hegemonic role of political parties in general over Italian society is unlikely to diminish in the foreseeable future either.

## References

Allum, P. (1973), *Italy: Republic Without Government?* London: Weidenfeld and Nicolson

_____(1979), 'Italy', in S. Henig (ed.), *Political Parties in the European Community*. London: Allen and Unwin

Anderson, B. (1983), *Imagined Communities: Reflections on the Origin and Spread of Nationalism*. London: Verso

Baldassare, A. (1983), 'Un nuovo partito di massa?', *Democrazia e Diritto*, no. XXIII (Jan./Feb.), pp. 41–64

Barnes, S. (1967), *Party Democracy: Politics in an Italian Socialist Federation*. London: Yale University Press

Barth, F. (1969), 'Introduction', in F. Barth (ed.), *Ethnic Groups and Boundaries*. Bergen: Universitetsforlaget

Bloomfield, J. (1985), Review of D. Forgacs and G. Nowell-Smith 'The Cultural Conditions for Political Transformation', *Marxism Today*, vol. 29, no.6 (June), p. 40

Christian, W. (1972), *Person and God in a Spanish Valley*. New York: Seminar Press

Cohen, Abner (1974a), 'Introduction', in A. Cohen (ed.) *Urban Ethnicity*. ASA Monograph No. 12. London: Tavistock

_____(1974b), *Two-Dimensional Man: An Essay on the Anthropology of Power and Symbolism in Complex Society*. London: Routledge and Kegan Paul

Cohen, Anthony (ed.) (1982), *Belonging: Identity and Social Organisation in British Rural Cultures*. Manchester: Manchester University Press

Cohen, Ronald (1978), 'Ethnicity: Problem and Focus in Anthropology', *Annual Review of Anthropology*, vol.7, pp. 379–403

Epstein, A. L. (1978), *Ethos and Identity: Three Studies in Ethnicity*. London: Tavistock

*Espresso* (1983), 'Lottizzati di tutta Italia', *L'Espresso*, 13 February, pp. 6–11

Ferrara, G. (1983), 'Ma quanti soldi per i partiti?', *La Repubblica*, 8 February, p. 8

Galli, G. and Prandi, A. (1970), *Patterns of Political Participation in Italy*. New Haven and London: Yale University Press

Grillo, R. (1974), 'Ethnic Identity and Social Stratification on a Kampala Housing Estate', in A. Cohen (ed.), *Urban Ethnicity*. ASA Monograph No. 12. London: Tavistock

Kertzer, D. (1980), *Comrades and Christians*. Cambridge: Cambridge University Press

Kogan, N. (1983), *Political History of Italy: The Postwar Years*. New York: Thomas Cromwell Co.

McKenzie, W. (1978), *Political Identity*. Manchester: Manchester University Press

Nichols, P. (1973), *Italia, Italia*. Glasgow: Fontana

PCI (1983), *Statuto del Partito comunista italiano*. Rome: Iter

_____(1989), *Organizzazione, dati, statistiche*. Rome: Ufficio documentazione e analisi del PCI

Poggi, G. (1968), *L'Organizzazione partitica del PCI e della DC*. Bologna: Il Mulino

Pridham, G. (1981), *The Nature of the Italian Party System*. London: Croom Helm

Riccamboni, G. (1976), 'The Italian Communist Party and the Catholic World', *Social Compass*, vol. 23, no. 2/3, pp. 141–69

Sassoon, D. (1986), *Contemporary Italy*. New York and London: Longman

Scalfari, E. (1983), Editorial Comment, *La Repubblica*, 6 February

Sebastiani, C. (1983), 'I funzionari', in A. Accornero et al. (eds), *L'identità" comunista*, pp. 79–159. Rome: Riuniti

Seymour-Smith, C. (1986), *Macmillan Dictionary of Anthropology*. London: Macmillan

Shore, C. (1985), 'Organisation, Ideology, Identity: The Italian Communist Party'. Unpublished D.Phil. thesis, Sussex University

_____(1989), 'Patronage and Bureaucracy in Complex Societies: Social Rules and Social Relations in an Italian University', *Journal of the Anthropological Society of Oxford*, vol. XX, no. 1

_____(1990), *Italian Communism: The Escape from Leninism*. London:Pluto Press

_____(1991), 'Lenin and the Crisis of Communism: The View from the Inside', *Government and Opposition*, vol. 26, no. 1/2, Jan./Feb.

Silverman, S. (1975), *Three Bells of Civilisation: The Life of an Italian Hill Town*. New York: Columbia University Press

Smooha, S. (1985), 'Ethnic Groups', in A. and J. Kuper (eds), The *Social Science Encyclopaedia*. London: Routledge

Wallman, S. (1986), 'Ethnicity and the Boundary Process in Context', in David Mason and J. Rex (eds), Theories of Race and *Ethnic Relations*, pp. 226–45. Cambridge: Cambridge University Press

White, C. (1980), *Patrons and Partisans*. Cambridge: Cambridge University Press

Williams, G. (1960), 'The Concept of Egemonia in the Thought of Antonio Gramsci', *Journal of the History of Ideas*, vol. XXI, pp. 586–99

# 3

# Who Can Tell the Tale? Texts and the Problem of Generational and Social Identity in a Tuscan Rural *Comune*

## *Ronald Frankenberg*

In our halls is hung
Armoury of the invincible Knights of old:
We must be free or die, who speak the tongue
That Shakespeare spake; the faith and morals hold
Which Milton held. – In everything we are sprung
Of Earth's first blood, have titles manifold.

Wordsworth

… texts are worldly, to some degree they are events, and even when they appear to deny it, they are nevertheless a part of the social world, human life, and of course, the historical moments in which they are located and interpreted.

Edward Said, *The World, The Text and The Critic*

### The Divine Write of the Sovereign Observer?

The chariots of both social and cultural anthropology run on wheels of small diameter; they frequently turn full circle. A recurring theme, introduced by Malinowski, has been who has the right to retail (re-tale?) myths, to whom and in what circumstances of cultural co-presence and linguistic style. (Wholesalers like Lévi-Strauss were, even then, less respected in the anglophone world.) As a postgraduate student I was an innocent, fresh from a standard course on Natural Sciences and mainly unaware, like most in the modern (but not the post-modern) era, of the guiles and necessities of persuasive rhetoric. The name of Kenneth Burke was known to me from Goffman (1959) and I knew that shop assistants and others 'presented the self in daily life' but I took it for granted, at least in the writings through which I presented myself to my teachers, that Malinowski's right to answer this kind of question about Trobriander's tales, like Gluckman's on the Lozi's and Evans-Pritchard's on the Zande's, required no more justification than Newton's right to describe universal laws of motion, Einstein's to show how these descriptions needed to be modified and Mendeléev's to arrange chemical elements in the periodic table. Scientists, social or natural, like Trobriand Chiefs, Azande Nobles and Lozi Aristocrats seemed to me then naturally to know what was true in their own culture. Data were given, merely there to be intelligently observed and, despite their name, facts, like the talents that dis- or uncovered them, were born to conceptual analysis not made by it.

In recent years, largely unnoticed by each other, the linguistically aware scholars of Oxford, treading in the footsteps of Ardener (1989) on the rocky beaches of Northern Europe, and the literary aware students of the Californian seaboard, following Bourdieu's footsteps in the sandy deserts of North Africa (Geertz 1988: 91–7), have converged in a concern to legitimate not their élite informants' right to produce texts for the consumption of ethnographers and others but their own to produce textual writings. Indeed it was not until reading Geertz's *Works and Lives* (1988) that I became fully aware of the significance of such activity. However, it did not then come as a complete surprise, even if I treated my field notes and doctoral thesis (1954) as, so to speak, Rip Van Winkle texts talking to me across years between, imagined as empty of structuralism and post-structuralism; Sartre, Lévi-Strauss and Foucault. I could not fail to notice at the time and in the re-reading of my notes on the media aftermath of my study of conflicts between persons and groups of men and of women in a North Wales village that while one side in the dispute denied the legitimacy of my specific account of the local events of 1953, in which we had jointly shared, both sides hinted that reducing their (or even our common) social life to a written or typed, let alone a printed text was illegitimate in itself. Indeed, my later monograph sought to analyse, *inter alia*, how when written records of events were perceived as necessary, villagers 'lost' them or contrived to cause them to be written by 'strangers' (of whom the ethnographer was but one specific exemplar) who were in one sense within the processes of social and cultural action and in another, outside it (see Frankenberg 1957 and especially additional material in the 1989 reprint). The typewritten writings I produced as secretary of village activities owed their usefulness as a potential source of factional and individual power precisely to the fact that they were at once perceived as those of an objective outsider but could also be repudiated as coming from an incomplete insider who had failed adequately to understand both spoken Welsh and local values. For villagers to make their own notes at all, let alone to make them publicly available, was a multiple betrayal through petrification of the dynamic orality of both village life and the nature of spoken Welsh which, as I then argued, was in any case a final line of defence. Even an intelligent and determined Englishman who could learn to read and speak Welsh could only do so in the formal 'written' style of the 'crachach' (aristocracy?).

Unlike other European societies to which I refer below, the Welsh villagers I studied were only 'people of the book' in a very special sense. As on a wider scale, Italians, and especially Tuscans, recognise Dante and Manzoni and the British, Shakespeare and Milton, villagers of Llansantffraid Glynceiriog identified certain books as identifying them. They kept Welsh Bibles and folklore pamphlets like Mari Jones a'i Feibl on their dresser shelves below the print called Salem and alongside the works of their eponymous poets, Ceiriog and Eos Ceiriog, but these had been written by others long ago and no one after adolescence read them now. They were non-interactive talismans of Welshness and belonging in a situation in which shared identity in fact arose out of fluidly differential interaction between opposing, overlapping identities built from difference between men and women, church and chapel, Welsh- and English-speaking. Such interaction certainly should not be recorded in any detail in apparently indelible print.

## The Rewards of Writing-Up

The publication of my book about their village changed my identity in a way that, had they known of it, they would have found completely mysterious. For it (and therefore they) gave me a right, if not a prescriptive one, since I had not worked in a proper African society, to join the Association of Social Anthropologists, where I found that I was both allowed and expected to call by their given names those who, in our own field were, like Wordsworth, Milton and Shakespeare more widely, destined to be known to written posterity by their unadorned surnames. With more tact than honesty I described at the time ( (1963) 1989), echoing the novelist Barbara Pym, how the anthropologist talked of 'my' people and their views. I did not reveal that the surnamed ones, those who had most effectively written up at Oxford, Edinburgh, Cambridge, London or Manchester what they had written down in Sudan or on Pacific Islands, generalised the truths of the societies they had themselves studied. Barnes (1979) might go down in history as the scholar who both revealed that the prompt conversion of down- to up-writing was an ethical imperative of the field (or post-Field) and showed that New Guinea was not (necessarily) Sudan (1962,1971). While Gluckman (1965: 4) characterised Frazer as an 'If I were a horse ...' anthropologist, he himself and his senior colleagues sometimes seemed to their juniors to be 'If a Lozi were a Welshman' (or perhaps in a cyclical double translation, 'If the man in the Clapham Omnibus were a Lozi') anthropologists.

Listening at a conference of the African Studies Association called White Presence and Power in Africa convened by the Oxford historian of Africa, Terence Ranger in 1978, and attended by other historians of Africa, most of whom were not African historians, I learned that apotheotic surnaming was not, as I had supposed, irreversible even in the relatively short term. In this context (Brown 1979 in the special issue of *The Journal of African History* devoted to its proceedings) Gluckman became Max Gluckman (sometimes shortened but not made authoritative by surnaming) and a primary informant whose experiences as recorded in archives and court records were as or more significant than his own interpretations of them. I realised that the identities of anthropologists complemented those of the people they textually recorded and arose principally out of other scholars' interpretation of the nature and legitimacy of the recording. Their subjects might sometimes confirm this scholarly identity, as when the Lozi use Gluckman's book as a text for their law, the Lamba, their ethnographer, Doke's book to explain their kinship system to a new young scholar (Anna Wong: personal communication), or the Bemba, Richards's as a justification for their ceremonies. The subjects of ethnographic study, at least initially and often still, did not and could not have their own inscribed texts to deny the authority of their chroniclers.

## *Bei Uns* It Is Different?

The problem I wish to attack on the basis of my fieldwork in Northern Italy is whether the continual creation of texts there necessarily has to crystallise and unify local identities in such a way as to make them disappear through over-identification. I predicted in the 1950s that, once the people of Glynceiriog ceased to be united by their shared and comprehended divisions, their local identity would cease to be overtly marked and therefore, perhaps, to exist and this seems in fact to have happened.

When I went in 1982 to the small town on which the Comune of Tavarnelle Val di Pesa is centred to study the dramatisation of sickness in the context of the then recent Italian health reform, I was not surprised to find the people I met conscious of their general identities as Italians, Tuscans and Tavarnellini/e or of their specific differences in terms of social affiliation to Communist Party, to Christian Democracy or to the Catholic faith. I knew enough of Italian and local history to expect to find symbolised differential identity based on generational difference between those who had endured or enjoyed fascism, those who had fought in the Resistance and the generation of *sessantottini*, those whose sense of self had been fired, one way or another by the events of 1968 and the immediately following years.

I expected to seek the bases of community, as I had taught generations of students to do, in difference but also in commensality, common residence, communal attendance at worship, and common sharing of daily and festive leisure pursuits. Co-textuality as a creator of context took me by surprise. For the people of Tavarnelle are accustomed to inscribe and have inscribed their diverse and their shared consciousness in texts which sometimes, through the Assessore Culturale Comunale, are officially made available, at least in theory, to a wider audience. All events are preceded by bill-posted printed manifesti and few, even ephemeral, celebrations are left unrecorded in print. During the eighteen months that I lived full-time in the Comune, quite apart from letters and articles in the Florentine newspaper *La Nazione* and the regional paper *Il Paese*, the Comune published a sociological treatise on the social impact of the change from *mezzadria* (sharecropping) agriculture (De Martino 1982), a set of schoolchildren's essays about the lives of their grandparents (Cresti 1984), and an illustrated edition of the text of the play that I am here using as my central illustrative motif (Chiti et al. 1982). It was only the exhaustion of available funds which prevented publication of the following year's play as a written text in addition to the only partially successful videotape recording of its performance. Aesthetically rebellious young men and women organised, in the basement of the Municipal Library, with Comune support in cash if not entirely in spirit, an Art Gallery and a Dada Art Society which put on exhibitions and published printed catalogues of their own and other's avant garde work, *pour épater*, if not *le bourgeois*, at least *il Sindaco* – the mayor – and the committee of the Partito Comunista Italiano. The Comune published a detailed illustrated guide in Italian to the more orthodox treasures of art and architecture within the Comune. The wife of the Comune secretary, an official of the central state, known to be conservative and presumed under the rules of patronage to be Christian Democrat, published two books (Pini Duti 1981a, b), one in prose and one in verse, on her life and on her experiences as a cancer sufferer. Catalogued photographic exhibitions recorded traditional methods and social relations of olive oil and wine production and, separately, Partisan experience in fighting Italian Fascism and German Nazism. Printed press releases recorded Tavarnelle's establishment of a Toscanini Prize for the musician who in any year contributed most to peace, and the citations of its successive award to and acceptance in person by Zubin Mehta and Ricardo Muti. I began to feel that the description of ethnography as the collection and translation of texts was indeed apt.

These texts are, however, part of a continuing series, the meanings of which change over time. Such changes are related to and meaningful within social context and social interaction. They may be overtly addressed to the outsider and can thus be repudiated, if they prove over-divisive or too revelatory of unshared aspects of internal identity. Their significance within the community is felt only by the natives although it may be appreciated by an ethnographer. Indeed as I hope to show, outside observers, by being made aware of the contradictions, may, like Zande nobles, help to legitimate native interpretations which remain semi-opaque within the generationally and politically divided cultural discourse of Tavarnelle itself. The sovereign right of English academics and members of the ASA to publish and not be damned for their trouble holds partial and useful sway even in a remote Tuscan village. In a similar way, in a small town where little goes unnoticed, I was able to address the PCI Sectional Congress at La Rampa (general workers' club) and attend the welcoming party to the new provincial District Secretary of Christian Democracy at the MCL Cercolo (Catholic Workers' Club) without comment by townspeople or myself.

Had I commented, my actions could have been dismissed as those of an ignorant outsider, even a tourist. I was referred to in some public situations as 'L'Inglese' and in Communist Party functions as 'nostro compagno Inglese' – our English Comrade. My assumption that my English affiliations were so well known as to be mentionable to a Catholic professional friend in private led to a sudden but definitive loss of rapport. I had identified myself within the system and had accordingly aroused mutual expectations of associative and disassociative behaviour.

## Texts in Context: Place — Tavarnelle

Tavarnelle Val di Pesa is a long-established settlement in the Chianti region of the Firenze Provincia some 25 miles from the city of Florence. It became an independent Comune in 1893 and achieved its present name in 1909. There are three major concentrated settlements within the Comune. First, Sambuca, which has a population of 747 and is now adjoined by a small but important industrial estate. Most of the firms on this estate and indeed elsewhere in the Comune come within the legal definition of small, having fewer than ten employees, but there is a large co-operatively owned and run winery (the boundary of the Chianti Classico Area runs through the Comune). One of the major caravan manufacturers in Italy, Laika, is also on the estate. The two large firms employ on average 150 persons each. San Donato in Poggio (Calzolai 1983) is a small, picturesque walled village with 877 inhabitants. Despite its 'revival' of a supposed mediaeval pageant called La Bruscellata, under the auspices of the Chianti Classico Consorzio, and with a glossy brochure printed partly in English, it seems to have been founded in the eighteenth century. Behind its plain exteriors are concealed elegant villas and gardens which, it is said, were often used in the past as (not always legitimate) second homes by rich aristocrats from Florence, Siena and even as far away as Rome.

The largest single unit in the Comune is, however, Tavarnelle itself which houses around 3600 of the Comune's official population of 6400. Tavarnelle is the main commercial focus; a ribbon of shops, banks, houses and cafes stretching out towards Florence in the North and Siena to the South, along the Roman Via Cassia (now called Via Roma) and by-passed by a motorway link, the Autostrada del Palio. At its centre is the central market square dominated by the Municipio, the Carabinieri post, the former Fascist Headquarters used until 1983 as a middle school, and the Banca Toscana. Close to it is the Co-op and the other main Bank, now its subsidiary, the ancient Monte dei Paschi, and it is faced on the side furthest from the Via Roma by La Rampa, the Cercolo of the ARCI, which includes dance hall, bar and other facilities and is the centre of town life for young people of both sexes and for older men. On the other side of the square on the Via Roma itself is the principal cafe and bus stop and the barber shop, pharmacy and other principal shops including fashionable jewellers, a furrier and boutiques selling men's and women's leather clothes and Gucci and similar fashionware. A little, but significant, distance along the road away from the centre and towards Siena is the less popular MCL Cercolo, the Catholic Workers Club, adjoining the headquarters of the Christian Democrat Party. La Rampa, named after the long pile of rubble which it replaced when it was co-operatively built, is separated by the multi-purpose hall, both cinema and ballroom, from the Municipal Art Gallery, the Library and office facilities for the trade unions, the dominant PCI and the tiny socialist party (PSI).

Thanks to some serious errors of aim by the members of a New Zealand artillery unit during the Second World War, the central part of Tavarnelle has few buildings even as old as the nineteenth century. There is a very small and inconspicuous chapel not far off near another cafe and 'neutral' cinema. There are, however, no other overt symbols of Christianity in the town centre. The cinema, lacking political affiliations to either ARCI or MCL, is also used for cross-sectarian gatherings and by the socialists if they invite a guest expected to attract a large enough audience. Funeral processions of native inhabitants usually traverse three sides of the square on their way from house to church to cemetery. Each end of the ribbon is punctuated by ancient churches. The one at the Northern end is a fine Romanesque Pieve, San Pietro in Boscolo, the courtyard of which was the setting for the second year's play. The more popular parish church of Santa Lucia al Borghetto is set to one side at the other end of the through road and was entered for the first time by many communist villagers when it was the setting for an orchestral concert in the first Festa del Paese in 1983. There is another even more attractive Romanesque Pieve near San Donato, and a mediaeval monastery in the hamlet of Morrocco in between has recently been re-occupied, for the first time in many centuries, at the invitation of the late Cardinal Benelli, by a group of, as it happens Australian, Carmelite Sisters. Sambuca has its own modern church, its more ancient and remote predecessor having been deconsecrated and converted to a dwelling house.

Many crossroads in the rural part of the Comune are, as would be expected, marked by crucifixes or Marian shrines. The ancient and famous Badia a Passignano monastery lies just within the boundaries of the Comune on the hill road towards Greve. When I lived in Tavarnelle it belonged to a foreign syndicate who hoped to turn it into a hotel but the refusal of local architects to plan the alterations led to its purchase by the Italian government and its return to the Church and its ancient monastic use. It is now possible, with some negotiation and careful timing, once more to visit the Comune's greatest, but least advertised, art treasure, one of Ghirlandaio's three Last Suppers.

One of the major aristocratic houses of the neighbourhood is now occupied by a Hare Krishna settlement, but their impact on the spiritual and other life of the Comune is purely visual and commercial. The nucleus of Tavarnelle which I have described is surrounded by stark new apartment houses, mostly blocks of flats, built within the last few years. Various peripheral services were built or refurbished by the Comune during 1982, 1983 and 1984. These include at the north end, near the parish church, a gymnasium, a new middle school, a new nursery and infant school and the playing field. There is also a youth hostel adjoining a *Pineta* (pine grove), and a nineteenth-century hospital, and newly constructed old people's home and day centre. The Misericordia, an ancient church medical charity which is now independent, has its recently renovated 'sede' (seat), blood donor centre and ambulance garage near to the hospital.

## Texts in Context — Economic Change

All this development and prosperity is the consequence and culmination of the concentration of much of the population of the Comune into the three main centres, which happened throughout the 1970s and is continuing. An official census in 1981 showed a 66% increase in industrial employment, 42% in commerce and 177% in services over the 1971 figures (De Martino 1982: 13). Figures provided by the Comune to the PCI economic conference on Chianti in May 1982 suggested that 50% of wage earners came from within the Comune and another 30% from neighbouring Comuni. Only 10% came from outside the *provincia* altogether. In 1961, three-quarters of the population still worked in agriculture, overwhelmingly as sharecropping tenants – *mezzadri*, with a small proportion of *coltivatori diretti*, working on their own farms or as tenants, and a somewhat larger number of wage-earning labourers.

When large estates were sold by their often absentee landlords, the *case coloniche* (estate farmsteads) in the countryside were offered for rent or sale to their occupants who showed little enthusiasm for their retention. Remotely situated and without services, their picturesque situation was scant recompense for the bitter cold of winter and the lack of water supply in summer. Now that it was possible to find other employment either as the proprietor of, or a wage earner in, a small business, there was no incentive to stay in them, especially since it was often possible to retain, rent or buy enough land nearer to the village or the main road to produce wine and olive oil for the household. Former peasants could not afford the electrification of farmsteads, the subsequent installation of water pumps and telephones and the purchase of cars for shopping in Tavarnelle, or even Florence or Siena. Some romantic urban Italians and numerous Germans, Swiss and the occasional Englishman could afford all this especially since the asking price of *case coloniche* was so reasonable. Many have also been acquired and furnished for occasional holiday use by companies as well as by wealthy individuals from different parts of Europe.

It was surprising to me, at least before I saw the play to be described, that there appeared to be little resentment amongst local people about this situation, since there were many young couples without the prospect of acquiring a house in which to start married life. Even for these, apparently, the memory of the hardships of rural life is still sufficiently fresh, and the knowledge that *case coloniche* were temporary residences for *mezzadri* families and the inconvenience of their position made foreigners welcome to them. The foreigners in question were, of course, also potential customers, employers, entrepreneurs and sources of amusement. Since many of them were artists and intellectuals their presence was a source of prestige, and provided custom for certain kinds of fashionable business enterprise and potential patrons of local arts and cultural performance. Despite housing shortages few workers leave and as we have seen, there has been little other in-migration to the area, especially of directly competitive workers. There is in fact real resentment against poorer immigrants from the South, Sicily or Sardinia who have spilled over from the immigration into the larger scale industrial area of Poggibonsi on the way to Siena. People from the Mezzogiorno with whom I was friendly were well aware of this and it emerged frequently in conversation with those on both sides of the divide. One very right-wing farmer, who had nevertheless been a Partisan hero, told me in explanation that he liked to shoot foreigners whether they were

Tedeschi – Germans or, as he called immigrants from the south, Africani. The expression of such extreme hostility was unusual but animosity in general was enhanced when in 1983 a Mafia 'hit squad' descended briefly on the Comune by way of Pisa airport and successfully gunned down the distant cousin of a 'traitor' Palermo boss as part of a long drawn out campaign to shame him into returning home from the United States to his promised death.

## Texts in Context – *Feste*, the Yearly Round

There is in no sense a regular integrated annual cycle of activities in which all or most Tavarnellini/e are involved, but the various overlapping identities within the Comune are regularly symbolised by the dedication of time and the use of space. The most frequent example of this is the weekly market-day invasion of the space in front of the Banca Toscana by farmers from the outlying areas. Sixty-seven per cent of the voters of the Comune voted Communist in the early 1980s and the number was higher in the wards of Tavarnelle itself. The Comune council of twenty members had a permanent Communist majority leavened by one Socialist, an outsider in many different ways, and four Christian Democrats. The three *sezione* of the PCI organise during the year three separate *Feste de l'Unità* in the Comune in Sambuca, in San Donato and in Tavarnelle itself. The one in Tavarnelle is the major event and occupies and dominates the central market square from dawn to past midnight for seven to ten days each year. During this time the sight of its stalls, flares, dancing and banners, the smells of outside cooking and the sounds of speeches, vie with each other to remind supporters and enemies alike of the importance of the PCI to the past, present, and it seemed in 1982 and 1983, to the future of Tavarnelle and its people. Funerals, traffic in general and the sleep of foreigners and Christian Democrats are seriously disrupted.

In 1982, it was opened at 9.30 on a Thursday evening in early September by a brass band parade and concert in the central square. It closed about midnight on Sunday, ten days later, with the last waltz of a *Ballo Liscio* – open air ballroom dancing – to a live orchestra, also in the square. In between there had been model car and aeroplane competitions in the stadium, several films, a choral concert and a duo playing Vivaldi in the cinema cafe. Two public discussions had been held on 'What does and does not go in Tavarnelle?' and 'The future of the sliding scale of Wages'. There had been Cabaret performances in the square and in La Rampa, and so-called 'animazione' workshops for children with clowns and actors on stilts provided by members of the group who put on the play to be discussed below. There were pizza and kebab stalls and wine bars available virtually all the time as well as open air dinners for 50–80 people each evening. The dance on the final evening was preceded by a political meeting with local and national Communist speakers. There was an early evening athletics meeting and stalls at which one could buy books and posters or enter competitions for bottles of wine or children's toys. The *Festa de l'Unità* obviously adds up to more than this bare account of events describes. It brings families together and out of their homes, not merely into public spaces but into the public space, which except on weekly market days and for promenading on Sundays, is used mainly as a car park and usually merely passed through by women on the way to shops and lingered in by older men and adolescents. Its invasion by expressively labelled members of the PCI and its supporters is a demonstration of power denied, as we shall see, to the Socialists and Christian Democrats. The *Festa* expresses support for, and its profits go to, the PCI newspaper, *L' Unità*. It also indicates solidarity with and participation in a national movement. Every locality in Italy has its *Festa* and there are apical *feste* at Florence, Siena and a national fortnight-long event in alternating years in Northern and Southern Italy. Coachloads of Tavarnelle PCI members and their families and friends go to these and their language, experience and symbols set the pattern for and are the inspiration of local organisation (Ferrara and Coppola 1983).

As it happened the news of the assassination of General Alberto Dalla Chiesa and his wife by the Palermo Mafia broke during the opening evening meeting of the *Festa* in 1982 and gave both the distant event and the local celebration of solidarity added meaning. So also did the funeral of a young communist militant and councillor, for which proceedings were interrupted on the first Saturday. He had been an active participant in organising the kind of leisure activities associated with the *Festa* before he succumbed to kidney failure and was reported to have asked that the event be neither cancelled nor postponed. It is not uncommon for families and friends from other parts of Italy and abroad, and especially the twinned town of Gagny in France, to time their visits to coincide with the *Festa de l'Unità*. (Tavarnelle is also twinned with Sutton in Surrey, but perhaps as markedly non-identical twins it is not surprising that official visitors from Sutton and Cheam are less in evidence.) The 1983 *Festa* was even more elaborate and advertised by a very glossy, A4-sized programme with 26 pages of advertisements for local businesses, by no means all of them run by Communists. I knew that several of them were indeed owned by Christian Democrat supporters. It was held much earlier and, surprisingly, in July, for the reason I later discovered that it was planned to hold a general festival for all the people of the Comune, *Tavarnelle in Festa*, at the usual September date.

The annual *Festa de l'Avanti* organised by the Socialists (PSI) is an altogether more modest affair. The only sign of its existence in central Tavarnelle is a handwritten notice pointing towards the Pineta on the southern outskirts where it is held. Leading Communist councillors do put in an appearance as a matter of courtesy, but its general attendance figures are relatively low and it has little overall impact or visibility. There are a small number of highly respected people, especially from surviving farm families, who are known to have been PSI supporters for many years and whose older members fought as Partisans under that banner. The leader of the PSI in 1983 was a councillor and a white-collar worker originating outside the Comune, a disability which he compounded by publicising his local discontents in the Florentine newspaper, *La Nazione*. This solution for his very real political frustrations upset the local feelings and loyalties of Christian Democrats as much as, or perhaps even more than, the Communists. The activities of these *feste* are very much scaled down versions of the *Feste de l'Unità* and virtually confined to the Pineta itself. The PSI's most successful public event in 1982-3 was a public meeting held in the cafe cinema and addressed by a 'turbulent priest', Gianni Baget Bozzo, then under Vatican interdict for trying to combine membership of the European Parliament with the exercise of his sacerdotal functions. Although effectively excluded from real political participation in Tavarnelle, the PSI exercised considerable provincial, regional and national power by the skilful exploitation of their minority Tertium Gaudens position led by the Machiavellian Prime Minister Craxi.

Christian Democracy in Tavarnelle is practised by consenting adults in private and indoors. Their one public meeting during my residence in Tavarnelle was public only in the sense that it was advertised by printed posters, quickly covered up everywhere except in the glass case outside the MCL Cercolo in the upstairs room of which it was held; and that I joined those few members who attended it. To my embarrassment, the speaker was introduced to every member of the audience individually. DC members do, however, attend *Feste de l'Amicizia* elsewhere and some also attended national celebratory meetings of the more right wing Catholic political action group, CL, *Comunione e Liberazione*. Quite apart from those Christians who covertly or overtly support the PCI and PSI, many other church members distance themselves from these semi- or officially approved political organisations. The Church has its own sacred spaces indoors, already described, and of course its cyclically repeated sacred times. An important one of these is Epiphany when children may receive gifts at home and themselves go into the streets to give adults gifts of sweets. By and large, however, the church members claim space in the public domain only through processions and, except for funerals, after dark. The candles of the Corpus Domini procession are answered by candles and illuminated flowering plants in the windows and on the balconies of the houses it passes and it is joined by both political and non-political believers. Once a year extra priests are called from retirement or elsewhere to bless each house individually. Neither the majority of local communists nor visiting English anthropologists fail to prepare their houses to receive this visitation. The more personal celebrations of the Church, like weddings and first communions, are attended by all. In the case of the latter it was possible to grade the degrees of belief, agnosticism or principled unbelief by whether relatives of celebrants sat or stood in the body of the church, stood at the back, stood *ad limen* in the covered space between consecrated and secular ground within the double doors, or remained, still dressed in their best clothes like full participants, in the small square outside.

From the children's point of view, the major annual festival is that of Carnival. The schools run trips to Viarreggio and while there is no Carnival procession in Tavarnelle itself, shops are stocked with masks, streamers and cheap sweets and toys. The two clubs co-ordinate their film programmes of animated cartoons and the children of militants on either side are 'licensed' to visit the others' club to see them. The visiting children in each case are easily identified by their hesitant appearance and their stationing themselves not too far from the door.

## A New *Festa*, A New (?) Text, A New Context

In 1983, as we have seen, the Comune initiated a Festa self-consciously intended to symbolise the unity and achievement of all Tavarnellini/e. It was, as I have said, to be held in September at the time usually set apart for the *Festa de l'Unità*, and a committee was set up to organise it which cut across usual divisions by including representatives of both clubs and of the Misericordia. The Communist council were not abdicating but they were not being exclusive either. In the terminology of their Catholic opponents they were not indulging in sectarian *triomfalismo*. The committee was chaired by a Communist councillor, it is true, but a man of national fame and standing. He was national full-time President of the Lega (of Co-operatives). Although he comes from the third or fourth generation of a well-established and respected Tavarnelle family, he has lived for much of his working life in Milan. The enemies which his militancy have made him, if such there be, are away from the locality. It might well have seemed also to be an appropriate time in the history of the Comune, as may already have become apparent. The success of the industrial and development policies put in train by the former communist mayor, signor Biagi, who had unfortunately died in October 1982 genuinely mourned by all sections, had become apparent to all. His successor Marcello Morandi, with wide local support, notwithstanding some opposition from provincial authorities of both PCI and the Church, had successfully continued his predecessor's policy of development and co-operation, especially with voluntary efforts, whether of the Misericordia blood donor and ambulance service, local entrepreneurs or of the Tavarnelle Friends of Classical Music. The increased local vote in the national elections of June 1983 and the success of the *Festa de l'Unità* at its earlier date suggested that the local PCI had nothing to fear.

The Comune spread streamer banners across the main street and a competition was organised amongst shopkeepers for the best window displays (photographed and later printed as a glossy calendar). There was an exhibition of local lace in the MCL Cercolo and of photographs of traditional life in La Rampa. In the main square there was an exhibition of agricultural machinery and equipment and a stall displaying traditional and modern methods of olive culture. Extensive stalls in the market square documented the local activities of the Misericordia who showed videos and recruited blood and organ donors. The local herbalists, a husband and wife team formerly associated with the now dead, famous Priest-healer of Morrocco, who had enjoyed a wide reputation beyond the limits of the Comune, had a large stall of their wares. Other stalls displayed and sold Chianti wines, *olio extra vergine* and various cooked foods including charcoal-broiled chicken, pork and beef as well as freshly prepared and baked pizza.

The Festa began on a Saturday evening with an angling contest, the first round of a week-long chess tournament and ballroom dancing. It ended eight days later with a midnight display of fireworks. In between the format was not dissimilar from that of a *Festa de l'Unità* but without the banners, national propaganda and distribution of the paper, and with such significant differences as a full orchestral concert in the parish church by the prestigious Tuscan Regional Orchestra, usually based in Florence with successive resident conductors already referred to in connection with the Tavarnelle Toscanini Prize. The public meetings and debates covered overlapping ground: 'Tourism in Chianti'; 'Problems and perspectives for Artisan enterprises in the 80's'; and 'The value of blood and organ donation'. There was an exhibition of sculpture in the Art Gallery and a flower show in the market square. The final Sunday had a band concert in the afternoon, a troupe of folk dancers in the early evening followed by a more conventional dancing display, cabaret and the closing fireworks.

### The Play

It was against this background and as part of this Festa that two plays by the Tuscan playwright Ugo Chiti were performed under the general title *Alfabeti e Segni di un Fantastico Rituale Contadino*. The first was put on by a group of professional actors from outside Tavarnelle called Teatro Arkhe. The play illustrates Chiti's general concern with the nature of myth in partial contrast with his specific concern (elsewhere and in the second play) with the persistence of the Tuscan and Chiantigiano past into the present day, as lived and reconstructed, rather than merely conserved, folklore; and as language. The play was a ritual theatre performance of the Epic of Gilgamesh given in the restored remains of a small mediaeval courtyard surrounded by houses just off the Via Roma. There was room for an audience of just about 100 for a floodlit performance on the same evening as the late afternoon play which is my main concern. It attracted a small local audience and a number of outside spectators and was afterwards seen as having been handicapped by the cramped performance space and the intemperate weather. It was not recorded, filmed or published locally as a written text or as a videotape and it was seen as no different from the other entertainments provided except as bringing cultural prestige and in being less accessible and possibly less entertaining.

*Volta La Carta … Ecco La Casa* was in sharp contrast. First it was in dialect and performed in an abandoned *casa colonica* which stands in isolation within the boundaries of the part of Tavarnelle Comune known as Noce. The spectators, limited to twenty for each performance, had to find their way by car, without the benefit of direction signs, to a field near this house and wait at the end of a dirt track until they were conducted, still in daylight, to the place in the vicinity of the house where the performance was to begin. Second, although one major part was played by a member of the Teatro Arkhe who had worked with them, the play was performed by a group of young Tavarnellini/e who worked together all the year round at Il Laboratorio Teatrale del Comune di Tavarnelle Val di Pesa – Tavarnelle Comune Theatre Workshop. The leading spirit was Massimo Salvianti who, like other members of the group, was not a professional in the sense that he worked for the theatre as such. He was, however, qualified as an *animatore* and worked on a freelance basis in local schools, encouraging pupils in the use of their bodies and voices in aesthetic performance. Third, although there were posters and the opening performance was attended by critics from *La Nazione* in Florence and from the Rome press, it clearly, given the circumstances, could not be envisaged that the play would draw any considerable audience from outside. There were other obstacles to attending the play since a would-be spectator had to call at or telephone the Library in advance, and when the librarian was there, and make an appointment to see a performance which had not yet achieved its maximum of twenty subscribers. This had the effect of confining those who were able to get to it to a local and privileged elite. I had intended to attend as a member of the paying public but in the event I was invited by the mayor, Marcello Morandi, to be his guest at the première – Anteprima Nazionale. He said, with justice, that as a student of current attitudes to sickness and as an English Comrade, I needed to try to understand the Tuscan past as a component of the Tavarnelle present. After the performance, which on this special occasion was followed by participation in wine denied in the play to the simulated wedding guests, he remarked that he hoped that I had enjoyed and appreciated the quality of the playing. He suggested that I could not have understood much of the performance in itself because of both the archaism of the language and the remoteness of the experiences from my own. He went on: 'To us, it represented our childhood and our past. You cannot as an outsider realise what we suffered.' It was only when I later read the full text and then my Keele student Elisabeth Gnecchi's translation that I fully appreciated the subtleties that he realised that I had missed in the performance.

### *The Play Summarised*

(My interpretations, discussed with Elisabeth Gnecchi, now a research Fellow at the Australian National University, and a Keele honours workshop on the sociology of drama, are in italic type in square brackets. The original English versions of quotations from the play are the joint responsibility of Gnecchi, who learned Tuscan dialect from her grandmother, and myself. I have revised them again for this paper.)

The title itself defies simple translation. In this context carta means an invitation as to a wedding, and a kind of stone with a particular form of traditional decoration. Once the spoken play is elevated or reduced to a written text, it might also mean paper or page. Similarly casa, the simple dictionary translation of which is 'house', is used in speech to describe a building, a household, a set of relatives or associates, the process of living, the rural way of life. Turn over the Card. Here is the House, or more figuratively, 'Look what you might find on the underside of an innocent illustrated stone!'

The audience was assembled and conducted along a farm lane towards a farmhouse yard. There they found Sassaiola – literally a hail of stones – sitting on a heap of stones with his back towards them rhythmically beating two stones together. [*If as guests they come seeking bread, they are to be rewarded with stones. Just in the same way as they will realise later that that was the reward reaped by the farm gaffe – il capoccia – in his search for food from the inhospitable soil*]

When they reach him he rises and accompanies them to the threshing yard, where Pacioso sits on a cage with a pig in it. To one side, half covered with oat sheaves, lies Maggio – May – asleep in front of a carpet of flowers. Sassaiola continues to beat time in the background with the stones and on a tin [*emphasising still the stony obstacles to peace and love*]. Pacioso – goodwill or quiet life – is the spirit of seedcorn and is the propitiatory god of the house who will invite the spectators to follow Maggio.

Pacioso welcomes the guests with promises to entertain them as lovers do each other in May with songs and jokes and with a blasphemous magical incantation. He then draws attention to the stone 'cards' he is holding and chants

> Turn the card, here's the house
> with the house you do it.
> Turn the card, here's the bride
> with the bride there is a wedding.
> Turn the card, here are all the evils.

After putting the stones down he goes on:

Today, you've happened on a good thing!
Today is a day of celebration of a wedding,
inside it's like jubilee

At the word 'jubilee' all the windows of the house are flung open and the guests hear the women inside chatting while they set the tables [*the women's work and talk about poverty and sacrifice sets the context for the next scene*]. After a warning from Pacioso to the guests not to eat too much and thereby upset the bride's father, he takes them to Maggio who leads them into the hay barn where they are greeted by April, the spirit who guards the intimacy of lovers whom May stirs into action. April recites the equivalent of encouragement to make hay while the sun shines to the lovers and shoos the guests away to leave them in peace. Maggio, playing his violin, leads the guests to the threshold of the house where he lists the callers who might, in the past, have been found there [*bringing news and requiring to be given money from the farm's meagre profit*]: the ropemaker who is related to the chairmaker, to the draper, to the smith, to the basketmaker, to the tinker, to the shoemaker, to the hanger-on of the priests – *pretaio* – and finally to the foxman [*in former times foxmen toured farms with a fox in a box as a symbol of their power over the animals and were paid to keep foxes and other misfortunes away by magic*].

The foxman then appears in person, beating a drum and describing at length the terrible bloodsucking, milk-stealing, calf-killing nature of foxes and asking for a gift of eggs to keep the beast at bay. The foxman beats his drum and the Woman in Black appears from the house, her face hidden, and picks up a bundle of faggots. There is a crescendo on the drum and a few chords on Maggio's violin, then silence which Maggio also enjoins on the guests.

He then recites:

This is the woman black from the fire,
Don't look her in the face
because you could even die.
At midnight she stokes the coals,
sleep children and be good.

[*The fox represents all the burning threats to male prosperity which come from outside the house. It has previously been said to have collided with a comet, so that its coat is fiery and its muzzle coal black. The woman controls the fire within the house and her power for evil*

*and for good derives from this. It later emerges that the Woman in*
*Black is unmarried and therefore a source of evil alone. She will be*
*seen to be driven from the bridal chamber.*]

The Woman returns to the bake house and, at Maggio's invitation,
the guests follow. She opens the oven, puts the faggots inside and turns
her back on the spectators. Three women in white are squatting in front
of a large mound of flour. They stand up, turn round, search under their
skirts and hide something under the floorboards. They rise spreading
flour onto their chests and laps and join the Woman in Black.

FIRST WOMAN:

In the bread of the bride we've put
a white sewing thread
because in the new house,
she will count for little or nothing,
the mother-in-law will always say the last ten words.

SECOND WOMAN:

In the bread of the bride we've put
a big clean handkerchief
because after the first kisses, the husband will hardly notice her
except when things go wrong to point a finger.

THIRD WOMAN:

In the bread of the bride we've put
a dream of when she was a child
because in the new house
between the field, the chicken run, the stable,
the rabbits, the children, she will hardly have time to sit in the kitchen

WOMAN BLACK:

In the bread of the bride we've put hope,
so that in the new house
between lowered eyes and bolted food
she will still be able to forget that things will always be so

Taccino [*a farm servant, poor relation, who out of 'charity' and in*
*return for his keep was allowed to do the rough work of the farm and*
*the demeaning tasks for a man of helping the housewife. His total*
*poverty and lack of earnings meant that he had no prospect of forming*
*a family or having a holding of his own*] now enters and tells Maggio

to bring the guests upstairs to the kitchen where the bad-tempered mistress of the house – *la Massaia* – is cursing fit to scare the devil with a set of rosary beads custom-made for this blasphemous purpose. Maggio and Taccino sit bickering on the sink and then recite:

> When the flour comes into the kitchen, the Taccina puts it into the cupboard to rise, and when the bridegroom takes the bride into the bedroom, the birds on the roof stay quiet all night, and when the housewife looks around her, it means that she will be swelling all day long.'

while the women lead them and the spectators upstairs, tracing the route by sprinkling flour as they go. They enter the kitchen and find that the housewife is in front of ten tables signified in outline by white pebbles on the floor. She abuses Taccino, who has put a pot of wild flowers on one of them, and describes how she has borrowed the tables from various named families and, with various graphic metaphors, relates in a thoroughly bad-tempered way how much the wedding is costing and how hungry the family will be as a result for years to come. She hopes that the food will make the guests ill and choke them and Taccino both, leaving fewer people to feed. Maggio leads the guests away hoping that at least the host will welcome them.

They find Il Cappoccia – the gaffer – in the store room with his back to them, looking at a crack in the wall and complaining that although he mends it every year, after winter it always shows through the whitewash again. He then moves to the centre of the room where piles of wood powder reveal the effect of woodworm and the death watch beetle. He compares them to the guest come to eat him out of house and home. Small evils and great evils come together. Nothing is worse than having three fields full of stones, the landlord of the vineyard will come back to renew the tenancy in three years' time and will only do so if they have been good years.

Taccino opens the door of the room and summons Maggio to spy on the bride while she is still naked before the women have had time to dress her. He turns back towards the room, puts his back against the door and looks shyly and confusedly at the guests while he tells Maggio the depths of his sexual frustration. He asks Maggio to swear secrecy, which he does in coarse terms. The housewife appears and says she could have sworn she'd seen a man. She goes back into the bedchamber and the guests follow her, beckoned on by Maggio. The trail of flour leads across the room to the feet of the Bride who is sitting with eyes lowered on the edge of the bed. The housewife complains about the quick growth and sexuality of Taccino and his burgeoning manhood.

The programme notes describe the bedchamber scene of dressing the bride as the central focus of the play: 'this room is the site of thought and bitterness; a peephole on the hard life of women within the hierarchic structure of peasant life.'

The women in white gossip in a conventional way, all talking at once, about how recently the bride was a girl and has now grown and is about to get married as they all have. The mistress of the house takes the bridal veil from the bed and says it is time to put it on, the Woman in Black snatches it from her and puts it on the bride saying that if she doesn't keep her head still she will hurt her with the pins. The housewife comments that she should put it on well so that the bride's hair cannot be seen. She had typhus a year ago and it has only just grown long again. Once the veil is on, the women say that now she is a real bride and coo over her praising her beauty and skill with the needle. The Woman in Black causes consternation by picking up a mirror from the bed and handing it to the bride, which the other women try to snatch away from her saying that it will bring bad luck.

The bride looks at herself, first in silence and then, covering her face with her hands, bursts into tears. The mirror is passed from hand to hand, 'all the women look at themselves as if recognising their common destiny', and each says something about the unpleasantness of married life. When the mirror reaches the Woman in Black, she also begins to cry and says

> I don't care … I want a husband,
> without it's even worse.
> They put you aside and that's it.
> At home nobody looks at you anymore,
> but everyone keeps calling you all the time.
> Then the children of the house are always teasing.
> Although it's the adults that set them off.
> And you, you have to join the game and laugh,
> and supposing I don't want to laugh.
> Why should one be forced to laugh?

She replaces the mirror in the bride's lap and continues:

> I want a husband.
> Tonight, I shall dream that I was in your place,
> and … that …

While she is speaking the other women arrange the bride's trousseau of household linens on the bed. The mistress of the house drives the Woman in Black from the room, telling her these are concerns for married women, she should make herself useful helping preparations elsewhere. She then drives the audience out as well.

They find themselves in a corridor where Maggio plays a few chords on the violin and sings:

> Maggio crowns the heads of lovers with garlands of stocks.
> As for widows and maiden aunts, Maggio seizes up their joints.

Taccino reappears cramped into his best jacket, kept from his first communion long before. He is tipsy and singing. He presents a picture of despairing happiness or happy despair born of wine and unrequited love. He leads the guests into the cellar where there are totemic masks of Bacchus – Bacio – and Solatio, the joyful and slovenly deities who preside respectively over good and bad wine and good and bad vintage years. They intone a duet about good and bad wine which is also replete with double meanings about male sexual activity and which is brought to an end by the housewife's abusive request to bring up more of the good wine adding: 'as far as God is concerned we are all mud.'

Maggio invites the guests to follow him out of the cellar and into the porch where they are met by Sassaiola – the hail of stones – in contrast to their original welcome by Pacioso. Sassaiola relates the myth of the Fall in terms of the coming of stones.

> As soon as man and woman were created,
> they were given a good farmstead – [*podere*] – on which to stay,
> there was good, soft, soft earth,
> it could be worked with a finger,
> a twig, or a bird's feather.
> The man and woman stayed there,
> sitting all day long,
> gazing, stroking, caressing,
> kissing one another, they lacked for nothing:
> figs, peaches, apricots,
> plums, jujubes.
> There were rivers of milk and honey,
> and the trees were full of bread and good things to go on it.
> All in all there was great delight.
> One day the woman found a nut.

'This must be good,' she said,
'Crack it with your teeth for me.'
The man tried, but he broke a tooth.
'We need a stone' said the woman who was the more ignorant
of the two.
And that's how the stone came about!

Sassaiola drops his pile of stones on the doorstep of the house and
then, picking one up again, continues:

Stones grow with the moon,
they double always doubling,
doubling, … stones

He puts the stone into Maggio's hand and runs off laughing. Maggio
takes up the story:

the stones filled the field,
and the man and woman stood up from sitting,
they had to make shoes to walk,
and then dress themselves because
they couldn't look at each other
wearing only shoes.

Sassaiola returns and threatens the guests with stones:

Stunted, lumpy, foreshortened.
I am Sassaiola,
with me it is always winter.
My stepmother, the moon, sows me in the fields,
my twin brother is couch grass,
with it I couple up on a bed of curses,
I hope you all get gallstones and piles
the word of Sassaiola who of all devils is the hardest.

He moves off again and squats in a field.

The guests, by literally following the action, now find themselves
once again in the threshing ground. Taccino comes out with a bucket of
water, notices them as if for the first time, and asks if they have come
for the wedding, and if so, they have left it too late; it was yesterday

and there's nothing left but the dirty water from cleaning up. He throws it on the pile of stones. The windows of the house open suddenly and women hang out sheets and linen. The mistress of the house comes out and shoos away the chickens and the guests. She goes back in, followed by the Woman in Black. Taccino closes the door and the women close the windows letting the white sheets fall to the ground.

## Looking Backwards, Looking Forwards

The published text of the play (Chiti *et al*. 1984) is prefaced by an account of the problems of representing Tuscan dialect, and the book concludes with an article by Paolo De Simonis on the roots of the play in popular literature and performance and their limitations. There is in fact, or was in the past, in Tuscany a tradition of peasant popular drama and indeed, according to Alessandro Falassi (1980), one of the last such performances was given in San Donato in Poggio as recently as 1974. De Simonis reports also that in the same year, a conference was held in Montepulciano to find ways and means of reviving the folk culture of the region. But as he points out, after ten years it could be seen that the participants suffered from well-intentioned illusions. The mode of production and the way of life which gave form and content to peasant drama, the *veglia* and other popular forms have disappeared. The actors I have been describing are young intellectuals and not peasants any more than are, as it happens, the farming advisers they acknowledge having consulted. This family which, in terms of internal social relationships, lives the most traditional life in the most traditional *casa colonica* in Tavarnelle, are self-conscious socialists whose life and methods of work are as modern as any urban innovator. The father and his wife, his three sons and their wives and families, shared in 1983 household, finances, a communal life and table but also agricultural machinery, cars, television and video recorder and their own disco light show in the traditional downstairs barn. Nor, of course, did Ugo Chiti live a life approximating to that he portrayed.

The audience knew that the house where the play was performed had been a real lived-in and worked-in *casa colonica* and many knew the last family who had lived there. They also knew that it was no longer and was very unlikely ever to be so again. It had been liberated from mundane reality to become a symbol and its layout, style of decoration and situation are residual reminders of perceived past truth that make it symbolically effective as a setting for performance. The spectators also knew that the players were acting, what Schechner

(1985) calls the incomplete transformation which excitingly makes players at once not-themselves and not not-themselves. But in this case there is an added dimension. Their names and their known relationships tell the knowing spectator that, but for the grace of God and historical circumstance, they could in fact have been similar to the characters they portray and still be living a similar life. They have escaped from filiation but voluntarily resubmit to it not only by acting their own imaged past and the present that failed to come about, but also by learning to do so in a dialect which is no longer current. The generation who intervene between them and the grandparents whose way of life they are critically seeking to portray also chose, or were forced to choose, affiliation to new values and identities and rejected (or were denied) ascribed filiation, but only in part. For the actors are not only the grandchildren of *mezzadri* but also the children and grandchildren of communists and militant socialists who had been committed not merely to enduring, but also to bringing about (often by force of arms) social change.

The performance as an event and the totality of its organisational timing, placing and context asserts common identity between generations at the same time as it emphasises difference. Young people please their immediate forebears by learning their dialect and re-presenting their past. The older generation provides ideological approval, finance, publication and a permanent record of an activity which they might normally be expected to regard as avant-garde and perhaps frivolous. Identities of values derived from descent and from shared political goals are made to appear congruent. I think that this may be particularly important in areas of Italy like this one where left-wing politics are dominant but where for the intermediate generation Socialist or Communist Party membership is an embraced value, but one which is associated with neither clear national policies nor with classical proletarian status. The individual and social policies of the middle-aged leaders of the Communist council were to create the conditions for themselves and other Tavarnellini to become successful small-scale entrepreneurs within a co-operative framework, if possible but by no means necessarily.

Their children had quite a different formation and outlook. They, unlike their parents, had not been drawn into the PCI or the PSI through the need to oppose and eventually to fight against Fascism, to resist and overcome oppressive and absentee landlords, or to counteract the national corruption and nepotism of Christian Democracy and the consequent stagnation of many other parts of Italy. They find the overt ideals of the left easy to support but its organisations bureaucratic, male, middle-aged and difficult to join with any enthusiasm. Younger members of communist families expressed approval at the break with the Soviet Union – *lo strappo* – and PCI general secretary Berlinguer's official pronouncement, long before Gorbachov, that the revolutionary spirit of the USSR was exhausted; but like the left itself, they were clearer about what it was against than what it was for.

The play and its performance, as I have already suggested, was not a naturalistic representation of the past. The rituals of the past were re-presented and re-contextualised by players of this hereditary left with an intention of demonstrating a critical realist position which was fundamentally anti-romantic in relation both to the position of women and, less overtly and directly, received wisdoms, especially of religious belief but also of party 'dogma' about the heroic past. In this respect it differs sharply from the kind of folk revival drama, sponsored by the Church, which I have seen (and enjoyed) in Eire. Religion, as such, features only briefly as a lumping together of priests and friars as kin to the other trade parasites on the peasants' production and in the inverted forms (a custom-made rosary for cursing, for example) historically associated with folk anti-clericalism in many parts of Catholic Europe. (As a partially assimilated, detribalised Jew formed alongside English public school and university Anglicanism, I was always (not necessarily unpleasantly) aware of the pervasiveness of Catholic culture even, or perhaps especially, for the great majority of the most apparently and determinedly atheistic communists. Chiti illuminates this in the following year's play to which I hope to return in a later article.) As far as women were concerned, the players, explicitly but perhaps vainly, hoped to encourage older males amongst their audience to look at their own lives and ask whether, even if the extreme poverty had gone, gender relations had not survived virtually unchanged. The only women present when I saw the play were the wives of the principals and the performers; like the women in the *casa* presented, the married women of modern Tavarnelle, like my own wife, had other things to do between four and six on a weekday afternoon.

## Conclusion

A final comment on the play returns to the meaning of *la casa*, the key to the power of the piece. Both in answers to De Martino's questionnaire and in the responses to my interviews a persistent theme emerged. Social change and communist policy had been successful because they had brought industry and trade to Tavarnelle itself and enabled Tavarnellini/e to find work *a casa* – at home. This meant in the Comune but also, in the case of many women, in the house itself as outworkers in the *Lavoro Nero* – black economy. The common phenomena elsewhere of *pendolarità* (commuting) and *precarietà* (temping) had been reduced to a minimum as had outright migration. So there was a paradox: the viability of *la casa* had been preserved at a cost of the death of *la casa*. For Tavarnelle, the situation had been inverted: trade no longer seemed to be parasitic on workers on the soil. But in traditional Tuscan thought, and in current attitudes to the family house which lie just below the surface, *la casa* is also associated with the body (cf. Anne Parsons 1966) and the play accurately portrayed local values in seeing penetration of the house, penetration of the family and penetration of the body as a continuum of dangers rather than as threats of different orders of meaning. The negotiations necessary to organise house-to-house interviews had earlier made this apparent to me.

In Victor Turner's terminology (1982), the physical body passage, of both actors and spectators through the symbolic house and the associated performance created a liminoid space, which made it possible for them to transcend the barriers of structure set up by party, unshared aesthetic assumptions and intergenerational conflict and emerge into a kind of *communitas* which, at least for some, made new structural forms and ways of reconciling generational difference of values more feasible. A combination of a wedding and a house, their temporary exposure to strangers and the successful humiliating expulsion of the strangers initially by the least comfortable of the insiders is a powerful reinforcement of the unity of past and present. The past is recalled, apparently but ambivalently glorified, and then exorcised. New forms of affiliation are presaged but not by the rejection of filiation. The second and third generation of heirs to the left (or for that matter to the right) have not that option. On the contrary, the presentation by their descendants of a symbolic but critical appreciation of their parents' and grandparents' past, in the language of that past, mobilised filiation to restate and reinforce the twin identities derived from birth and derived from rational choice. This is especially important because in Tavarnelle, *la casa*, family/household, remains unchallenged as the arena of production, whether of goods, of services, or the values of overt and shared, but only partially consensual, identity. The multiplicity of texts and the polysemicity of some particular texts, including this play, preserve identity by almost acknowledging difference. Tuscans are 'people of the book' and sophisticated villagers, whether players or councillors, know what they are about and welcome licensed strangers, whether they be playwrights or ethnographers, as legitimate scribes into their midst.

## Acknowledgements

An earlier version of this paper was given as a joint presentation with Dr. Libi Grecchi-Ruscone who, when an undergraduate in the Department of Sociology and Social Anthropology at Keele, assisted me with translation from Tuscan dialect. I am grateful for this and her other helpful suggestions. My stay in Tavarnelle was supported by SSRC grant no. G0023/0016

## References

Ardener, E. (1989), *The Voice of Prophecy*. Oxford: Blackwell
Barnes, J. A. (1962), 'African Models in the New Guinea Highlands', *Man*, vol. 62, pp. 5–9
_____(1971), *Three Styles in the Study of Kinship*. London: Tavistock Publications
_____(1979), *Who Should Know What? Social Science, Privacy and Ethics*. Harmondsworth: Penguin
Brown, R. (1979), 'Passages in the Life of a White Anthropologist: Max Gluckman in Northern Rhodesia', *Journal of African History*, vol. 20, no. 4, pp. 525–542
Calzolai, C. C. (1983), *San Donato in Poggio: le sue glorie, le sue tradizione*. Florence: Venturine Editore
Chiti, U., P. De Simonis and P. Lucchesini (1984), *Volta La Carta … Ecco La Casa*. Comune di Tavarnelle Val di Pesa: Biblioteca Comunale
Cresti, P. (1984), *Vicende Vissute: Episodi di vita Contadina*. Tavarnelle Val di Pesa: Biblioteca Comunale e Scuola Media, 'Il Passignano'
De Martino, S. (1982), *Famiglia Contadina e Classe Operaia nella Campagna Urbanizzata del Chianti: Il Caso di Tavarnelle VP*. Tavarnelle: Comune di Tavarnelle Val di Pesa
Falassi, A. (1980), *Folklore by the Fireside; Text and Context of the Tuscan Veglia*. London: Scolar Press
Ferrara, F. and Luigi Coppola (1983), *Le Feste e il Potere*. Rome: Officina Edizione
Frankenberg, R. (1957, 1989), *Village on the Border* (reprinted with additional material). Prospect Heights, Illinois: Waveland Press
(1963, 1989), 'Participant Observers', *New Society*, 7 March 1963, reprinted in Frankenberg 1989
Geertz, C. (1988), *Works and Lives: The Anthropologist as Author*. Oxford: Polity Press

Gluckman, M. (1965), *Politics, Law and Ritual in Tribal Society*. Oxford: Blackwell

Goffman, E. (1959), *The Presentation of Self in Everyday Life*. Garden City, New York: Doubleday Anchor

Malinowski, B. (1922, 1983), *Argonauts of the Western Pacific*. London: Routledge and Kegan Paul

Parsons, A. (1966), 'Is the Oedipus Complex Universal? The Jones-Malinowski Debate Revisited and a South Italian "Nuclear Complex"', in W. Muensterberger (ed.), *Man and his Culture*, pp. 331–84. London: Rapp and Whiting

Pini Duti, R. (1981a), *Al di là del Male del Secolo*. Florence: Editrice La Ginestra

_____(1981b), *Una Vita in Versi (prima scelta)*. Florence: Editrice La Ginestra

Schechner, R. (1985), *Between Theater and Anthropology*. Philadelphia: University of Pennsylvania Press

Turner, V. (1982), *From Ritual to Theatre: The Human Seriousness of Play*. New York City:Performing Arts Journal Publications

# 4

# At Play with Identity in the Basque Arena

## *Jeremy MacClancy*

' dentity' is a catch-all term of our times. It is an empty
vessel which can be filled with almost any content. As a
quick perusal of recent volumes on European communities shows,
astute anthropologists can use identity as a general framing device for
a surprising variety of ethnographic data. In these books discussion can
range from the individual to the regional to the supranational, from
styles of dress to modes of cuisine to religious faith. The range of
possible topics seems to be limited only by the imaginative power of
the compiler. The worry, of course, is that we anthropologists may
well impose a notion of identity upon unmarked aspects of others'
cultures. The danger is that we may extol or assiduously analyse a part
of others' lives which they themselves regard as of little importance, or
as not just restricted to themselves but as common to many. We start to
find symbols where none at present exist. The resulting ethnography
may tell us more about the classificatory ingenuity of its author than
about the way the people studied regard themselves. In these
conditions identity begins to seem primarily an anthropologists'
category; it appears to be an unjustifiably arbitrary manner of
delineating others' lives in academic terms.

For instance, Anthony Cohen, in his recent ethnography on a
Shetland community, *Whalsay*, worries about the implications of
anthropologists inferring symbolism in other people's behaviour. He
argues that in the analysis of others' social identity the interpretations
he makes are the ways that he, rather than they, makes sense of what
they do. The reasons they give for their action need not coincide with
the explanations he proffers. He suggests that the only defence of an
interpretation can be its plausibility.

> What [an anthropologist] calls 'symbols' are the constructs of meaning
> which he sees surfacing repeatedly and which are thus commended as
> significant to the analysis. While this apparent consistency may itself be a

figment of the analysis, it is the only basis on which interpretation can proceed. (Cohen 1987: 94)

Cohen's problem arises because Whalsay folk do not have a strong, collectively acknowledged sense of identity; there is usually no need for them to agree publicly on what being 'Whalsay' means.

But Cohen's qualifiers, doubts, and self-imposed restrictions have no place in the analysis of politicised ethnicities. In these ethnographic situations, there is no need to posit an identity, to classify these people according to one's own criteria and then worry about the status of the construct. Local political parties or energetic factions which claim to speak for an ethnic group organise their own symbolism; in their speeches, writings, and graffiti they provide their own exegeses of their own actions. In this sort of contested social arena an anthropologist has the privileged opportunity to see the game of identity at play. And the rules are openly discussed as each side attacks the strategies and manoeuvres of the other.

In my present fieldwork I am attempting to elaborate an account of the confrontation between Basque nationalism and the regionalism of Navarre, a northern Spanish province. This ideological battle provides differing conceptions of prehistory, history, race, religion, territory, language, and political destiny. Identity and ethnicity cannot here be taken as ethnographic givens as Navarrans argue over who they are: Basques or Spaniards? Clearly in these sorts of context ethnicity is a mutable *strategy* grounded in historical circumstances, not an unchanging datum coasting in some timeless ethnographic present.

Where divisive politics permeates so much, people are made much more sensitive to their acts – no matter how seemingly 'trivial' – and of the possible political meanings that these can be given. Their lives become more dense and their behaviour takes on tones of significance absent in more peaceful provinces of Spain. Thanks to the elision of politics and ethnicity in northern Spain, people are being reminded and are reminding one another of their ethnicity far more frequently than, say, Oxford postgraduates. Adults living within the geographical area where Basque nationalism is a political force may have organised their way of life so that they can avoid being charged or charging others of being Basque nationalist or Navarran regionalist, but the point, of course, is that they have had to *organise* their lives that way by deliberately avoiding certain places, turns of phrase, and habits. A Basque patriot friend mentioned that my yellow lighter with its red top had the same colours as the Spanish flag; others said that my red braces reminded them of Manuel Fraga, the highly patriotic right-wing leader who sometimes sports Marylebone Cricket Club suspenders, bought while he was ambassador to Britain in the days of Franco. A mother sharply tells her son to turn off the radio, because the gentle love song broadcast is being sung in Basque. During the annual fiesta of the village that I lived in one ardent Basque patriot criticised the playing of the hired Zaragozan band. 'They're just bloody *españolistas*!' he cried. Politicos can make their nationalist or regionalist strategies apply to any aspect of culture. Anything can become marked politically and so be regarded as positive or negative by different factions. Nothing escapes the political eye.

The accepted context for the rise of Basque nationalism in the late nineteenth century is the alienation in 'their own land' of rural migrants to the newly industrialising Basque towns. Its first major ideologue, Sabino Arana-Goiri, defined the Basques nominally, anthropologically, and linguistically. Basques were those who had four Basque surnames, were intelligent, spoke Basque, and clearly did not look or act so stupid as the Castilian migrants. The next major definition of the Basques was by ETA (Euskadi eta Askatasuna, 'the Basqueland and freedom'). Originally (i.e. in the 1950s) a broad cultural and humanist movement, it has evolved – after passing through a period of great popularity – into a terrorist organisation with nationalist, separatist, irredentist, and revolutionary socialist ends. Members of ETA ignore people's surnames, do not look at the shape of their heads nor at the colour of their eyes, but stress the central importance of speaking Basque. To them, the Basque language is the main cultural prop, a besieged form of distinctiveness which must be maintained. Marrying nationalism and socialism they define a Basque as someone who sells his labour in Basqueland. The point of this shift in definition is that it includes migrants from other parts of Spain who work in the Basque area.

In Navarre most Basque nationalism is revolutionary socialist. Its main organisation is Herri Batasuna ('Popular Unity'), a radical coalition of small political parties, most of them originally splinter groups from ETA. To members of the coalition, Basque patriots are *abertzales*, a status not defined by birth but by performance: an *abertzale* is one who actively participates in the political struggle for an independent Basque nation with its own distinctive culture. You are not born *abertzale*. You make yourself one. I have met people whose parents emigrated from southern Spain and who, though not born in Basqueland, identify with the Basque movement, learn Basque, and join demonstrations against the latest threat to the integrity of the

Basque people. One told me, 'Not being *born* Basque doesn't matter. I *feel* Basque.' His gathered friends nodded agreement. To be *abertzale* is defined both prescriptively and proscriptively. *Abertzales* must totally shun *chivatos* – 'informers, people thought to have any connection with the police'. My first month in Pamplona, friends of my Basque flatmate told him I was a *chivato* because they had seen me chatting (innocently) to an armed policeman during a small riot. He corrected them, saying I was just an ignorant foreigner newly arrived in town. Later, angrily, he put me right about local rules of life. Locals recognise the danger of being branded *chivato* by their own peers and that it is necessary to demonstrate the unfounded nature of the charge as quickly and as effectively as possible. People branded *chivato* can be so ostracised that the only community left in which they can find friends is the police. The *chivato* is pushed into becoming a real informer, sometimes with fatal consequences, for ETA gunmen shoot informers dead.

Radical ideologues speak of *la gran familia abertzale*, a social unit where political attitudes are often inherited and one broad enough to accommodate both militant nationalism and revolutionary socialism. Members of Herri Batasuna have so successfully appropriated left-wing metaphors that in Basqueland it is now difficult to be left-wing but not *abertzale*. (In the dying days of the dictatorship, being a member of ETA was a way to assert opposition to Franquism and members of the opposition looked well on ETA because it helped their aims. Anti-Franquism and armed Basque nationalism were seen to go hand in hand.) Almost all left-wing issues are discussed within a Basque frame. To *abertzales*, *el Pueblo Trabajador Vasco* ('the Basque Working People') is a *raza* ('race'), or *pueblo* oppressed by the occupying forces of the Spanish state and exploited by centralist capitalists. Following their line of metaphors, the Basque people is already a 'nation' with its own 'popular army' (ETA) and whose gunmen are its 'best sons'. Basque politicians who do not advance the Basque cause are 'traitors', the attempt to build a nuclear power station on the Basque coast becomes 'genocide', and the entry of Spain into NATO is damned as subversion of 'Basque sovereignty'. In this way radical Basque nationalists have created an explanatory world-view with great interpretive extension.

This rhetoric can turn deadly, for when gunmen recently put two bullets through the head of an ex-leader who had renounced terrorism and returned to a quieter life, a Batasuna leader argued that 'an army cannot allow deviations, and even less so from one of its generals who appears strolling through territory occupied by the opposing army'. The quite literal appropriative power of radical nationalism was exhibited at the funeral in 1987 of the first ever gunwoman to be shot in a police action. Though the funeral was the usual mass event such occasions are, her father (a well-known nationalist moderate) removed the Basque flag draped over the coffin, and tried to prevent radical militants from entering the graveyard, raising their fists over the descending casket and singing 'Eusko Gudari' ('The Basque Warrior'), the popular song to ETA gunpersons. He was strongly criticised in *Egin*, the Batasuna organ, which stated that the corpse belonged to the 'people' and not to its father, and that the 'people' could not be stopped claiming political kinship with their fallen sister. In dying for the cause, she had forfeited the rights of her family for those of *la gran familia abertzale*.

*Abertzales* wish to increase the number of Basque speakers, to extend the range of occasions on which Basque is spoken and thus, if necessary, to create social events in which Basque is the language of communication. In an attempt to 'Basquise' Castilians *abertzales* impose Basque orthography on Spanish: tx is used in place of ch (e.g. *txorizo*, 'sausage, thief'), b instead of v (Nabarra). Where possible Basque rather than Castilian terms are used (e.g. *arrantzale* 'fisherman'; *irrintzi* 'a cry, radio'). Political slogans are preferably shouted in Basque, words for new Basque institutions came from the Basque, not the Castilian, lexicon (e.g. *ikastola*, a Basque school), and parents give their children Basque names – a practice banned during Franquism. In Basque-speaking areas place signs are often bilingual, and with the Castilian toponym usually painted out by some midnight *abertzale*.

In this general context learning Basque becomes an exercise in left-wing politics for politicised youth, and speaking Basque in non-Basque-speaking areas (police stations, for instance) becomes a political statement. In the intensive course of Basque I attended in the municipal School of Languages in Pamplona, posters used in the class often centred on political themes: pollution, demonstrations, dropping flower-pots on policemen, etc. Every soldier or policemen in these pictures looked distinctly ugly and clearly had not shaved in the last few days. In reaction to political events outside the school, teachers staged (bilingual) democratic assemblies in which people decided what action was to be taken: our commitment to the cause was unquestioned. Bars run by radicalised youth are given Basque names and barpersons will reply in Basque if spoken to in the same tongue, though neither they nor their clients may be able to utter more than a few phrases. In one new bar I saw the sign 'Castilian is also spoken'.

In fabricating their own social events, their own fiestas, and, to some extent, their own language, *abertzales* create a novel, functioning sub-culture of their own, one broad enough to include urban activists, punks, young villagers, and skinheads. (Some *abertzales* are particularly proud of the fact that Basque skinheads, unlike their bald counterparts elsewhere in Europe, are not automatically associated with the violent end of the right wing.) Students of Basque collectively camp out for days, and sponsored thousands run in marathons pacing out the extent of Basqueland, all for the sake of raising money to promote the teaching of Basque. They also participate in fiestas celebrating marked aspects of 'Basque' culture, such as wood-choppers, stone-lifters, dancers, troubadours, Basque musicians, and the *olentzero* (the Basque equivalent of Father Christmas). In fact there are so many of these modern fiestas that committed nationalists can spend many of their spring and summer weekends going from one event to another. Public gatherings held in homage to murdered Batasuna leaders, to dead gunmen (or their mothers), or to *abertzales* killed by police in demonstrations become the frequent occasion for further, congregated celebration of the radical version of how to be 'Basque'. The range of this constructed culture is shown by the articles in the Batasuna newspaper, which may laud the pre-capitalist way of life of Basque villagers in the nineteenth century, or describe the latest developments in 'the Basque novel', 'Basque painting', 'the Basque cinema', 'the Basque video', 'Basque sports', 'Basque cuisine', or (very popular) 'radical Basque rock'.

Herri Batasuna coined the phrase 'el rock radical vasco' in 1983 as a categorical strategy to give shape to, to stimulate further, and to politicise a previously uncoordinated collection of Basque rock bands. This was a way for the *abertzale* organisation to reinforce its connection with energetic youth and to radicalise rock-concertgoers. The coalition gave consistent publicity to these rock groups in a weekly *Egin* section devoted to their music and repeatedly hired them to play in Batasuna fiestas. *El rock* is seen as a direct result of the contemporary sociopolitical situation in the Basque country. And this makes it different from, if not also superior to, rock movements in other regions of Spain, which are regarded as but mere imitations of fashionable transatlantic music, not reflecting the life in their own towns. *El rock radical* is loud (often very loud), not at all subtle, and the sense of protest is meant to be clear. One band, *Hertzainak* (the

Basque term for the Basque autonomous police), sing all their highly charged numbers in Basque, though none of the group can speak the language. The songs of *el rock* concern the level of unemployment, the pervasive drug culture (especially the heroin flood), the lack of change, the chances of revolution, the hatred of state militarism, the oppression by the forces of legitimate violence, and the need to act. Sex is a more common theme than love. With their pounding rhythms, high decibels and frenetic lead singers these locally produced bands are seen to be one way of carrying on 'the struggle'.

A comic strip in a special issue of the *abertzale* newsmagazine *Punto y Hora* issued in August 1986 summarily depicts most of *el rock radical's* rebellious aspects. The lead singer of the fictious band, 'Txakurrack' ('dogs' in Basque) is first shown in bed with a woman, making love and smoking joints. Praising marijuana he complains about the hallucinations produced by heroin, the irritating tickle in the nose on sniffing cocaine, and the stomach indigestion caused by amphetamines. He is next seen on stage, singing 'We're going to give *hostias* [a swear word referring to the host used in Holy Communion] without pause to the national police'. His simulation of anal intercourse with a guitarist of his band while singing, 'Don't worry. All this about AIDS is a lie' provokes the arrival of the police whom he single-handedly beats into submission. The strip ends with the protagonist joining his friends (a punk, a rockabilly, a skinhead, and a rocker) in what promises to be a violent demonstration.

This music is seen as specifically Basque both because it is made by Basques and because it sometimes blends Punk, New Wave, Heavy Metal, and Ska with strands of traditional Basque music. Leading *abertzales* regard these groups as a part of the emerging self-created Basque society, one generated 'from below', not imposed 'from above'. *El rock radical* is played in the bars run by Basque youths, it is produced by independent Basque record companies, it is discussed in the numerous fanzines published in the area, and it is broadcast by the plethora of pirate radio stations found in almost every Basque (or Navarran) town of any size. This is a world which Basque youth can regard as having been effectively constructed by themselves. In the words of one irreverent musician, speaking against the perceived oppression of the Basque land,

> What we say is that we would like to change it all. And if we could write and make a free and tropical Euskadi [the Basque Country], we'd like that because it would be more amusing. The problem is that we can't. What we

can do is to try to tell the people to raise their consciousness, to break the seat in which they are sitting, and to move themselves. If the people move themselves and search, they will find something good. If they go out into the street, we'll see one another there. The unity of our movement is based on action in the street.[1]

The members of these groups are not mere puppets of experienced politicos, being cynically manipulated for political ends. In the best anarchic tradition of rock and roll rebels, some are uneasy being associated with a political label and some reject any association with *el rock radical vasco* – they do not want any ties to a particular political project. But the attitude of rebellion controls the stage. When the promoters of one concert learnt that the Galician rock band they had hired was made up of national policemen, the event was hurriedly cancelled.

At about the same time as the creation of 'el rock radical vasco', Herri Batasuna began to use the slogan 'Martxa eta borroka' (perhaps best translated as 'liveliness and struggle'.) This rallying-cry connoted both the need for young *abertzales* to enjoy themselves while still working for the cause, and their need to remember the cause whilst enjoying themselves in town and village fiestas. 'Martxa eta borroka' is a way both to enliven the struggle for Basque independence and to politicise traditional fiestas in a radical mode. For, as so many examples show, these collective parties of sanctioned licentiousness with excited and inebriated crowds filling the streets can easily turn into major demonstrations. The bloody conflict between the festive participants and massed groups of the police in the Pamplonan fiesta of 1978 was so sustained that the municipal council was forced to stop the festivities after only two days of the week-long event. In the same fiesta eight years later two hapless *nacionales* who had to change the wheel of their police car in the main Plaza were surrounded for the duration of the operation by some sixty whistling youths. Since they were not being violent, the police did not reply. They did not want to provoke a major riot. Outside of fiestas, the same scene would have been unthinkable; the police vans would have arrived in minutes to clear the area of the disrespectful whistlers.

Though *abertzale* culture is a mix of modern events and a selective taking-up of former ways, it gains prestige by association with the glorious past of Basque culture and history. But by claiming to be the

---

1. 'Hau dena aldatu nahi nuke', *Punto y Hora* monograph, August 1986.

rightful heirs to Basque tradition, nationalists can be criticised by others for acting inconsistently. When I watched a display of Basque dancing in an anti-war fiesta, one Pamplonan friend said to me that it was good dancing, but what was it doing here in Pamplona? The dances performed came from a fishing village miles north of Pamplona. Traditionally it would not have been staged in Pamplona, and certainly not by Pamplonans. Though the annual festival of Basque dance brings together performers from many different areas, it also decontextualises and reduces the distinctiveness of regionally based dance routines by making them all assimilable parts of a generalised 'Basque culture'. The confusion here is between culture as a static bounded entity, its content legitimated by traditional use, and culture as a dynamic, interpretative product, its content continually redefined by its present practitioners. *Abertzales* want the reflected prestige of the Basque past: they do not want to be confined by it. The culture they manufacture is a modern mix of the present and the past in the present, a continuing construction. Here, marked 'cultural' events are appropriated by a party programme which, in turn, is judged by political effectiveness.

An integral part of this nationalist culture is political demonstration, and I must emphasise the frequency, size and often spontaneous nature of these gatherings. Since elected representatives of Herri Batasuna do not attend any of the national or regional legislative assemblies, they manifest their political clout by the number of activists they can rapidly mobilise into the street. These demonstrations could be seen as doubly democratic because they are a way for 'the people', without the aid of any political representatives, to state their politics with their feet, and because everyone within the demonstrating crowd is equal – there is no apparent hierarchy within their number during the event. When units of the newly formed Basque Autonomous Police first went into action against a riotous assembly, journalists in *Egin* asked what these men were doing. Did they not realise they were part of the Basque people themselves, and why were they trying to prevent fellow members of the Basque people from expressing their grievances?

The street is openly recognised by all politicians as urban territory to be contested. As the Batasuna newspaper said, demonstrating is almost the duty of an *abertzale*: it is part of their performance. It is also acknowledged as a necessary *rite de passage* for radicalised teenagers. In the words of one: 'You have to suppress your fear.' Participants discuss these demonstrations in the same terms and phrases used to talk about the bull-running in the Pamplonan fiesta made famous by Hemingway. People ask beforehand, 'Are you going to run?' and afterwards, 'Did you run? How often? Where? How long? How close did the bulls get?' (for the police are sometimes called 'bulls'). And people run, in both occasions, along the same narrow streets of the Old Quarter in Pamplona. This conjunction was exploited in the Navarran television advertisement put together by Batzarre, a hard left radical nationalist coalition separate from Herri Batasuna. The beginning of the advert interspersed clips from violent demonstrations in the Old Quarter with shots of the crowd being chased by the bulls in the fiesta. One leading member of the coalition told me these two aspects were juxtaposed 'because they show the reality of Navarran life today'.

When a member of ETA died in prison (of natural causes) *Egin* followed its usual pattern of devoting several pages to the life of the dead man. Amidst the general panegyric typical of such events, the paper emphasised the athletic ability of the late terrorist. He had been nicknamed 'El Olimpico' ('The Olympic runner') because, in one well-known demonstration seen on television, an armed policeman swinging a truncheon had chased him for several hundred yards but had been unable to reach his target. By participating in the demonstration and getting so close to the police that one of them singled him out, El Olimpico had acted like a true *abertzale* and had done so in an exemplary, swift-footed manner.

The meeting between the police and the crowd is almost as ceremonialised as the encounter between bulls and people in the annual Pamplonan fiesta. Demonstrators provoke reaction by spilling the contents of bottle-banks across one entrance to the main Plaza. The police arrive, to the expectation of their opponents. I once heard the crowd *cheer* when the vans belatedly turned up, and others have seen demonstrators impatiently stamping their feet while waiting for the opponents to show themselves. The police push open their van doors and charge towards the fray. The demonstrators run to the relative safety of cars pulled out across the street, or stay behind smelly barricades of burning bags of rubbish. The police use tear gas, rubber bullets, and long rubber truncheons. Those behind the barricades shout slogans, whistle, maybe let off firework rockets, and smash small drain-hole covers against marble shopfronts to make stones for throwing: windows of banks are a common target for these fervent anti-capitalists. The taunting, challenging nature of their jeers is patent. I have heard demonstrators cry, '!Vago! !Vago!' ('lazy, indolent') when the police paused in their firing. The police charge again, their opponents retreat, and so on, until the crowd is dispersed. Both police and people recognise the similarities between bull-running and demonstration, but the unpaid participants in these duels emphasise that they run because they are against the police. If they enjoy it, then that is merely a secondary benefit. The fight may have ritualistic elements: it is still a fight for political ends.

The demonstrators do not just aim at any cop in uniform: their target is more specific. Members of the armed forces, the National Police and the Civil Guard, are the focus of their assaults. It is in their stations that suspect terrorists are questioned, are tortured, and sometimes die. Municipal police do not usually carry arms and are not normally concerned with maintaining the peace in the face of violent disorder. On the whole they are left alone by *abertzales*. When a mob of two hundred used a heavy log to smash their way through the locked entrance of the Pamplona city hall, they were disappointed to find just a few municipal policemen inside as the only guards. It was not worth their while fighting these relatively untrained officials, and they turned away in disgust, in search of a more suitable, more qualified foe. But the agitated youth on the streets still recognise the official nature of the '*munis*' position: one municipal policeman told me how he had come upon a riotous gang who had just started to tear up the street to build a barricade. As he walked towards them, they quietened down, only to start up again as soon as he had gone a distance past them. Both sides in this casual encounter knew the *nacionales* would have to deal with the situation but the barrier-builders still made their token gesture in order not to compromise the *muni*.

Historically *navarrismo*, or Navarran regionalism, is a reaction to Basque nationalism. It is a reactive ideology which is forcefully restated whenever Basque nationalism appears threateningly strong. *Navarristas* have no desire to *change* the configuration of the Spanish state. Their stated aim is merely to increase the autonomy of Navarre within the broad national frame. Hence they do not have so developed a world-view since they do not radically stress difference, nor are they trying to change fundamentally the political order of society. Basque nationalists underline the Basque nature of Navarre, historically, linguistically, and culturally. They argue a unitary view of the whole Basqueland. They want 'their' ethnic region treated as a single unit. *Navarristas* stress a plural view of their province, linguistically, culturally and ethnically. To them, the unity holding this diversity is the *fueros*, antique particular rules of self-government granted to communities at the village, urban, regional and provincial levels. They claim Navarre is the only Peninsular example of a province (once an ancient kingdom, mentioned by Shakespeare and Dante, home to Chaucer for two years) which has kept its *fueros*. Such a central concept is open to several different interpretations and when the *abertzales* are attacking the *navarristas*' version of them, the Basque patriots deride the *fueros* wholesale as 'antediluvian privileges' which do not respect the popular sovereignty of the Basque people. Similarly, they crab any institutionalised extolling of Navarran identity, such as the newly created 'Day of Navarre', any tentative proposals about establishing any sort of 'Community of the Ebro' (i.e. a superordinate organisation co-ordinating particular services between the three provinces, Navarre, Rioja, and Aragon, which border on the river Ebro), and the activities of the Principe de Viana, the cultural wing of the Navarran Government. Just as *abertzales* see their fight in both nationalist and socialist terms, so they crab *navarristas* as being both reactionary regionalists and members of a controlling élite. For committed patriots these enemies within their geographical camp are not merely anti-nationalist but also members of an exploitative class. And they are to be hated for both reasons.

Politics also pervades human geography for Navarre is one of the geographically most varied provinces of Iberia, descending from the snowcapped peaks of the westernmost Pyrenees on the border with France down through successively shallower and wider valleys to the Ribera, the visually dull flat plain that borders the river Ebro. Support for Herri Batauna comes mainly from the hilly north and industrial centres while the regionalists rely on their support in, above all, Pamplona and the southern half of the province. *Navarristas* play up the stereotyped psychological differences between those of the mountain and those of la Ribera. *Montañeros* (who fit almost all the criteria of most definitions of Basqueness) are said to be withdrawn, grave, quiet and not very sociable. They are men of the mountain. But when they finally offer you friendship, they give it completely. *Ribereños*, however, are said to be loud, joyful, gay, boastful, and extremely friendly. *Abertzales* acknowledge these temperamental differences but call the *montañero* sincere and truthful, the *ribereño* insincere and often deceitful. They are said to lack manners, have an unlikeable sense of humour, and at times are to be considered animals. One Saturday night, in a village bar in the middle of Navarre, I saw the local dwarf using a towel to bull-fight with a dog, to the hoots and laughs of his inebriated friends. On throwing in the towel he turned and farted loudly into the faces of two sitting men, both *abertzales*. 'Oi!' one of them responded, 'That's done in the Ribera!' i.e. not here, not in the village. *Navarristas* do not denigrate *ribereños*. In fact, many of them are *ribereños*.

In this factious context the ambiguity of almost any image is exploited by both parties. Nationalists put forward the independence of mountain-dwelling Basques from invading Romans as the reason for the successful maintenance of much of their distinctive mythology. To them Basque Christianity is both distinctively fervent and neo-pagan in many aspects. But to the distinguished Spanish historian Sanchez Albornoz this same lack of romanisation explains Basque 'backwardness' and their 'irrationality': it is only the descendants of cave-dwelling pagans who could be prepared to shoot or blow up so many Spanish policemen.

The limit case to the pervasiveness of nationalist politics is the highly popular Navarran football team, Osasuna, normally to be found in the lowest ranks of the First Division of the Spanish league. For financial reasons (it's a cheap way to get players) the Osasuna Football Club supports juvenile football teams throughout the province. Until 1984 all its players were born and bred in *la cantera* ('the quarry'), i.e. the province itself. In a recent effort to end the seemingly constant threat of relegation to the Second Division, the club has started to buy in players from overseas, predominantly England. Some supporters reacted immediately, claiming that the ideals of the club, as a representation of Navarre, were being betrayed. But as the new players have improved the team's game, the opposition has quietened. The owners of the club have taken particular pains that the team not become politicised. Unlike their peers in leading football teams in the Basqueland, players for Osasuna do not appear in newspaper advertisements recommending that people respect their heritage and learn Basque. (The term *osasuna* is Basque for 'health'.) But if the players do not actively support Basque nationalism, nor are they criticised politically in *Egin*. It seems that the *abertzale* parties recognise the broad popular following of the team and so, in an effort not to alienate potential support for Herri Batasuna from among the ranks of fans, they succumb to the apolitical stance of the club. However, nationalist friends in Pamplona, grumbling quietly, have told me that the players are *fachas* (a derogatory term with the same significance and political accuracy as the British 'fascist'). If they're not with us they can only be against us.

There is no neat end to the political wrangle over the status of Navarre, no tidy conclusion to the enduring debate. Though the self-government of the province and its independence from the Basque Autonomous Area seem more and more assured with each year that passes, fervent *abertzales* will not let the issue die down. And so long as the nationalists remain a threat, *navarristas* will not let their constituents forget the singularity of their province. The contest of identities continues.

## Reference

Cohen, A. P. (1987) *Whalsay, Symbol, Segment and Boundary in a Shetland Island Community*. Manchester: Manchester University Press

# 5

# Good To Be French?
# Conflicts of Identity
# in North Catalonia

## *Oonagh O'Brien*

n France, to work for the state means to be French. That being
so, then what does it mean for a Catalan to work for the state
– to be a *fonctionnaire*[1]? In popular discourse in France a fonctionnaire
is no longer Catalan (or indeed any of the other so-called minority
ethnic identities which exist within the French state, such as Occitan,
Breton, Flemish or Basque). However, I found while doing fieldwork
in North Catalonia[2] that it appeared to be exactly this fonctionnaire
group within the community which was most actively Catalan. After
some time it became clear that even those fonctionnaires who were not
actually more active in Catalan activities were perceived to be so by
the rest of the community.

In order to understand this, it is necessary to clarify the workings of
the fonctionnaire system, and to specify who the fonctionnaires in the
community are. It is not sufficient to consider only the present
fonctionnaires; their parents and grandparents are also part of the
explanation. The fonctionnaires are the fulfilment of the previous
generations' dream – they are French and that is good. They represent
the struggle of a whole family over two or three generations to educate
and improve conditions for their children. The parents and

---

1. A *fonctionnaire* is not the same as a civil servant, and as I do not feel that the literal
translation, 'functionary', conveys any meaning in English, I use the French throughout.
I have left the name of St Llorenç de Cerdans, El Principat and the term *Catalanista* in
Catalan, but Catalonia and North Catalonia are referred to in English as these terms are
widely used in English language literature.

2. There is some debate over the use of the name North Catalonia, with arguments that
it refers to Barcelona and El Principat as a geographical centre and that the older and
more popular usage of Roussillon should be used. However, strictly speaking, Roussillon
is only one *commarca* (traditional Catalan county) out of the four in North Catalonia and
so I use the name North Catalonia.

grandparents of fonctionnaires in this study are overwhelmingly industrial workers, and a particular sequence of inter-generational socio-economic mobility has contributed to the current position of the fonctionnaires.

Social anthropology has traditionally examined rural communities, and examined them in isolation. Mediterranean anthropology is no exception despite the proximity of huge urban centres to many of the chosen villages. It is not just that the wider region is often ignored, but also that the state and the effects and interaction of state bureaucracy with the local community are rarely discussed (Grillo 1980: 21; Llobera 1989; Davis 1977). While it has often been pointed out that those who become educated intellectuals, or who leave a community, become the most actively identified with the ethnic identity in question, there are few ethnographic studies which examine the process those individuals undergo. This paper focuses on those members of a community, St Llorenç de Cerdans, who are themselves members of the state bureaucracy. In so doing my concern is not with a pre-formed dichotomy between community and state: instead my aim is to show how the relationship between the two plays a role in ethnic identity.

## Ethnic Identity in St Llorenç de Cerdans

St Llorenç de Cerdans is a centre of rural industry in the mountainous border province of Vallespir in North Catalonia, a region which was ceded to the French State by the Spanish Crown in the Treaty of the Pyrenees, 1659. It is part of the *Paisos Catalans* (Greater Catalonia) which also includes *El Principat* (the Catalan term for the major part of Catalonia in the Spanish state), Valencia, the Balearic Islands and Andorra. There is a long tradition of small-scale industry in the community, dating from forges in the fourteenth century, to the production of rope sandals and textiles from the mid-nineteenth century. At the height of industrial prosperity in 1911 the population was just over 3,000; in 1982 it had fallen to 1,613. The highly divided class structure is going through a period of change: as industry declines the industrial working class is decreasing, and the multi-status socio-economic group of state employees, fonctionnaires, is increasing.

St Llorenç de Cerdans is considered a particularly Catalan community, with a high standard of Catalan widely spoken and Catalan traditions and festivals maintained. The established Catalan ethnic identity within the French state is reinforced in St Llorenç de Cerdans by constant in-migration from El Principat; the migrants being of the same ethnicity but from a different state[3], that is, from Spain. The French state has been much more effective in diluting minority ethnic identities than has the Spanish state, and at least one effect of this migration is to reinforce the Catalan ethnic identity of the community. This places St Llorenç de Cerdans in rather a special position *vis-à-vis* the rest of North Catalonia, or indeed *vis-à-vis* other ethnic areas in France, some of which straddle the border but are not necessarily recipients of in-migration.

At the outset of fieldwork, my proposal was to study the extent to which Catalan ethnic identity had been maintained or eroded in the community. However, this was extremely problematic as I would have needed some kind of estimate of how 'Catalan' the community was before French rule, as well as some way of measuring changes in ethnic identity. What was more, it was not possible simply to label people 'Catalan' or 'not Catalan', as for the most part ethnic identity in St Llorenç de Cerdans is what I shall term 'dualistic', that is, it incorporates elements of both 'French' and 'Catalan' identities. There are other ethnic possibilities too, especially Spanish and Moroccan, although French and Catalan are dominant. Within the community it is not the case that one identity is more highly valued than the other in all contexts. Rather, there appears to be a value placed on achieving an 'appropriate' balance between them. Achieving and maintaining the balance is difficult, however, not least because members of the community differ over what is 'appropriate', an evaluation which also depends on socio-economic status, age and gender. Being an ideal – or set of context-dependent ideals – the balance appears to be more or less unattainable. Although many individuals may subjectively feel that they have sorted out issues and conflicts for themselves, it is clear to the observer that the precarious peace is easily disturbed when new or additional factors are introduced into their lives.

In the community of St Llorenç de Cerdans, I suggest that the nature of the boundaries between ethnic identities is not the same for all social groups. For some, they are flexible and permeable. For others, they are relatively fixed. The relative flexibility or fixity is related to power relations. Ethnicity may be perceived as a 'resource', but this is largely

---

3. These 'migrants' who have moved to St Llorenç de Cerdans have come from an area using the same language and having the same customs, traditions and beliefs. In some cases they have travelled a distance of only 15 km. Nevertheless they have crossed an international frontier and are classified as foreign workers in the French records.

the case with the fonctionnaires, who are the group with least constraint on movement across ethnic boundaries. However, there is a constant danger for fonctionnaires that their behaviour will be judged as not 'in balance' by the rest of the community. On the one hand, because of the link between their employment and a French identity, the fonctionnaires may be judged too French. Being too French involves being regarded as an outsider and in a negative way as socially superior. On the other hand, fonctionnaires risk being labelled Catalanistes, a title which implies that they are Catalan nationalists. This, too, is generally regarded negatively by the majority of the community.

During the late 1970s and early 1980s there was a resurgence of ethnonationalism in France which, fuelled also by events in El Principat, spread to North Catalonia. The result of this was to challenge French centralism in a manner which would have been inconceivable twenty-five years previously. Although the ethnonationalist resurgence affected the community of St Llorenç at the level of cultural consciousness, the majority of the population did not become involved in ethnonationalist politics.

Active participants from St Llorenç de Cerdans in *Catalanista* politics are to be found among those who have left the community in order to work elsewhere, and particularly among young fonctionnaires, both male and female. By no means all fonctionnaires from St Llorenç are *Catalanistes*. The fonctionnaires are also those who have taken most advantage of the recent growth in Catalan activities which has been taking place in Perpignan and North Catalonia in general; activities which include teaching Catalan, and participating in Catalan television and radio programmes.

The reason for this more active participation in Catalan politics and culture, I suggest, is that young fonctionnaires have to exaggerate their 'Catalan-ness' in order to retain their Catalan identity. They become expert at changing, not just from one language to another, but from one ethnic identity to another.

## Problems of Analysing Ethnic Identity

Ethnicity is notoriously difficult to define and to quantify. Its daily manifestations are intangible, and this intangibility increases the longer one lives with a group of people whose replies consist so often of 'that's the way we do it' or, worse, 'that's the way we've always done it'. The anthropologist is in the unenviable position of having to tease out the strands of ethnicity, and identify the patterns and symbols that are tightly woven throughout the community. A number of critics have pointed to the naivety of early anthropologists who assumed ethnic identity to be unproblematic and who used the term 'tribe' so incautiously (Abner Cohen 1974: 51; Southall in R. Cohen 1978: 382; Jenkins 1986: 174). Despite the recent anthropological interest in the situational approach to ethnicity (see Enloe 1973: 20; Smith 1981: 66; Vermeulen 1984: 7) which emphasises the fluctuations and response to shifts in circumstances, the divisions within the ethnic group itself still tend to be ignored. It is not only a case of ethnic identity changing in response to external factors, but also of ethnic identities shifting within the group. As Anthony Cohen has put it: 'We seem generally to have assumed that individuals bearing the "same" culture have imprinted the same meanings to their shared linguistic and behavioural forms. When our ethnography has been able to identify differences, we have treated these as exceptional and, therefore, of special significance' (1986: 11).

However, if the focus on internal divisions is taken to its logical conclusion, it can lead to the kind of individually orientated perspective of rational choice theory that is now being proposed by Hechter and Levi (1985), Hechter (1986), and Banton (1977, 1980, 1985). This assumes the primacy of individual actors in making choices. Individuals are seen to act rationally to maximise advantage, preferences (wealth, power and honour) are assumed, and it is argued that behaviour can be predicted in a given cultural situation.

Much of the debate around rational choice theory is about what constitutes a 'rational' choice, and more importantly what constitutes an 'irrational' choice. It has been argued that there is no such thing as an irrational choice, as every choice, given a certain set of constraints, can be explained as rational, in which case there is no value in the term (e.g. Mason 1982: 422).

Given the problems with assumptions of homogeneity in ethnic groups and with an individual-led approach, a solution may be to look at broad-based divisions within the ethnic group. To some extent the empirical material must dictate this, and the group's own perceptions are of crucial importance. In the case of St Llorenç de Cerdans ethnic identities cannot be fully understood without taking into account the stratifications of gender, class and generation. A crucial stratification for fonctionnaires is that of class, as I illustrate below.

## Stratification

Largely due to its industrial economy, St Llorenç de Cerdans has a clear-cut class structure. The class divisions are not so apparent in the rest of North Catalonia, which has a mixed economy based on agriculture (particularly viticulture on the plain), tourism and a high proportion of pensioners from all over France. St Llorenç de Cerdans cannot be seen in any way as typical of the region, in fact rather the opposite; it is an exceptional case (apart from the neighbouring community of Prats de Mollo) in having had a flourishing, if small, industrial economy.

Since the advent of the textile factory and the *espardenya* (rope sandals, known as *espadrilles* in French) factories and workshops which it supplied, there has been a small group of *industrial bourgeoisie* or owning class, which replaced a landowning group based in El Principat. The growth of the factories was influenced by the prosperous textile industry in El Principat, the proximity of the border to St Llorenç de Cerdans, and smuggling.[4]

The *petty bourgeoisie*, made up of those who own small businesses, is a stable group. Economic interests have shifted over a period of 400 years along with changes in the local economy. This group currently owns small artisan workshops producing *espardenyes*; small timber yards; cafés and shops.

The third class in St Llorenç de Cerdans is the working class. Members of this class group all work in the factories or agriculture. Agriculture has not been of primary importance in the area surrounding the community for about 200 years, and possibly longer. In the French census of 1982, approximately 6 per cent of the population was recorded as being *actifs agricoles*, that is actively working and earning a living from agriculture. St Llorenç de Cerdans differs from both the region and the rest of France in this low participation in agriculture. Land ownership is in large units and there is a high turnover of agricultural workers, most of whom move on rapidly to work in the factories. All workers originate from El Principat or other parts of the Spanish state[5] within about three to four generations. Indeed, it is extremely rare to find families in the

4. See Saquer (1970), Brunet (1986) and Sahlins (1989) for excellent studies of smuggling on this section of the French/Spanish border.

5. It is interesting to note that people from El Principat, i.e. Catalonia in the Spanish state, are called 'Spaniards' by those from North Catalonia whereas people from other parts of Spain are labelled according to their region, i.e. Galicians, Basques etc.

community that do not have kin within two generations from *l'altre costat* ('the other side', i.e. the other side of the border in El Principat). Those who have family going back two generations or more on the French side of the border only are more likely to be petty bourgeoises.

Lastly, there are the fonctionnaires who cannot accurately be called a class group, as they come from widely varying class backgrounds and represent a broad spectrum of status and economic remuneration. However, in the context of ethnic identity this group has some very specific characteristics, and therefore I will discuss it as an entity, although it is by no means without internal differentiation.

## The Fonctionnaires

The fonctionnaire group has similarities with the British category of civil servant, but there are also important differences. The French system of state bureaucracy has been classified as a Doctrinaire System and the British as a Pragmatic Scheme (Piquemal 1986: 44, my translation). A doctrinaire system is imposed by statute, that is, laws are passed to define exactly the role, loyalty and salary of a public agent. A pragmatic scheme harnesses a class of workers and converts them into public agents through a looser, decentralised system.[6] The doctrinaire system in France has a central body of legal documentation, and categories of status which cross-cut all the different sectors (there are four levels of employment, A, B, C and D) which have both pay and obligations attached. Security of employment for fonctionnaires was granted in 1880 for some of the higher grade posts, and spread down through the other grades until in 1945 it was granted to all fonctionnaires (Zeldin 1973: 120). One consequence of these laws is that some fonctionnaires are employed without there being a specific job for them to go to. When someone becomes a fonctionnaire it is for life, something which implies not only job security but a reciprocal relationship with the state whereby the worker will always be at the disposition of the administration. The administration will become a 'carer' of the worker, ensuring his or her well-being, continuous employment, long holidays and a good pension.

An explanation of the 'spirit of public service', as it is called in France, is necessary to clarify that what is being discussed is not a

6. Although aspects of the British civil service are dealt with legally (i.e. many civil servants have to sign the Official Secrets Act) conditions of employment are usually related to the category of work and are often established by that employment sector and their unions rather than through the law-making bodies of the land.

simple socio-economic category but a form of identity that is a 'way of life' for those concerned. There is a state-wide understanding of this identity. Whatever it means to the individuals concerned, they present an external image that is understood (even if perceived differently) by everyone in France. The state-wide understanding has varied over time, as Zeldin (1973) clarifies. In contemporary France, however, it is reasonable to say that to be a fonctionnaire means to be French.

A high proportion of the employment for intellectuals in France is as fonctionnaires, although it is certainly not the case that all fonctionnaires are intellectuals. Much of the literature on ethnicity points to the important role of intellectuals in nationalist movements (e.g. Gellner 1964, 1983; Smith 1979, 1981; Nairn 1981). The role of teachers in particular has been pointed out (Beer 1977, 1980)[7]. It is certainly the case in St Llorenç de Cerdans that many of those who are most 'ethnically active' are intellectuals, though it seems to me that it is not so much the fact that they are intellectuals that is the common denominator as the fact that they are fonctionnaires.

It is worth noting at this point who the fonctionnaires are in the community, their class origin and their type of employment. In St Llorenç de Cerdans there are three types of fonctionnaires. Firstly there are those who have come to the community from elsewhere to work; these include members of the police, customs officers (mostly men) and teachers (both men and women). One of the characteristics of the fonctionnaire system is the geographical rotation of jobs which was established for *représentants en mission* in 1793, whose job it was to quell resistance to the Revolution in the provinces. Job rotation and reporting to the committee every ten days was introduced to ensure unity and loyalty to the administration system. Discussing the establishment of the *représentants* Wright says: 'A France brought to the verge of disintegration by the federalist revolt was to be forced into acceptance of administrative uniformity so that resources could be co-ordinated for the war effort. To resist a *représentant* was to resist the sovereign will of the people' (1978: 76).

The system of job rotation was later applied to the fonctionnaires, and in contemporary France certain higher grade fonctionnaires are still not

---

7. In a study of ethnic activists throughout France, Beer gives a total of 37% of respondents being teachers. Professionals – of which teachers are only one category – account for only 5% of those actively employed in France, suggesting a particularly high proportion of activists among teachers. Beer's sample of Northern Catalonia is, as he points out, problematic in that the official statistics used are those of the region, not the departement, which means that four 'non Catalan' *departements* are included in the figures, and the sample of ethnic activists brought only seven replies. However, from my observations I would suggest that the percentage of activist teachers appears to be plausible.

expected not to work in the area from which they come. Job rotation is also designed to avoid allegiances building up in the more sensitive political posts such as that of *prefect*, and those concerned with law and order. Consequently the French language has been obligatory between locals and incoming fonctionnaires, something which has caused tensions regarding language use. Some of the teachers whose origins are from outside Catalonia have become involved in community activities, but no one in this group is involved in Catalan politics.

Secondly, there are those from St Llorenç de Cerdans who work elsewhere. Many fonctionnaires in France are sent to Paris for the first years of employment. Most of those from St Llorenç de Cerdans request a move nearer home as soon as they go to Paris although it can take about ten years to be transferred, as many people in France want to move south. The status of work varies greatly and includes post office workers, police, teachers, mechanics, secretaries, social workers, and customs officers. As far as I am aware there are few from St Llorenç de Cerdans who are in the élite administrative jobs and it is probable that this is due to the class background of most of the fonctionnaires from the community. It is this second group of fonctionnaires which is perceived as being most active in Catalan activities, and which appears to contain the highest proportion of women. Exceptions here are the police, customs officers and mechanics.

Thirdly, there are those from the village who are employed in the locality. A number of posts, particularly those of lower grade (C and D posts), do not require job rotation. D posts are basically manual labour. For example, there are eleven municipal workers in the village, all men, who repair roads, collect the rubbish, and do general repairs, and the female cleaner of the *Mairie* (town hall) is also a fonctionnaire. However, the employees who work in the offices of the *Mairie* are higher grade, as are the health workers in the old people's home, post office employees, and the new post in a recently opened museum of the community which also acts as a tourist information service. A small number of teachers are also from the village. These teachers had to work elsewhere before getting a transfer back to St Llorenç de Cerdans or the vicinity. Some fonctionnaires live in the village and commute daily to a neighbouring town, or weekly to Perpignan.

I have said that the fonctionnaires cannot be called a class, and have gone into the differentiation of posts in some detail in order to show this. It is, however, useful to look at the class background of fonctionnaires in the community. The industries of St Llorenç de

Cerdans have not been able to withstand the rationalisation of the 1980s and, after surviving, with a number of serious crises, a hundred years, the factories are now closing. At their height (from 1900 until the early 1970s) there were eight factories and an average of twelve small artisan workshops functioning in the community. During the 1970s most of these closed and in 1990 there were two factories operating with only a few personnel, and three workshops. The workers as a class are disappearing. The fonctionnaire group, however, is increasing.

It is clear from data on the community that the workers are becoming fonctionnaires. This change is complex; it is not possible for someone to become a fonctionnaire just because there is no work at the factory.[8] The change is part of a long term-process of shifting employment whereby workers moving out of their class occupations have been replaced by migrants from 'the other side', firstly from the Spanish state and, when this source of migrant labour dried up,[9] from Morocco. As employment in St Llorenç de Cerdans has declined, the chain of migration has stopped, and there are no more migrants coming in.

The result of this is that there has been long-term linear change in the community with increased social mobility for migrant workers. The French administration has 'served as a major avenue of social mobility' (Zeldin 1973: 115; McPhee 1980). Employment as a state employee must be preceded by at least one generation of residence in the French state, and more usually two or more. As the factories are declining a generation of young people are being prepared for a 'life of public service'. Young people from the petty bourgeoisie are also becoming fonctionnaires, although the proportion is substantially smaller than from the working class. For the petty bourgeoises, the administration is not so much a form of social mobility as an employment resort for offspring who do not inherit the family business. It is perhaps because of this that becoming a fonctionnaire does not seem to affect their ethnic identity in the way that it affects that of fonctionnaires from

8. The applications for fonctionnaire positions demonstrate this: in 1984, 724,469 applications were made of which 46,856 were successful (approximately 6%).

9. The number of people from Spain has decreased because of an improved economy and better employment opportunities within Spain since the late 1960s. This was particularly the case with work of a similar nature in espadrille and textile production in the nearby villages in El Principat. In general the 1960s was a period of slowing emigration from Spain, and even the return of some migrant workers, including some from St Llorenç de Cerdans.

working-class backgrounds.[10] There is not room to explore this in detail here, but it appeared during my fieldwork that the petty bourgeoisie were much more secure in their balance of ethnic identity than were the workers.

## Shifting Ethnic Identities

The fonctionnaires of St Llorenç de Cerdans, then, constitute a group of both men and women, whose origins are largely based in the working class and who, within three to four generations, have come from the 'other side'. How are the fonctionnaires perceived within the community, particularly by other young adults of working-class origins? To answer this question it is necessary to examine briefly the chain of social mobility for the workers, from migration to state employment, and the concurrent shifts in ethnic identity.

While in the past the factories in St Llorenç de Cerdans provided plentiful employment for many workers, that work was far from being continuous or secure, and most summers there were lay-offs for a month or even two. Workers moved from one factory to another depending on demand and on their own reputation for hard work and/or political militancy. While it is true that during the twentieth century many workers were able to accumulate money, this was only due to sustained simultaneous employment of many members of the family, and temporary work such as grape-picking on the coastal plane of Roussillon, or even factory work as far away as Perpignan, to supplement lay-offs. The workers' aim was that their children would not be subject to the same economic insecurity as themselves. However, alternative employment in St Llorenç de Cerdans was extremely difficult to find. The petty bourgeoisie had an iron grip on the small industries and cafés, and other work required unavailable capital. The only feasible improvement in employment was to become a fonctionnaire, which demanded good spoken French, and the completion of at least the first stage of schooling. At a deeper level it required a shifting of ethnic identity from being Catalan to being French. This triggered a language shift in the family whereby the parents spoke Catalan to each other and

---

10. So far I have no record of offspring of any of the industrial bourgeoisie group becoming fonctionnaires. However, with the rapid decline of the factories, this may happen as the group are faced with the choice of moving or changing socio-economic group unless new economic interests are developed within the community, which at the moment looks unlikely.

French to the children. Until approximately the mid-twentieth century it was difficult for workers to have the opportunity to learn good French. It was not generally spoken in the village, and few families could afford to keep their children at school beyond the minimum age of 13 rather than work in the factories. A whole family contributed financially over two or three generations before there was enough material security in the family to allow a child to stay on at school.

The process of social mobility through education is common throughout Europe, and indeed many parts of the world. However, here – because of the associations of improved employment with the dominant state ideology – it is linked with ethnic identity. To become a fonctionnaire the children of workers adopt a French identity, and this is recognised state-wide. This entails a danger of being rejected from the community, of being seen as 'French', something which implies a series of meanings. These seem to include at least the following: being an outsider, being to a certain extent of a 'superior' social status, being part of a modern and urban life, and being part of a dominant culture and language. These qualities are all potentially double-edged – they can be regarded either positively or negatively. The problem for fonctionnaires is not to be too French and not to have their Frenchness viewed in a negative light.

It is perfectly understandable to the community when fonctionnaires no longer return to St Llorenç de Cerdans and leave their Catalan identity behind; something not infrequent among fonctionnaires. However, during my period of fieldwork, a sizeable number did not reject their Catalan identity. Rather they were perceived in the community as *having a choice* of identities. The ethnic boundaries had become permeable to them through their occupational status, though this permeability was not without its problems. For the fonctionnaires themselves the way to ensure that they were not rejected from the community was to maintain Catalan activities. However, because of the element of choice available to them, the rest of the community tended to categorise them as being more actively Catalan than was necessarily the case. They were even labelled *Catalanistes* (Catalan nationalists) which is on the whole a pejorative title suggestive of a lack of the balance in ethnic identity which is so valued in the community. Although other people in the community might also fall short of this balance, they are more likely to be excused because of locally recognised constraints which are not applicable to fonctionnaires. Constraints do apply to fonctionnaires, in that they themselves sense that the French identity they have struggled to achieve is only semi-successful. Such is the ambition for economic security and social mobility among the workers that this aspect of what could be called 'identity conflict' is overlooked by the community as a whole. It is largely the fonctionnaires of working-class origin who have to grapple with it.

Although many workers in St Llorenç de Cerdans would claim that it is 'good to be French',[11] those who become French do not always see it in those terms. While seen as clearly French in the community, they are not quite so French in Paris or other parts of France. Their accent and vocabulary is noticeably different and often classified as Spanish. The way they eat and the music they listen to also marks them as different from other French people. On the whole a Catalan identity is regarded within France as a social stigma.

Gellner (1964, 1983) attributes the development of nationalist movements partly to the alienation which rural workers may feel when they move into the city, something which forces them back to the secure solidarity of their ethnic group. Although this can be the case, the analysis must go further in order to explain why such solidarity takes on a specifically 'ethnic' perspective. Power relationships, which determine the dominant ethnic identity, also restrict access to it. Those who are struggling to be accepted into the dominant ethnic identity can be classified as having a 'marginal' identity, as opposed to a 'central' identity; for example, people from North Catalonia have a 'marginal French' identity, while people from the Parisian Basin have a 'central French' identity.[12] Fonctionnaires, however, find themselves somewhere

11. This phrase has been adapted from Brand (1985). That article, which has been an important influence for the ideas in this chapter, compares Scotland and Catalonia and says 'For the Scots, it was good to be British', referring to the place of Scotland within the expanding British Empire.

12. I have adopted this differentiation between types of ethnic identity, although there is not space to discuss it fully here. As a brief definition, it is assumed that any one 'ethnic identity' is not necessarily uniform but can be *centralised* or *marginalised*. It is proposed that a marginal identity occurs where there is:

1. A strong centre (core) to the state (i.e. Paris).

2. A detrimental economic relationship with the core for the periphery, particularly where there is an exportation of labour to the core, and an importation of tourists and pensioners to the periphery.

3. Inferiority is attributed to the periphery by the core, regarding factors such as language use, customs, value for employment, and generally negative stereotyping. Following this we could say that El Principat does not have a Marginal Spanish Identity, but that North Catalonia has a Marginal French Identity. French Catalans feel a need to express their French identity but feel out of place in the core where a sizeable number of them go to work. They are often called Spanish and their accent and manner of speaking are a cause for jokes. French Catalans may deal with this by reinforcing their own identity in Paris. For further discussion, see O'Brien 1990; forthcoming.

in between. A fonctionnaire from the village described it as follows: 'You see, when I am in Paris, I don't feel *chez moi* [at home], and when I am in Barcelona, well I don't feel at home there either. We are stuck in the middle, we are in a sandwich.' It is in order to feel at home in Catalonia that fonctionnaires may emphasise their Catalan identity by becoming involved in political mobilisation or by being a member of, or showing support for, a party that is clearly a Catalan nationalist party. In other cases the label *Catalanista* is applied for activities which are exactly the same as those of non-fonctionnaires. Special significance is read into the fact that fonctionnaires choose Catalan at all.

Even fonctionnaires who are not involved in any way in nationalist politics may still be labelled *Catalanistes* by the community. Non-fonctionnaires and fonctionnaires alike may speak Catalan, dance the national dance (the *Sardana*), eat traditional food, participate in festivals, and so forth, but only a fonctionnaire is likely to be labelled a *Catalanista* for so doing. Fonctionnaires' use of Catalan may be ridiculed for it will be said that they 'can speak lovely French', and 'what did their parents sacrifice themselves all those years for in order to send them to school to learn French, if all they want to do now is to speak Catalan?' This contrasted with the reaction to my speaking Catalan, which, although the residents were rather incredulous that I should want to learn the language at all, was seen as a functional part of my studies – and, of course, there was only my unlovely French to compare it with. What emerges here is that it is not the speaking of Catalan that defines the speaker, but rather, who speaks it and in what circumstances.

As previously mentioned St Llorenç de Cerdans has no tradition of Catalan nationalist politics, but there is a long tradition of trade unionism, left-wing political allegiance and a strong co-operative movement. To complicate the situation further, a left-wing political perspective in St Llorenç de Cerdans is associated with the concept of 'France' and being 'French'. There is, of course, an obvious link between a French identity and the French Revolution, which can provide the association between the left and a French identity.[13] Trade

13. The link between the Revolution and French identity is felt strongly in the community, and is given as a reason why the strongly left-wing population should espouse a French identity. Interestingly enough the community did not support the early stages of the Revolution, and in fact the Spanish anti-revolutionary troops entered France through St Llorenç de Cerdans, some would suggest at the invitation of the locals (see Brunet 1986). It should be said that the permanent supply of workers from the Spanish state, and particularly El Principat, probably contributed to the political consciousness of the community, due to the active workers' movements there.

unions and workers' rights are also associated with France: this is in contrast to Spain. From the point of view of the left, there is also a negative association of the Church with a Catalan identity in North Catalonia. Within the context of being from a working-class background and being politically active, then, there are a number of constraints against involvement in Catalan nationalist politics.

Despite the lack of political nationalism, there is a strong sense of identification with being Catalan and with the village itself, and since my first visit there has been a growing reflection on the history of the community as embodied, for example, in the museum established in 1981. The museum is situated in the oldest *espardenya* co-operative factory and exhibits *espardenya* production in general, as well as the co-operative in particular. Since 1981 it has expanded and could now be seen as a record of the major events of the community. People take much pleasure in visiting and seeing their history, as well as in recognising their own family and friends in the photos exhibited and in the short film that is shown daily during the summer. Part of this new reflexivity is an awareness of the strength of the Catalan identity of the community compared with that of the rest of North Catalonia. This is expressed as the difference between what is locally called a 'real' Catalan and a 'superficial' Catalan. In recent years a choir singing traditional Catalan songs and a Catalan theatre group have been set up, both of which receive a lot of support. Another example of the new ethnic consciousness is a book that has been produced in the local Lycée at Ceret, attended by children from St Llorenç de Cerdans. This book concerns a period of local history during which there were rebellions against taxes imposed after the treaty of the Pyrenees. Some have interpreted these rebellions as being not just a tax revolt but an attempt to assert a Catalan identity. The writing of this book has been seen in the community as an important process in the reclamation of local identity. Supervised and edited by a teacher resident in St Llorenç de Cerdans, the book is written in such a form as to be highly accessible to the local population (Sala and Megevand 1985). Catalan traditions and identity are being reassessed. Traditions are in a process of being turned from events central to everyday life into folklore; events and activities are being actively preserved because of their local authenticity and interest.

While political mobilisation around a Catalan identity is not to be found in the village, it can be found elsewhere in the region and in Paris. There is no strong politically nationalist party demanding autonomy or re-unification with El Principat,[14] though there is a consensus that North Catalonia is getting a raw deal within the French state. Economically, North Catalonia is an impoverished province, and suffers many of the socio-economic problems that commonly occur in areas of mass tourism. There is an ageing population, an influx of pensioners, depopulation of the young (particularly from the mountainous areas), and a lack of economic dynamism. The fact that these problems were not tackled after Mitterrand and the Socialist Party came into power in 1981 has led to a growing disillusionment with the left, particularly among the young. Tacit support for regionalist politics and Catalan Nationalists is a form of protest that a small but growing number are willing to give within limits. The slogan 'Volem Viure al Pais' ('we want to live in our land') used throughout North Catalonia (and Occitania) by parties otherwise categorised as extreme nationalists, has entered the popular discourse and awakened an awareness of 'enforced exile'. The teaching of Catalan language in schools is now much more acceptable to parents throughout the province than it was during the 1970s and early 1980s. There are local Catalan radio stations and a local Catalan newspaper, all started up in the late 1980s, and which appear to be supported in principle by many who do not even speak, read or understand Catalan.

Fonctionnaires have long been aware of 'enforced exile' and it is during that exile that their Catalan identities may be reinforced. In Paris there is a Catalan radio station run by people from North Catalonia, and some of the fonctionnaires from St Llorenç de Cerdans are active in it. There is a centre of Catalan Studies in Paris which again is supported by fonctionnaires from the village. In Perpignan a small number of fonctionnaires from St Llorenç de Cerdans are active in *Catalanista* parties as well as in radio stations and in the teaching of the language.

## Conclusion

I have argued that ethnic identities are complex shifting phenomena. They may shift alongside a whole range of social and economic

---

14. To list all the parties in North Catalonia would take a long time. Suffice to say here that there are many, they are split largely over the question of allegiance to the *Paisos Catalans*, and there are frequent re-alignments. While there is no overwhelmingly powerful party, the different alignments appear to be willing to co-operate over presenting 'Catalan lists' in the elections, which do not win many votes.

developments. Not only may ethnic identity be experienced differently by different members of what is assumed to be an 'ethnic group', but individuals may experience conflicts over the nature of their own identity, as has been illustrated here with regard to the fonctionnaire group within the North Catalan community of St Llorenç de Cerdans. The conflict they experience has been shown to be embedded in the social and economic structures of the community as well as in the administrative organisation of the state.

What becomes apparent from close observation of activities and labelling in St Llorenç de Cerdans is that different meanings are attached to certain activities according to the perception of the actor. Fonctionnaires are particularly subject to differing perceptions, and as I have suggested in this paper, are rarely seen as having their dualistic identity 'in balance'. In a community where there is no tradition of political mobilisation around ethnic identity, the few *Catalanistes* do come from the fonctionnaire group. Their involvement appears to commence when they are away from the community, and therefore particularly affects exiled fonctionnaires. *Catalanista* politics are not generally supported in the community and many people find it difficult to sympathise with or understand these exiled or returned fonctionnaires. The question I have asked here is why the fonctionnaires should find it necessary to give support to *Catalanista* politics. There is no clear answer but I have suggested that, firstly, the marginal French identity that fonctionnaires discover they have on arrival in Paris, or any other French town, encourages deeper examination of the 'good to be French' ideology; and secondly, although this political activity is not supported in the community, the fonctionnaires themselves feel the need to exaggerate their Catalan identity to remain in any way part of it. They have already been classified as French and the links with the community have been weakened, ready for severance.

To understand why the fonctionnaires are even concerned about this break from the community, it can be useful to look at the close-knit networks of the working class in St Llorenç de Cerdans from which this group of people largely originate. Families, neighbourhoods, work colleagues, political affiliations and language use criss-cross this class group in a tightly bound network. Even before migration to St Llorenç de Cerdans there are connections from the villages of origin in El Principat. An example of these close networks is the marriage some years ago of someone whose grandmother left the village, to someone whose father left the village; the marriage took place in northern France. Neither party had lived in St Llorenç de Cerdans and yet the community was clearly the connection between them. None of these explanations can give the whole answer to the contradictory situation of the *Catalanistes* in St Llorenç de Cerdans. However, they do indicate some of the issues that I consider relevant.

Despite the negative associations the community attributes to the label *Catalanista*, if the fonctionnaires do not assert their Catalan ethnic identity they will be excluded from the community and categorised as French. For the fonctionnaires who return to St Llorenç de Cerdans with their French identities assured, it is their Catalan identity that is in danger of disappearing and which they struggle to maintain. Those who do not question the 'good to be French' ideology find this difficult to understand. The fonctionnaires may have flexibility in shifting their ethnic identities but the price they pay is that they are never considered to be in balance – in Paris they risk being peasants, and, in St Llorenç de Cerdans, nationalists.

## Acknowledgements

The research on which this paper is based was supported by an SSRC studentship and a grant from the University of London Central Research Fund which I gratefully acknowledge. I also thank Sharon Macdonald for helpful comments on the paper.

## References

Banton, M. (1977), 'Rational Choice: A Theory of Race and Ethnic Relations', *Working Papers on Ethnic Relations*, No.8. SSRC Research Unit on Race Relations

_____(1980), 'Ethnic Groups and the Theory of Rational Choice', in *Sociological Theories: Race and Colonialism*, pp. 475–83. Paris: UNESCO

_____(1985), 'Name and Substance: A Response to Criticism', *Ethnic and Racial Studies*, vol. 8, no. 4 (Special Issue on Rational Choice Theory)

Beer, W. R. (1977), 'The Social Class of Ethnic Activists in Contemporary France', in M. Esman (ed.) *Ethnic Conflict in the Western World*, pp. 143–58. Ithaca and London: Cornell University Press

_____(1980), *The Unexpected Rebellion: Ethnic Activism in Contemporary France*. New York: New York University Press

Brand, J. (1985), 'Nationalism and the Neocolonial Periphery', in R. Rogowski and E. Tiryakian (eds), *New Nationalisms of the Developed West*, pp. 277–93. London: Allen and Unwin

Brunet, M. (1986), *Le Roussillon, Une société contre L'État 1780–1820*. Association des Publications de L'Université Toulous le Mirail, Editions Eché

Cohen, Abner (1974), *Two-Dimensional Man*. London: Routledge and Kegan Paul

Cohen, Anthony (ed.) (1986), *Symbolising Boundaries: Identity and Diversity in British Cultures*. Manchester: University Press

Cohen, Ronald (1978), 'Ethnicity: Problem and Focus in Anthropology', *Annual Review of Anthropology*, vol. 7, pp. 379–403

Davis, J. (1977), *People of the Mediterranean*. London: Routledge and Kegan Paul

Enloe, C. H. (1973), *Ethnic Conflict and Political Development*. Boston: Little Brown

———(1980), *Ethnic Soldiers*. Harmondsworth: Penguin

Gellner, E. (1964), *Thought and Change*. London: Weidenfeld and Nicolson (1983), *Nations and Nationalism*. Oxford: Blackwell

Grillo, R. D. (ed.) (1980), *'Nation' and 'State' in Europe*. London: Academic Press

Hechter, M. (1986), 'Rational Choice Theory and the Study of Race and Ethnic Relations', in D. Mason and J. Rex (eds), *Theories of Race and Ethnic Relations*. pp. 170–86. Cambridge: Cambridge University Press

———and M. Levi (1985), 'A Rational Choice Approach to the Rise and Decline of Ethnoregional Political Parties', in R. Rogowski and E. Tiryakian (eds), *New Nationalisms of the Developed West*. London: Allen and Unwin

Jenkins, R. (1986), 'Social Anthropological Models of Inter-Ethnic Relations', in D. Mason and J. Rex (eds), *Theories of Race and Ethnic Relations*, pp. 170–86. Cambridge: Cambridge University Press

LLobera. J. (1989), 'On the Myth of Primitive Spain', *Anthropology Today*, vol. 5, no. 5, pp. 24–5

Mason, D. (1982), 'Race Relations, Group Formation and Power: A Framework for Analysis', *Ethnic and Racial Studies*, vol. 5, no. 4, pp. 420–36

McPhee, P. (1980), 'Internal Colonization', *Review*, vol. III, no. 3, pp. 399–428

Nairn, T. (1981) *The Break Up of Great Britain* (2nd edn). London: Verso Editions

O'Brien, O. (1990), 'Perceptions of Identity in North Catalonia', in J. Llobera (ed.), *Family, Class and Nation in Catalonia*, Special Issue of *Critique of Anthropology*, vol. 10, nos. 2 and 3

———O'Brien, O. (1992), 'Sisters, Parents, Neighbours, Friends; Reflections on Fieldwork in North Catalonia (France)', in D. Bell, P. Caplan and W. J. Karim (eds), *Gendered Fields*. London: Routledge

Piquemal, M. (1986), *Les Nouvelles Fonctions Publiques*. Paris: Berger-Leurault

Sahlins, P. (1989), *Boundaries; The Making of France and Spain in the*

*Pyrenees*. Berkeley, LA: University of California Press

Sala, R. and R. Megevand (eds) (1985), *Els Angelets de la Terra; La Guerra de la Sal*. Perpignan: Sofreix

Saquer, J. (1970), *La Frontière et la Contrebande avec La Catalogne dans l'histoire du département des Pyrénées-Orientales de 1814 à 1870*. Toulouse: D.E.S.

Smith, A. D. (1979), *Nationalism in the Twentieth Century*. Oxford: Martin Robertson

_____ (1981), *The Ethnic Revival*. Cambridge: Cambridge University Press

Vermeulen, H. (1984), 'Introduction', in J. Boissevain and H. Vermeulen (eds), *Ethnic Challenge – The Politics of Ethnicity in Europe*, pp. 7–14. Gottingen: Herodot

Wright, V. (1978), *The Government and Politics of France*. London: Hutchinson

Zeldin, T. (1973), *Ambition, Love and Politics, 1848–1945*. Oxford: Clarendon Press

## 6

# Becoming Celtic in Corsica

## *Rosemary McKechnie*

This paper is about Corsica, Scotland and looking for ethnic identity on the peripheries of Western Europe. The thread linking these concerns is my own experience as an anthropologist from one peripheral area carrying out research in another. The path taken may appear circuitous, not only travelling from the North to the shores of the Mediterranean, but covering the internal journey I embarked on as I moved from Scotland to Corsica via Oxford. However, in retracing the development of my own understanding of what I was studying, and the problems I encountered on the way, I hope to be able to offer some insights into the nature of what has become a common pursuit, that is the definition of peripheral ethnic identities. In articulating some of the questions that have come to trouble me about aspects of Western European interest in peripheries and 'minority' identities, I would like to raise some problems I believe have to be confronted if anthropology is to render fruitful its new role at home.[1]

The geographical distance covered here does permit some consideration of the framework of shared ideas that shape the way we categorise ourselves and others in Western Europe. Ardener (1987) has underlined the necessity of critically examining the ideas that we have about such 'remote areas' and the identity of those who live there. We can no longer innocently take a positivist approach, finding a remote area, noting language and cultural differences then reading them back and forwards in history (McDonald 1987: 121). Research concerned with identity benefits from textual examination of the historiography, the development of imagery defining an area, from realisation that the whole of society participates in the creation of peripheral identities. McDonald (1982, 1986) and Chapman (1978, 1982), by looking at the

---

1. Many of the issues addressed in this paper follow on from themes first raised in the ASA volume *Anthropology at Home*, A. Jackson (ed.), London, 1987

textual recreation of Celtic identity, and the symbolic appropriation of this construct by, amongst others, the educated activists who speak and act on the behalf of minority areas, have thrown light on one important facet of the puzzle. However, it is still true that using ethnographic techniques we are limited to consideration of one small group, usually a village or town in the peripheral area, usually focusing mainly on the indigenous population. This can make it difficult to get a clear view of the relations that recreate identification in the everyday. Anthropologists interested in the way cultural difference is established and reproduced in Europe face a double challenge as the body of ideas involved in the generation of symbolic boundaries are increasingly complex. As Maryon McDonald points out, the general process of definition and self-definition is one in which 'categories of identity are constructed and come alive, not in isolation or in nature or in the mists before time, but in specific, and changing contexts. The identity of a people is a product of the contemporary structural context in which it exists' (1986: 333). One problem arising from research that focuses on small communities is bridging the apparent gap between the textual reproduction of imagery and the experience of those we study. The story we tell concerns that gap.

Including the ethnographer herself in the picture does several things. To begin with, reflecting self-consciously on my own perceptions of how being Scottish was interpreted, both in Oxford and in Corsica, brought home how what is left unsaid concerning ethnic identification can be more important than what is said. The stereotypical terms in which we often appear to see ourselves and others, which we talk in terms of, often mask much more complex communications. I also gained insight into how the process of identification works in establishing or blocking relations with others. Reflecting on what was read into my own ethnic status uncovered an *ad hoc* bricolage of ideas about identities in Western Europe that allowed considerable latitude for interpretation of my presence in both positive and negative terms.

Perhaps the most important result was that people's interpretation of my nationality gave me some indication of what identity meant to them. It became clear that people were more or less self-conscious about identity, that it could be more or less significant in their lives. In Corsica I found that some were very aware of being Corsican, of retaining their Corsican character. Others were very much less so, but nevertheless being Corsican was something that everyone was conscious of. The political situation, and the nationalist violence that was prevalent at the time of my fieldwork, put a particular stress on definitions of identity, adding to what Ardener (1987) has termed the 'event richness'[2] of this particular 'remote area'. The nationalist vision of what it meant to be Corsican as opposed to French had entered into everyone's life in a way that could not be ignored. I found that accounts of 'real' Corsicanness were already theorised, already contrived. My own conceptualisation of what was 'really' Corsican was different again, and here I was forced to confront several problems for which I was unprepared. These problems concerned my own conceptualisation of identity and the reasons I had chosen to approach fieldwork with identity as guiding precept. But here I am pre-empting the narrative structure of the paper, to begin at the beginning, I should say something about why I chose Corsica.

## Celts and Corsicans – On Common Ground?

Corsica appeared to be an eminently suitable location for an ethnographic study of identity. Not only was it a peripheral region of the French state, it was geographically separate; an island surrounded by the Mediterranean sea. Corsican, an Italianate language, was still spoken by many of the population. There was an active nationalist movement, one that had resorted to violence. In addition, the island had a history of colonisation that marked the shift of dominant power from the Orient to Western Europe – the Phoenicians, the Greeks and the Romans, Pisa, Genoa and finally France held sway there.[3] The last region to be integrated into France, and then by force, the island had in the seventeenth century experienced a brief period of independence. Under the 'enlightened' leadership of Pascale Paoli, who invited Rousseau to draft a constitution, Corsica had been, in theory at least, a precursor of the modern state. Corsicans embodied Rousseau's vision of noble savagery able to realise a free and egalitarian society.[4] At the same time it was the birthplace of modern France's most famous son, Napoleon, as well as several leading statesmen in the centuries that

2. Kirsten Hastrup has succinctly summarised the theoretical underpinnings of Ardener's term 'semantic density' (1989: 225).

3. This is, of course, a simplification of the relationships that existed between these powers and the island, a simplification that has become reified in histories written through the centuries. Pomponi (1979) probably gives the most thorough evaluation of the roles played by each.

4. See Rousseau, *The Social Contract*, 1973, p. 203.

followed. Not only was there an interesting relationship to the state, there was a plethora of imagery constructed around notions Mediterranean honour and shame, and personal violence. This imagery of violence and passion, though rooted in the past, has been translated into the present with Corsicans' perceived predilection for posts in the armed services and the police, their involvement in organised crime and nationalist activities. Last, but not least, Corsica was almost virgin territory in terms of British anthropology.

One aim of this paper is to explore some aspects of the mapping of the definitional structure that organises space and population, that sets out relational similarities between peripheries in opposition to the states that they are part of. It may seem far-fetched to posit any similarity in the tenor of representations of, respectively, the Gaeltacht and a Mediterranean island, emanating from the dominant societies they are part of. However, if the brief description given above has accentuated the particularities of the Corsican case, here I come back to the observation that certain congruences do emerge from a comparison of the two. This is true over a long historical perspective. The descriptions of Corsicans found in classical texts, for example, are very similar to the descriptions of the Celt made by Greek and Roman authors detailed by Malcolm Chapman (1982: 124–6).[5] Even early classical descriptions reveal much about the relationship between the centre of power where text was produced and the margins of their dominion. Then, as now, no observation was free of theoretical prejudgements.

We should not be surprised, then, that descriptions of one sort of barbarian should be like another, nor that there should be marked continuity in ideas about marginal peoples over time. In some ways the metaphorical distance between Greece or Rome, and Corsica or Scotland is very similar, as is that between London and the Hebrides or Paris and Corsica. The same process of definition is at work in, for example, the description of Corsica written by Seneca when exiled there and the accounts of French officials sent there at the end of the eighteenth century.[6] Images of 'otherness' located in the peripheries have played a definitional role for centres of power in Europe down the centuries. The process of ideas shaping observation, giving rise to

---

5. Badouin (1967) compares the observations of Herodotus, Diodorus (V., xiii. 1–14) and Strabo (V. ii. 6–7).

6. Seneca, *De consolatione ad Helviam*, vii, 8; vi, 5. The most comprehensive analyses of eighteenth-century officials' accounts can be found in Desideri (1981: 5–23).

further ideas has continued, despite shifts in the geographical location of power or ideology. Here I am concerned with the image of peripheral populations that has gelled in modern Europe, as power bases have settled in the North-West, within a specific theoretical structuring of the world and humanity.

Travellers of the modern period have certainly found similarities between Corsica and Scotland. By coincidence, one of the most widely read was himself Scottish. The young James Boswell, seeking fame and fortune, visited Corsica on Rousseau's recommendation, and subsequently wrote a glowing account of Paoli's free state and the Corsican rebels (1768). Unlike members of earlier French expeditions, Boswell did not find the Corsican population particularly barbarous. He went prepared to find a people untainted by civilisation and he was undismayed by the rough manners and rude material conditions he encountered there. He drew several parallels between the peasants of his own land and those he came across in Corsica. That Boswell should also have contributed to British society's vision of the Celtic fringes, after his visit to the Western Isles with Dr Johnson is ironic, but not perhaps completely fortuitous.[7]

The comparison has been made explicitly by the writer Joseph Chiari, a Corsican who lived for many years in Glasgow. He wrote describing the nature of his own and his adopted people's character, finding common Celtic inheritance at the root of many similarities (1960: 93–7). The idea of 'common Celtic roots' may appear to stretch the imagination beyond acceptable limits when forced to encompass a Mediterranean island with no linguistic or historical links with Gaelic-speaking areas. However, it is one that appears to have been, with some modification, relatively acceptable to a wide reading public in Corsica and elsewhere.[8] That the idea that Corsicans and Celts are in some way related, or even the same, is acceptable to many Corsicans is an illustration of the way we think about ourselves in Europe.

---

7. There is perhaps a parallel to be made between Boswell and a young ethnographer taking her first steps in academia. Boswell's pursuit of the primitive in the wilder reaches of Europe was far from disinterested. If he chose to vary the route of his 'grand tour' it was because he realised that there was a curious public that would remark on his writings. The contrast between his Rousseau-esque vision of Corsica, and the down-to-earth depiction of the Western Isles written with Dr Johnson, encapsulates the geographical and epistemological framework of European self-understanding of his time.

8. Dorothy Carrington's popular works, based on a lifetime's archaeological and ethnographic work on Corsica, have claimed common megalithic origins for Celtic and Corsican cultures (1984: 50–1). See also Chiari (1960).

The particularities of each regional characterisation are clear, but the similarities are also present: both are rural, passionate, violent, poetic, uncivilised, clan-centred, and impatient of authority. The framework of opposition to the dominant society is one that works spatially no matter how the peripheral area is orientated towards the dominant centre, as the parallels between two regions, one Mediterranean, the other Northern, show. This is not to say that analyses that have followed the oppositions in one direction are faulty, but there is the risk that previous academic representations will be reified and the dynamic of the definitional process lost. The strength of this process is that it is flexible, that each case can be backed up by all sorts of auxiliary theories that apply to a particular area and that can be used in an *ad hoc* way.

The definitional process is not restricted to the level of academic discourse; it also takes place 'on the ground', in everyday social interaction. Fitting the historical/textual background together with empirical observation of how people's ideas about themselves and others are recreated in the details of everyday life, is the problem facing anthropologists looking at identity. As Ardener points out, individuals are defined by the social space but they are also its defining consciousness (1987: 28). There is no one Corsican identity. People see themselves as individuals and as Corsicans in a variety of ways, and their shifting perceptions are constituted in the self, in context, in their relationship to those around them. One of the focuses of this paper is how the sense of self is bound up by imagery, and vice versa; the fuzzy area where the work of identification is carried out.

## Becoming Celtic in Corsica

My choice of research area was partly due to my own perception that there were similarities between the Celtic fringes and Corsica. The possibilities for contrast and comparison were amongst the factors that made the island attractive to me. I was, however, surprised that such links were made by Corsicans when I arrived on the island. Some of what follows concerns how my own presence was interpreted by people in Corsica. Although the focus of the paper is ethnic identity, many of the observations relate to carrying out ethnography close to home. First, being there as an anthropologist might have been strange, but being there at all was not very odd. As Kirsten Hastrup (1987: 100) has pointed out, the anthropologist herself is a sign to be interpreted, and close to home the sign is far from meaningless; my gender, age, training, even the clothes I wore, all meant something. Here I am concerned particularly with my nationality, and my role as ethnographer. These two aspects to a great extent shaped the way in which people thought about me. They found contrasts and similarities to structure ideas about their own setting and mine, their own character and mine. The categorisations involved were at the same time mutually comprehensible while never completely mapping one over the other. The gaps and misunderstandings that gradually came to light between their interpretation of what it was to be Scottish and my own, provided me with both insights into what it meant to be Corsican and questions about my own conception of 'identity'.

During my first fieldwork experience on the Isle of Man I took it for granted that people would accept me more easily because I was Scottish; that having 'an ethnic identity' made studying identity accessible. However, on Corsica I was forced to re-evaluate this assumption. To begin with, those who were conversant with nationalist theories but opposed to them, tended to see me, a member of another ethnic minority 'interested in nationalism', as a sympathiser myself: someone to regard with suspicion. My nationality provided a reason to suspect me of complicity with those involved in violence. One woman openly confronted me, asking why I claimed to be Scottish: what was wrong with being English? Was I another trouble-maker?

Less obvious perhaps were the difficulties engendered by the way some nationalists perceived me. Several times I found myself in uncomfortable situations, hearing things I did not particularly want to hear – my allegiance was taken for granted simply by merit of my nationality. Maryon McDonald has described how she came to be redefined as Celtic by Breton militants once her Welsh ancestry was established, and how being seen to be on the side of 'the oppressed' was in many ways more comfortable than the converse (1986: 341). This had been my own expectation in Corsica. However, after some time it became clear that there were some drawbacks involved, particularly in the light of the activities of some of the 'oppressed' there. I was faced with moral dilemmas long before I left the field as to whether I should simply 'go along' with the views and the actions of this particular group. In the reality of a fieldwork situation where I was moving between different groups, including the activists and the French professionals who were the potential victims of nationalist violence, the complexities introduced by the way these groups perceived my ethnic identity were factors I could well have done without.

Amongst the keen young activists at the university I was at first put in the same basket as 'the nice chap from Ireland', whom I had just missed. Very soon, however, questions as to my command of Gaelic, my ability to dance the Scottische (most young nationalists could manage a Scottish country dance or two), my own involvement in and views concerning nationalism in Scotland, began to raise doubts. It became clear that, for some, my minority status was of inferior coin. This gave rise to some uncomfortable situations which were, it seemed, much to do with what I was supposed to be but wasn't. The usually easy elision from simply being Scottish to being 'really Scottish' when the situation required it, was not so easily made in such a demanding situation. I began to avoid allusions to my nationality and even resorted on occasion, when I could foresee difficult times ahead, to describing myself as '*Brittanique*'.

One nationalist spent much time and effort showing me the 'real' Corsica. He was sure that I, as a Celt, would be able to understand as no other outsider would, the greatness and tragedy of the Corsican people and their struggle. I did try to clarify my own point of view, to point out that his expectations of what I might produce were likely to be disappointed. He shrugged off my reservations, however, insisting that he could feel that I was in tune on a mystical level with what he showed me. Corsica may have been geographically, linguistically and historically quite a distance from the Celtic fringe, but brotherhood with fellow oppressed minorities created strong ties in the face of the common enemy of, respectively, France and England. Many similarities between the two areas, and the characteristics of the two peoples as warriors, rebels and poets were pointed out to me. He believed that my Celtic character would make Corsican life accessible to me, and would shape the way I went on to write about it, even in spite of myself.

Outside the context of mainly middle-class nationalists and anti-nationalists Scottishness was less of a problem, but it remained intriguing. Though being Scottish seemed immediately appealing, it was somehow insubstantial. People who would on first meeting wax enthusiastic about the beauties of the Highlands, salmon and bagpipes, would ever after refer to me as *l'anglaise*. England was solid if uninteresting, while Scotland was a puzzling phenomenon for most. I was asked time and again, whether Scotland was a country, or a nation, why its parliament was in England and then what about the queen? If England is interchangeable with Britain most of the time, why isn't it all of the time? My answers failed to satisfy, in that they did not really relate directly to the questions posed. The British constitution in all its intricacies and contradictions just does not correspond to the way society and space are organised in France.

My explanations did little to enlighten anyone about the Scottish. Corsicans are as well versed in national stereotypes as the inhabitants of any Mediterranean island where tourism is the principal economic mainstay. Germans, Italians and Dutch could all be described in familiar stereotypical terms. The imagery associated with the English was particularly finely tuned – there was fish and chips, afternoon tea, cricket, and royalty. The English were always calm, well-mannered to the point of insanity, and invariably badly dressed. The category 'Scottish', although undoubtedly evaluated positively, was, in comparison, rather empty; it did not really go beyond men wearing skirts, and drinking whisky (Chivas Regal of course), in the midst of some hopelessly exaggerated mountains. Within a Corsican-speaking context the problem was compounded by there being no word in Corsican for Scottish, or if there was no one knew of it. So that in the context where people were most likely to wish to refer to me as Scottish, that is in the nationalist context, it was most difficult to do so. On one occasion, for example, I was taken to visit an old lady who smoked ham in the traditional way. We sat in a smoke-filled room, around the steaming cauldron, poised on the edge of a rather difficult introduction. 'Well, is this another *pinzuti*?'[9] she asked with a sneer in her voice. 'Oh no' replied my gatekeeper, 'she's...' and after trying a few variants on the Italian, he shrugged his shoulders and uttered the word '*Inglese*'. This led to a rather long apology later, for the insult he had been forced to inflict on me.

My presence often gave rise to *ad hoc* theorising. Sometimes this took the shape of mapping French/Corsican characterisations over English/Scottish ones. Hence statements that took the form of ' . . . yes you are like us, we are warmer/care more about our families/are less arrogant, than the French and English', came up often. At other times incomprehensible actions of my own were explained in a way that opposed Southern and Northern characteristics. My clumsy attempts at ritual embraces were attributed to the undemonstrative nature of Northern peoples, my execrable dress sense was considered a generic British trait. A friend once rose, with creative aplomb, to the occasion of explaining my *faux pas* of kissing a baby on the mouth (when the kiss became inevitable I shut my eyes, smacked and hoped for the

---

9. The French were labelled *Pinzuti*, literally 'pointed ones' because of the tricorn hats worn by French soldiers at the end of the eighteenth century.

best). 'Oh,' she said, 'don't you know they are very socialist in Scotland' (she was herself at odds with her family in being a staunch socialist) 'it's hardly surprising she kisses like a Bolshevik'.

Europeans do share a common body of ideas. We are all aware of characterisations of ourselves and others, and able to use them in a creative way. The strength of ideas about ethnic identity lies not in their coherency, but in their flexibility. That being said, these categories do carry a certain amount of determinacy. Some symbolic boundaries are easier to cross than others, and the primary identification of those with whom it is desirable to establish a relationship, and those with whom it is not, is certainly an important feature of identity, as will be shown later in the paper.

To be Scottish, then, meant more than I bargained for in some contexts in Corsica and less in others. I had first consciously begun to reflect on the fact that my origins might have some bearing on the study of identity at a seminar I attended in Oxford before embarking on fieldwork. It was a seminar about things Celtic. Some friends warned me that I might find it upsetting, and afterwards enquired solicitously if I had been shaken by the presentation. I was puzzled by this superfluous attention. Why should I be upset? What did the deconstruction of imagery concerning the Celts have to do with me? I was taken aback to find out that it was assumed that I really identified with this construct in a way that differentiated me from others in the seminar. For some reason I had not expected anthropologists studying identity to assume that being Scottish meant identifying with Gaeldom. I had felt that I was an anthropologist amongst anthropologists. However, I was used to my Scottishness becoming more Celtic and romantic, or kilted and haggis-eating, the further I got from Scotland. Though I was a stranger to the romantic Scotland that stereotypes portray, like all Scottish, I was familiar with passively accepting being drawn into its glamorous embrace; familiar with the privilege of being Scottish. I had long grown to expect my accent to provoke enquiries as to my birthplace and for people's response to be positive. I always nodded my head and smiled without any sense of contradiction, despite the fact that this was not really the case.

For the first time I began to examine my own uncritical acceptance of the way others identified me as Scottish. It was clear that though there was dissonance between what 'Scottishness' meant to others and to myself, my own and other Scots' responses hid this. This might seem to be a rather lengthy navel-gazing exercise about what is, after all, an everyday phenomenon. However, as I went on to carry out fieldwork in

Corsica, the disquiet that resulted from this incident began to assume wider dimensions. I realised that looking at how people see others, and themselves, is more complex than it might first appear. Eliciting stereotypical categorisations is one thing, but it is necessary to get beyond the way people talk about themselves and others to what they do not say. I too was participating in the identification of myself. I was participating in the etiquette that allowed relations to be woven around the basis of identification. Self-conscious reflection on my own actions and interpretations, my own compliance and silence, made me aware of just how much can be concealed. It is easy to decide to get beyond stereotypical categorisations but, in practice, penetrating the surface appearance of relations and understanding what people don't say – 'reading the blank banners'[10] – presents some difficulties. As Becher, following from Yates, has pointed out, the distinguishing feature of anthropological research is the fact that anthropological fieldwork is about experience rather than gathering data: 'for anthropologists methodology is the internal apprehension of relationships and their transformation through cultural meaning … what is of significance is the competence of introspection' (Yates in Becher 1989: 39). My understanding of identification on Corsica came to depend less on what people were saying, than on my personal knowledge of their situation and their relationship to those present and myself.

Having reflected on what Corsicans read into my Scottishness it seemed a strangely empty category, open to arbitrary, contradictory interpretations. And yet it was important. Identification enabled people to categorise me in a framework in relation to themselves and others. Any of my actions could be explained in the light of my being Scottish, as could my personality, and my relationship with others. Beyond that, it carried with it implied moral obligations and political affiliations. None of these were fixed, all could be interpreted according to the standpoint of the observer. It coloured any observation regarding me in a situation where people did think in terms of identity quite a bit, some of them self-consciously. What it meant to be Corsican was important in Corsica.

### 'Real Identity' and the Ethnographer

There are two terms denoting 'Corsicanness'. The first, the French *Corsitude*, is used mainly in the French press, but seldom in

10. Edwin Ardener gives a full explanation of 'blank banners' in his introduction to *Social Anthropology and Language* (1971: xliii–xlv).

conversation. *Corsitude* is usually left undefined, but often has negative connotations. The Corsican *Cursichezza* on the other hand, was often used in activist circles; it was much more closely defined and positively evaluated by those who used the term. In fact, defining 'real' Corsicanness or *Cursichezza* was a nationalist preoccupation. Temporally, *Cursichezza* was spoken about as characterising life on the island before the First World War. It was located spatially on the island in the mountains, particularly in the Niolu, which was generally represented as the most 'remote', untouched region of Corsica. Unlike other French regions, the shepherd rather than the peasant was perceived to be the last living embodiment of traditional Corsican life.[11]

Amongst educated activists there was despair at the consumerism of modern Corsica, the obsession with turbo-drive cars and designer clothes.[12] Nationalists did not absolve themselves from these ills, and would point out to me how they themselves were tainted by modernism, indicating examples of purer Corsican character in comparison. The idea that in the past all Corsicans were close to nature, to the land, and that those living on the island today have lost touch with some indefinable way of being, was often discussed. This image of identity on the brink of destruction is familiar, it is in the nature of 'remote areas' and nationalist discourse.[13] Here, having already raised some questions about stereotypes and identities, I would like to go on to examine more closely how *Cursichezza* was related to the way the self and others were conceptualised in Corsica.

Amongst young nationalists, the keenest young men grew beards, wore waistcoats and dark wool 'Corsican jackets', symbols emblematic of their serious intent. Discussions of family origins could degenerate into a sort of competitive Corsicanness, as they vied with each other to establish whose Corsican roots went furthest back, whose family had maintained a traditional life-style for longest. Individuals told me of how they felt much closer to grandparents than parents who had 'sold out' and gone to work in France. Some did speak Corsican with ease, others wrestled in conversations, falling back into French when emotions ran high. It was agreed that some ways of life provided the

---

11. A comparison can be made with Herzfeld's account of how the shepherds of Crete are seen as primitive and backward, yet also as the embodiment of essential Greek characteristics (see introduction, 1985).

12. See Bellone, 'Crise d'Identite' in *La Corse et La Folie*.

13. See Chapman 1978: 18.

best basis for regaining what had been lost, and those who worked in agricultural communes or artisanal crafts were admired. It was generally recognised, however, that just staying on the island and finding any way of making a living was a positive contribution.

Despite their optimism and the constant recreation of the romantic ideal in conversation, it was clear that, for them, being Corsican was neither simple nor easy: it required dedication. Becoming self-consciously Corsican meant that many of the activities that other young Corsicans participated in every day had to be considered in a negative light, though not all avoided them altogether. Although most young activists enjoyed folk-dancing evenings, and there were 'ethnic' music discos (mainly reggae or Latin-American dance music) organised at the university, they, like others in their age group, could be found several evenings a week dancing to the latest disco music in one of the many *boîtes de nuits*.

The inherent paradoxes of their position were perhaps clearest in their perception of modern Corsican masculinity and femininity. Young men drove fast cars and drank in the same bars as their peers. One confessed to me that he went to bars with friends and picked up girls, hiding the fact that he was homosexual because he felt that it was incompatible with Corsican masculinity. Young women talked of how they did not know if they should see their university education as the basis of a career because they felt that the traditional role of women within the home was central to Corsican family life. Some worried about how far their participation in cultural activities should go; should women sing music traditionally sung only by men? The predominantly masculine vision that lauded the courage and honour of the Corsican male did not accommodate these young women easily. *Cursichezza* touched on every aspect of their life, and their consciousness of it served to highlight how far they fell short of it. The more dedicated they were the more their ideals set them apart, and the more militant among them were marked out from their peers to a certain extent. However, the university did provide a community for young activists facing these problems together. Most students were Corsican. Many had relatives in the town and knew young people of the same age as themselves. Their activities were accepted as part of the vagaries of student life.

Older activists expressed much more ambivalent feelings about their effort to be Corsican. For them, the late 1960s and the early 1970s had been a time of hope; the revolution seemed nigh and they felt they were at the centre of it. They were now resigned to the fact that revolutionary change was not going to take place, and the tone of their discourse was much more pessimistic about the future of Corsican nationalism as well as the Corsican way of life. They bemoaned the lack of interest shown by the majority of their fellow islanders. Several accepted, however, that their expectation that others would want to live their ideal had been unrealistic. They were critical of their own efforts to maintain it. As they had got older and acquired responsibilities, professional positions and material possessions, it had become more and more difficult to maintain their allegiance. When they measured their life against their youthful intentions, they were only too aware that in many respects they had fallen by the wayside.

Many activists also had to live with isolation. They recognised to some degree or another that they were viewed with suspicion and sometimes derision by the Corsican community of which they wanted to be part. Their espousal of an ideal of Corsicanness excluded them from Corsican life. Partly this was because of suspicions about their participation in violence, but local disapproval was not simply due to the means used to attain their aims. It was a rejection of their vision of Corsican life and also their assumption of a leading role. Even amongst those who were sympathetic to many nationalist claims there was little regard for educated activists. Their education, dress, and liberal ideals set them apart.

Some of the male activists made a point of drinking in a bar frequented by working men. They persisted in this despite the fact that their greetings were returned without enthusiasm, their invitations not rejected but simply ignored. I watched as one working man, plainly embarrassed, did talk to them, only to be ridiculed after they had left. I asked him about it later and he explained that he felt he did owe them some respect, that they had achieved something, but personally he too found them exasperating. They were not 'real men'. Their efforts to be 'more' Corsican only served to mark them as out of place, highlighting the aspects of their life that clashed with local understanding of what it was to be a Corsican man.

My presence as an ethnographer 'interested in identity' acted as a catalyst, it led to self-conscious reflection by activists on their aims and how they had shaped their life. This was in part due to their assumption that I must be searching for people who were 'really Corsican'. I suspect that their frank discussion of their feelings might have been more guarded had they interpreted differently my statements that I was interested in everyone and everything, themselves and their position included. It was always assumed that once I got to know some real

Corsicans *dans les villages* then I would shift my interest to them. They endeavoured to make clear to me how far I was from 'real' Corsica in their company, to point me in the right direction. They saw themselves as having failed in an endeavour that could never ultimately be achieved: *Cursichezza* by its nature could not be realised by educated professionals.[14]

The preoccupation with 'real' Corsicanness was not limited to nationalist circles. The anthropologist creates self-conscious thinking about ethnicity. My presence on the island was seldom thought to be particularly surprising, nor was the fact that I professed to be interested in Corsican identity. The concept of identity and the idea that Corsican identity was interesting were fairly familiar and acceptable. However, most people were surprised that I should want to talk to them personally. When I approached people their first reaction was often to point me in the direction of others they considered to be 'real Corsicans' either by merit of being old, of living in the mountains or of their occupation. Often I was told that there were no real Corsicans left. There always seemed to be someone, be it the last real bandit, or the last *strega*[15], who had died just a few years ago; someone who personified some aspect of Corsican life that had just passed.

Sometimes people would be critical of what they perceived as my lack of dedication. One woman refused to speak to me, telling me that she would talk to me when I got a bit more serious about my studies, and stopped wasting my time gossiping in coffee bars or shops. She considered that I should be spending more time in a nearby village, where a group of local artisans had recreated their vision of a real Corsican community. Their livelihood depended on attracting tourists in the summer. The self-consciously constructed Corsicanness that appealed to tourists was, then, also considered fitting for anthropologists. While it was regarded as unrelated to 'ordinary' life, it was at the same time respected as a repository of something that was essentially Corsican. People assumed that their own life today would be uninteresting to me, banal. It was much the same as life elsewhere.

14. Maryon McDonald (1987: 136) had a similar experience amongst the educated activists in Brittany. She has described how it was assumed that the true object of her study was 'real' Breton life. Activists took it for granted that she would eventually feel that she had done enough background research and would move to a village where she wold meet Breton peasants, apt objects of research.

15. The *strega*, or *streia*, a female sorcerer that sucks infants' blood.

For some, this tension between the 'real' and the 'ordinary' was directly relevant to their everyday lives. They were far from surprised that I should be interested in them and, in fact, assumed that they were apt subjects of research. These were those whose occupation was categorised as 'traditional': the chestnut miller, the shepherd or the stonemason. The shepherd is perhaps the most significant personification of the ambiguities involved in what it means to be 'really Corsican' today. The occupation is at once despised as physical dirty work (as in other Mediterranean areas agricultural labour has low prestige) while at the same time it is regarded as the last bastion of the 'real' Corsican way of life. Shepherds would point out traditional techniques still in use, explain cheese-making in detail or how to make snares from horse hair. They passed by new equipment with barely a comment, and when asked about it, talked about how life had changed from the old days. A miller, showing me how he ground chestnuts, was at pains to point out that the same wheel had been used by his father and his father before him, but he was clearly uncomfortable about the ingenious contraption he had rigged up to run the whole thing electrically. His pride was offset by awareness of the disapproval with which this innovation might be greeted by anyone interested in traditional Corsica.

Those whose way of life is defined as 'traditional' live with being perceived by others in terms of stereotypes. For them, the imagery is not just an abstract set of ideas contained by nationalist discourse or tourist brochures. It enters into their lives. Some were, of course, aware of the way they had to live with the reflections of others, be they positive or negative, though it is a difficult area to write about with any certainty. For example, one shepherd remarked with his tongue in his cheek that German women hikers, too, were always interested in visiting a shepherd's hut on the high pasture (the parallel with young women ethnographers remained unarticulated), presumably a positive aspect of personifying the unsophisticated and traditional. Just as the traveller gypsies are able to manipulate dominant society's imagery to their own advantage by being seen to fulfil stereotypical representations (Okely 1979), so too can goatherds on high pasture.

However, such confrontations with dominant society's visions are relatively infrequent. On a day-to-day basis, 'traditional' Corsicans live as part of the modern Corsican community. The same man prefaced telling me how proud he was to follow in his father's footsteps, that the pasture had been in the family for centuries, by remarking that he knew people might look down on him. He went on to point out that although he was not educated, his cousin, with whom he shared the flock, had been a teacher, indicating that he was not necessarily stupid just because he chose to work with animals. His difficulty in maintaining a positive self-image illustrates how the evaluation of traditional Corsican occupations did not necessarily carry much weight within the local community.

While imagery may be positively regarded as an ideal, in everyday life other sets of values cut across it. One couple on the verge of divorce provide a sad illustration of how the attraction of the traditional can fade when it moves from its 'remote' location. The educated wife who saw her husband as wild and natural while they lived on an isolated farm, found him uncouth and uncommunicative when they had to move to the town and he took up manual labour. Living with this sort of paradox was particularly difficult for younger people. Unlike the older generation, who were viewed as remnants of a lost past, they were evaluated in the same way as others of their age group: in terms of professional and economic status. Feelings of anger, pride, shame, superiority and inferiority were expressed about their own and others' perceptions of their position. It is too easy to make assumptions about the often contradictory relationship between the images of identification and life. Understanding what 'identity' means to people requires detailed ethnography, requires sensitive interpretation. I came to realise how my own conception of 'identity' in general and Corsican identity in particular were put under stress by the need to do this.

### *Outsiders Inside Identity*

One aspect of identity I had not thought very much about before arriving on the island was the role that non-Corsicans would play. Identity is often considered in terms of the community defending itself from the incursion of outsiders, and I expected that the increase in French residents on the island would provide some example of this. However, before moving on to look at the way Corsicans viewed these incomers, I would like to consider the case of another group: North African workers. It simply had not occurred to me that immigrant workers could have very much to do with Corsican identity, and it was some time before I revised this point of view. North Africans are to a great extent invisible on the island. They work in the countryside and many live there, often in barrack accommodation. They are seldom seen in shops, virtually never in the bars or nightclubs of smaller towns. They appeared to be outside the social life of the community.

I'm afraid that to begin with this was one aspect of identity I would rather not have had to think about. It would have been convenient simply to label perceptions of the migrant workers as 'racist', something present everywhere in our society, and then ignore it as another problem, unrelated to ethnic identity. In addition, it seemed impossible actually to make any other than the most superficial contact with North Africans. They were ignored, or actively shunned. The stereotypical representations of the Arab male included being dirty, dishonest, violent and sexually rapacious. Young women simply did not speak to an Arab man.

Through time, it did begin to dawn on me that the way the immigrant workers' presence on the island was perceived was crucial to Corsicans' self-image. The negative representations of North Africans were in fact almost exactly the same as those that had been applied to earlier Italian immigrant workers.[16] The *Lucchese* had also come to the island as labourers by dint of economic necessity and had occupied the same dilapidated flats in the oldest *quartiers*. Many had stayed on the island and had bought agricultural land at low prices. They were, themselves, now in a position to employ other workers, as were the *Pied-noirs* who had settled on the island after the Algerian war. The Maghrebian workers' position at the bottom of the social structure in Corsica was, in part, due to the distaste with which physical labour was regarded. To work on the land was considered inferior, to work for someone else even more humiliating. As a result many Corsicans had sold the land they owned, or let it lie fallow. These workers played a central role in the island's economy, simply because no one was prepared to do labouring work. They also played a central role in Corsican self-image by occupying the lowest rung of social and economic status, and by providing a 'pariah' group, defined in opposition to Corsican values of family, cleanliness, pride and intelligence.

The difficulties that this raises for nationalist ideology are obvious. Visions of Corsicans working close to the land do not hold much water in a region where the low esteem of agricultural work is embodied in negative representations of North Africans. Rhetoric of common

16. See Noiriel (1984) for consideration of this imagery in the South of France as a whole. Most Italian immigrants came from the region of Lucca, hence *Lucchese* came to be applied to any Italian labourer. France dealt with the influx of expatriate *pied-noirs* after the Algerian war of independence by offering grants to buy agricultural land in disadvantaged areas, Corsica amongst them. The one area of fertile agricultural land on the island is now profitably farmed by them (Brun 1969: 163–93).

'brotherhood' with other colonised peoples falls flat in a situation where anger at the French state could not translate for many into aligning themselves with people they consider inferior. The warmth extended to European minorities, the 'fictive' ethnic kinship that was often spun to establish a relationship with myself was never, in my experience, used to create any personal ties with North Africans. Their exploitation was ignored by the recently set up Corsican unions. The killing of two Moroccans by nationalists in Ajaccio was justified in terms of protecting Corsican youth from drug trafficking. However, the kind of support the act received shocked many nationalists. A statement explicitly denying that race had anything to do with the matter was published by the nationalists, but this repudiation only added to the confusion.

This being so, the conversation of a group of middle-class Corsicans opposed to nationalism can be put into context. One man was recounting a scene that he had witnessed in a shop. It concerned a Frenchman who had patiently waited to be served, only to be ignored as everyone else was dealt with 'even an Arab'. When he asked what was wrong with his money it was the Arab who answered: 'Listen, me, I'm at home here, it's you who is the stranger' ('Ecoutez, moi, je suis chez moi ici, et vous, vous êtes l'étranger'). It was disgraceful but true they agreed, even Arabs were treated better than the French nowadays on Corsica. This group viewed nationalism and the strengthening of anti-French sentiment on the island (as they perceived it) with some anxiety. One evening at the bridge club, the discussion passed from *attentats* (terrorist attacks) to the way people were much more aware of who was native Corsican nowadays, and who was not. The terms they used, *indigène* and *allogène*, were far from current in everyday conversation, as the puzzled expressions on several faces betrayed. They were determined to avoid the weighted distinction of *continenteaux*, for they too considered themselves to be French. Their values and position were vulnerable to attempts to devalue French culture. They considered being Corsican as one of many ways of being French, without there being any contradiction, the first simply being of less definitional importance than the latter.

Outside these circles there was surprisingly little discussion of the *attentat*s, or other anti-French activities.[17] The graffiti IFF (*I Franchesi Fora* – 'French get out'), that decorated many walls, was ignored. Individual French would be talked of as *continenteaux* or as *pinzuti* but

17. See Ramsay (1983).

the *continenteaux* as a group were seldom talked about. It was a subject that people were wary of, that they steered around in conversation. I was often told that the situation was exaggerated in media reports and sometimes it would be compared favourably with the near anarchy of the continent, where armed robbery,[18] rape and assault were everyday occurrences. Women and even children were constantly under threat there. The terminology used to describe the bombings minimised the destructive nature of such events. A whole vocabulary of euphemism was evolved from the root *plastique* (plastic explosive), hence *plastiqueurs*, committed *plasticages*. The efforts made by most Corsicans to minimise the violence extended as far as possible to not knowing about it, or appearing not to know.

Having any opinion on the matter implied taking a position. One conversation I was party to could perhaps serve as an example of this. I had just eaten with three friends, all in their fifties, and we were watching television. The atmosphere became uncomfortable as a news report on *attentats* began. There was a moment of silence. My presence clearly called for some comment to be made. I was asked if there was anything like that in Scotland. Choosing words carefully, one friend excused the perpetrators and the rest of the community: 'They're just a minority … young people, they don't do any real harm, they only blow up banks and cars, it's just silliness (*bêtises*).' This comment was supported by another who added that the youngsters would grow out of it. The third, who lived for most of the year in Paris, was astonished and indignant. She refused to agree it was harmless: 'Maybe they haven't killed anyone, but they have started this violence, and who knows where it will end. French people are going to stop coming to the island because of it.' Her friends were clearly unhappy with the topic and one wound up the conversation abruptly with the statement: 'Anyway we're proud of being Corsican but we're proud of being French too.' This assertion sounded more like a plea; such a balance was difficult to maintain when accepting violence implied anti-French feeling yet rejection of it implied lack of solidarity with fellow Corsicans. Apart from middle-class educated activists (both nationalist and anti-nationalist) most people were unwilling to take one line or the other. Avoiding the subject in public was the safest alternative.

18. However, armed hold-ups appear to the outsider to be common events on the island. During the fifteen months I spent in the Balagne region there were five. The perpetrators of these were generally viewed as young and inexperienced rather than hardened criminals.

Avoiding thinking about it at all may well have been possible for many.

This way of dealing with the situation led to an implicit division between French and Corsican within the community. It shaped the way French people in the town were perceived and acted towards. Most Corsicans did not know French people. Knowing them would be to know their fears, would make acknowledgement of the situation unavoidable. In order to carry on as if life was normal it was necessary to avoid those for whom it was definitely abnormal. When violence occurred in the Corsican community, support of perpetrators and victims was expected from friends and relatives, it was not accepted passively nor left to the legal authorities. Maintaining the silence that protected those participating in *attentats* did undoubtedly cause discomfort in many quarters. The conflict in loyalties that would have ensued (and sometimes did) if victims were integrated into the community would have been very difficult to avoid. It would have meant taking sides.

This sort of avoidance is similar to that described by Larsen in Northern Ireland (1982), but in Corsica not everyone participated. Most outsiders were at a loss, unfamiliar with the 'ground-rules'; they were grateful for any opportunity to air their views on the situation. One group that was targeted by activists were teachers at the lycée and university. Many of them shared the nationalist discourse of colonial domination, but they considered that they too were part of the struggle against state oppression. It was particularly shocking for them to find that they themselves could be seen as representatives of state power, and that they in turn could be cast in the role of victim. They found themselves isolated, not knowing who threatened them. Since everyone appeared to know everyone else, it seemed that everyone had to be against them. For them, the community appeared opaque, theories about Corsicans abounded, and stereotypical representations multiplied. Their observations fitted into pre-ordained categories, challenged by only the most superficial personal contact.

The boundaries between different groups in the town were strongly marked by the economic and political situation, and in the case of continental French by violence. As boundaries were reinforced, the strains put on categories relating to an individual's self-definition, on what it meant to be Corsican, increased. Differences amongst the Corsican population were also marked by differing interpretations of what it meant to be Corsican. Corsican identity did not preoccupy everyone to the same extent, but being Corsican was something of which people were highly conscious. Many resented the activists' assumption of high moral ground, of the right to speak for them. They did not always approve of the activists themselves nor did they agree with interpretation of their own lives. Perhaps this is exemplified by the outburst of one woman at a conference to which members of the public had been invited. Following one paper concerning the disorders that could result from the loss of Corsican women's traditional role coupled with their cultural and ethno-psychological inability to assume a fully modern role,[19] she stood up and said with obvious fury that she was perhaps too dumb to say what she was, but she was damned if she was going to have some psychiatrist come and tell her. My intuitions about the importance of identity on Corsica gelled around such incidents. The comparison with my own passive acceptance of whatever people wished to read into my ethnic identity before I came to the island, and the discomfort and increasing self-consciousness I had experienced there, mirrored that of people I was studying. I began to apprehend late in my fieldwork that the over-definition of identity common on all peripheries could result in real anxiety and tension between groups.

## The Ethnographer and 'Real' Identity

Apart from those groups which were particularly self-conscious about 'identity', people did not spend a great deal of time wrestling with the complexities of what 'real' Corsicanness meant: it was generally situated firmly in the past or on the mountainside. But as an ethnographer studying 'identity' it was not possible for me to leave it there. The dislocation between 'real' Corsicanness and self-image, the way tension between perceptions of being Corsican and of being 'really' Corsican shaped relationships, these things came to be central to my own attempt to understand Corsican identity. This was not the case at the beginning of my fieldwork. Having already benefited from work done by others in marginal areas of Europe I did have preconceptions concerning what I expected to find. I went *expecting* to be confronted with idealistic notions of what it meant to be Corsican, to be introduced to those perceived as traditionally Corsican. I firmly intended not to accord them a privileged position in my own construction of identity.

19. M Creixell (1984), 'Pathologie de transition chez la femme Corse'.

I steered clear of the 'real' Corsican village at first, and paid little attention to the local figures pointed out to me as interesting, such as the 'wise woman' whom people said I should talk to, while at the same time intimating that she was not quite right in the head. One old man in particular, whom everyone said I must see, came to symbolise my impatience with 'real' Corsicanness. 'L'Omu Còrsu', as he was known, could be found most days sitting on the marble steps of one of the town's modern apartment blocks. He wore a 'traditional' Corsican costume (velour trousers, bright shirt and waistcoat) and sported a carefully combed white beard, felt hat and pipe. He stared ahead, saying good-day to everyone who passed, conversing not at all. I found him perplexing, an out of place two-dimensional image. What could I say about this man, or what his silent presence meant to everyone else? I let him become part of the background, as he seemed to be for everyone else. I was determined to find my own 'real' Corsica, the Corsica of everyday life.

People would often describe aspects of their character and certain of their actions as Corsican. However, it was difficult to tell how 'natural' this was. My presence gave rise to some self-conscious reflection, a search for aspects that might interest me. Hence one woman in the middle of preparing dinner while I looked after her baby described how she was making a 'typically Corsican' dish. She went on, without any prompting, to remark that she always spoke to her baby and her dog in Corsican, though once the children started speaking she switched to French, and then describing a new outfit she had just bought, added that 'like all Corsicans' she loved clothes. When her husband was late, she shook her head, said he would turn up when he felt like it, expecting his dinner on the table because he was a typical Corsican man; his mother and sisters had always run after him and she did too. When talking about themselves and others, generalisations in terms of being Corsican were tagged on, without any attempt to elicit this sort of reflection on my part.

There was a discernible pattern to these generalisations. The closeness of the family and distrust of those outside it, preoccupation with politics, patronage, secrecy, envy, vengeance, as well as concern with appearance were again and again pointed out to me as typically Corsican. Some of this mapped over the more stereotypical *Cursichezza* imagery, but much of it did not. While the former was bounded off in space and time and beyond comment, 'ordinary' Corsicanness was open to positive, or more often negative, evaluation. There were similarities with French stereotypes of the 'Mediterranean' nature of Corsicans, that had been 'edited out' of nationalist representations, and attributed to the nefarious influence of the state. The tenor of the tags was often that of indulgent criticism, conveying that this Corsican trait was not necessarily attractive but that it was part of life: just there.

What did disturb me was how neatly their representations and the terminology people used to describe their own life fitted with academic constructions of identity. These versions of what it meant to be Corsican differed from educated, self-conscious constructions, but they were theoretically sophisticated. My own chosen ground for discovering Corsican identity, 'ordinary', modern life, was already packaged in the vocabulary of Mediterranean honour and shame. This was already familiar to me from the ethnographies I had read in preparation for going to the island. I had taken on board the debate that such terminology 'glossed over' the meaning of indigenous concepts (see Herzfeld 1981). It had not occurred to me that years of theoretical activity delimiting Corsican identity would have led to these glosses being tied down into people's own descriptive frameworks. When, for example, one man described his relationship with his patron to me at length, dwelling on the typical Mediterranean aspect of their relationship, I could have been listening to the rendition of several pages of ethnographic text. What had been ethnographic convention had become a tool for self-description.

Corsicans were quite capable of presenting an ethnographic account of themselves, perhaps lacking academic rigour and coherence, but disquieting in the frequency with which it echoed what I might otherwise have been tempted to say myself. I found myself trying to separate out theoretical influences, to free meaning from the definitional influences of the terminology in which they were wrapped. Marilyn Strathern writes of how, far from home, anthropological contrivance is transparent in the disjunction of cultural content, and that this leads to routine reflexivity. Analytical concepts are revealed as being context-dependent. When the anthropologist turns to home, however, 'contrivance … must take a different place … What comes over is an account of contrivance. Thus people's commonsense understanding of the roles they play and their place in society are shown themselves to be contrived' (1987: 28).

### 'Identity': Inside Out

The realisation that our techniques of theorising have much in common with those we study raises questions about the role of research (ibid.:

27). Our contrivance is not separate from the world we are looking at, it has already entered back into it. Attempting to 'save' an academic and objective meaning in text, separate from meaning in context, looks like a losing battle. We cannot write simply for our peers in the innocent assumption that our interpretation will not have repercussions in our chosen field of study, or for ourselves. Take the concept 'identity' itself. On Corsica I came across several interpretations of 'Corsican identity'. I perceived my aim as setting these in relation to each other within a framework that covered details of life not considered by actors themselves as important to their identity. Could this still be labelled 'Corsican identity'? I might be accused on the one hand of devaluing identity by those who see it as important in the fight against domination or simply to maintain heterogeneity, or on other hand of pursuing a chimera of 'identity' that in the end is everything; reminiscent of the paradox of the set that cannot include everything since it cannot include itself. There are politics involved in engaging in fieldwork and producing text close to home (see McDonald 1987). The boundaries between the ethnographer and the object of study are blurred, and if we do not recognise this others will remind us of it. The textual tradition we contribute to is already part of the field, as are members of our academic peer group able to contest our interpretation on our own terms. The assumptions made by people on Corsica, that I must be on one side or another, were in some ways eminently reasonable. Participation in debates concerning our interpretation brings us to an interesting point where another sort of fieldwork can begin.

Everyone I talked to had their own idea of what could be written about their community. The 'raw material' of everyday life was already theorised for me, demarcated for my benefit. People assumed that most of their life would be uninteresting to an anthropologist, if not to me personally. As with the nationalists, any vague assertions that I might make about being interested in everything carried little weight; it did not occur to people that all of their lives might be considered as ethnographic material. I did not at the time reflect much on this. I worried about getting as much information as I could. My conception of 'identity' encompassed 'private' details of their lives, their relationships, the clothes they wore, how they spent their free time, their economic situation. It also encompassed details of the historical, economic and political setting, that might have appeared distant or irrelevant to them. I was recreating around my observation of their life a structure they themselves would not recognise as their 'identity', and

I was using my personal relationships in order to gain insight into how they thought and felt about things they might consider were none of my professional business.

What is the point of further refining concepts already taken into popular description of the self and others and in doing so rendering even more complex the artifact of textualised identity? Like other areas where we go to look at identity in action, questions about identity are already important in people's lives in Corsica. Edwin Ardener described some of the consequences of the expropriation of imagery for the inhabitants of such areas: '[They] have had the privileged experience of being made, as collectivities, part of a similar process. They have become ... at worst "text", at best "art"' (1987: 44). He points out that people are still 'there' behind the textualisation of others: 'A lifetime of being in a remote area, turns you into an ordinary...? What?' (ibid.: 45).

Like other researchers, I naively imagined that I was going to be on the side of the oppressed. In the course of my fieldwork it became less and less clear where that ground lay. On Corsica 'the oppressed' was not a clear category as it can be in a community study that concentrates on one population: sometimes one group of Corsicans, sometimes another, North Africans or French, appeared to fit this category. It is difficult to escape becoming another voice used by the articulate and well-read to speak for 'the oppressed'. Whom we speak for and whom we speak to is not always clear. We have to realise the limits of control we can maintain over our work. We cannot dictate how it will be understood or used and by whom. But then, if this is a process in which everyone participates, we should perhaps accept that we can only contribute our own point of view in the expectation that this will enter a wider debate. This inevitably leads to unintended consequences, which, because 'we' have not conceptualised them, have implications for our subsequent understanding of our subject of study.

This is the point where a description of what happens inside Corsican identity could begin. It is here that an attempt to disentangle the metaphorical activity encompassing everything from the importance of the latest turbo-drive model to theoretical constructions of academic discourse could be turned into text about the material and abstract world bound up in Corsican self-image. The above may give the impression that I would approach this with misgivings, but this is not the case. The fact that fieldwork leads us to question our concepts, question what our text is going to mean to those we have studied, question whether our version of their lives justifies our intrusion, is, I think, good reason for carrying it out. The fact that it forces us to view research as a critical perspective on our own society, does make it worthwhile. In turn, questioning our own role, becoming aware of our own experience of identity, will give us a clearer perspective on how to do finely tuned fieldwork. To read what is unspoken.

## References

Ardener, E. (ed.) (1971), *Social Anthropology and Language*. London: Tavistock

_____(1987), 'Remote Areas', in A. Jackson (ed.), *Anthropology at Home*. London: Tavistock

Badouin, J. (1967), *La Corse dans les textes Latins*. Aix-en-Provence: La Pensée Universitaire

Becher, T. (1989), *Academic Tribes and Territories*. Milton Keynes: Open University Press

Bellone, H. (1984), 'Crise d'Identite', in *La Corse et La Folie*, pp. 49–64. Bastia: C.O.R.S.

Boswell, J. (1768), *An Account of Corsica, the Journal of a Tour to that Island and Memoirs of Pascale Paoli*. London: Dilly

Brun, F. (1969) , 'Le nouveau vignoble Corse', *Études et Traveaux de Méditeranée*, vol. 8, pp. 163–93

Carrington, D. (1984), *Granite Island*. Harmondsworth: Penguin

Chapman, M. (1978), *The Gaelic Vision in Scottish Culture*. London: Croom Helm

_____(1982), '"Semantics" and the "Celt"', in D. Parkin (ed.), *Semantic Anthropology*, pp. 123–45. London: Academic Press

Chiari, J. (1960), *Corsica: Columbus's Isle*. London: Barrie and Rockliff

Creixell, M. (1984), 'Pathologie de la transition chez la femme Corse', in *La Corse et la Folie*, pp. 90–102. Bastia: C.O.R.S.

Desideri, L. (1981), 'Les Corses et les sauvages dans les voyages du XVIIIème siècle', *Études Corses*, vol. 16, pp. 5–23

Hastrup, K. (1987), 'Fieldwork among Friends: Ethnographic Exchange within the Northern Civilisation', in A. Jackson, (ed.), *Anthropology at Home*, pp. 94–109. London: Tavistock

_____(1989), 'The Prophetic Condition', in E. Ardener, *The Voice of* pp. 224–8. Oxford: Blackwell

Herzfeld, M. (1981), 'Honour and Shame: Some Problems in the Comparative Analysis of Moral Systems', *Man*, vol. 15, pp. 339–51

_____(1985), *The Poetics of Manhood: Contest and Identity in a Cretan Mountain Village*. Princeton: Princeton University Press

Larsen, S. S. (1982), 'The Two Sides of the House: Identity and Social Organisation in Kilbroney', in A. Cohen (ed.) *Belonging: Identity and Social Organisation in British Rural Cultures*, pp.131–65. Manchester:

Manchester University Press

McDonald, M. (1982), 'Social Aspects of Language and Education in Brittany, France'. D.Phil. Thesis, University of Oxford

_____ (1986) 'Celtic Ethnic Kinship and the Problem of Being English', *Anthropology*, vol. 27, no. 4, pp. 333–341

_____ (1987), 'The politics of fieldwork in Brittany', in A. Jackson (ed.), *Anthropology at Home*, pp. 120–39. London: Tavistock

Noiriel, G. (1984), 'L'histoire de l'immigration en France: Note', *Actes de la Recherche en Science Sociale*, vol. 54, pp. 72–6

Okely, J. (1979) , 'Gypsy Women: Models in Conflict', in S. Ardener, (ed.), *Perceiving Women*. pp. 55–86 London: Dent

Pomponi, F. (1979), *Histoire de la Corse*. Paris: Hachette

Ramsay, R. (1983), *The Corsican Time Bomb*. Manchester: Manchester University Press

Rousseau, J. J. (1973 edn), *The Social Contract*. London: Everyman

Strathern, M. (1987), 'The Limits of Auto-Anthropology', in A. Jackson (ed.), *Anthropology at Home*, pp. 16–37. London: Tavistock

E. Tonkin, M. McDonald and M. Chapman (eds) 1989, *History and Ethnicity*. London: Routledge

**7**

# The Marching Season in Northern Ireland: An Expression of Politico-Religious Identity

## *Rosanne Cecil*

> ... as you move throughout Northern Ireland society you can *see* and
> *hear* the division, expressed through colours, objects and tunes
>
> S.S. Larsen, 'The Two Sides of the House'

This chapter examines the concept of 'identity' in terms of the people of one small town in Northern Ireland. The town, like many in Northern Ireland, is mixed in its religious composition. Religious affiliation is of paramount importance in determining identity, although elsewhere I have suggested that gender and kin ties also have an important role to play in identity formation by 'placing' a person within a known and generally accepted role (Cecil 1989). Ultimately, however, it is the religious affiliation of a person which matters in so many facets of life in Northern Ireland and it is upon this that I focus here.

Throughout much of Northern Ireland a person's religious allegiance is considered to be the most significant factor in determining identity. Assumptions about the association between religious identity and political allegiance are widely held in Northern Ireland. Protestants are generally assumed, by Protestants and Catholics alike, to have a predominantly Unionist outlook, and Catholics to have a predominantly Nationalist outlook. It is this association between the religious and the political which is referred to by the term 'politico-religious'.

The expression of a number of aspects of politico-religious identity is discussed; one focus of the chapter is upon the colourful ritual

146

display of identity which occurs throughout Northern Ireland during the summer months. The months of July and August, when this display occurs, are aptly known in Ulster as 'the Marching Season'. The celebrations of 'the Twelfth', along with the other events of one Marching Season in a small town in Ulster, are depicted here, in the context of a wider discussion of the issue of acknowledging, maintaining and expressing identity in a divided society.

## Religion in Glengow

The small town of Glengow[1] and its rural hinterland constitute the area in which fieldwork was conducted. To the east of Glengow lies good farming land with a scattered and mainly Protestant population: this region I call Cullydown. To the west, where the land becomes quite hilly (or what local people call mountainous), reside two predominantly Catholic communities, Killyullin in the north and Ballyreagh in the south. Between these two areas lies Magherahill where a scattered community of Presbyterian hill farmers live. This settlement pattern, with Protestants residing in the town and Catholics in the mountainous region, is fairly typical of those towns in this area which were founded during the period of the Plantation. It is a matter of some debate among contemporary historians as to whether the common settlement pattern associated with these towns was the result of a government plan or whether, as Macafee (1977) and Robinson (1984) argue, it arose spontaneously due to ecological and cultural factors.

Just over two-thirds of the 1,200-strong population of Glengow are Protestant. Glengow town is fairly representative of the religious composition of Northern Ireland with 64 per cent of its Protestant population being Presbyterian and 36 per cent being members of the Church of Ireland; in the surrounding rural area the proportion of Presbyterians in the Protestant population is somewhat higher. The provision of churches in and around Glengow reflects the religious constitution of the community. In the town itself there are two Presbyterian churches and a Church of Ireland church, while outside of the town are two Catholic chapels and another Presbyterian church.

---

1. 'Glengow' is a pseudonym, as are the names by which I refer to other towns and townlands in the region. In referring to the work of other social anthropologists, I follow their personal preference as to the use or not of a pseudonym for the location of their research.

Regular church attendance is the norm among the majority of Glengowers. In a situation where politics and religion are closely entwined, as is the case throughout Northern Ireland, observance of, and attendance at, religious festivals are acts of political significance. One of the Presbyterian ministers, discussing church attendance, commented that people in Glengow 'have this veneer of being fanatically loyal to the church. Note that I say "the church" for I wouldn't always say fanatically loyal to the Lord, but fanatically loyal to the church and to Protestantism', for in Glengow, 'you must keep the side up ... with regards to religion you don't rock the boat'.

In the face of Catholicism the Protestant churches present a united front, despite the fact that the differences between Protestant denominations are also of considerable significance in Glengow, certainly to the extent that intra-denominational endogamy, or marriage within the group, is preferred.

## Two Communities

The population of Northern Ireland is divided along religious grounds to the extent that it is common for politicians, people in the media and lay people to refer to there being 'two communities'. The social division between groups or communities is characterised by a boundary which delimits the extent of each. Whereas some groups or communities have geographical or physical boundaries, those that are discussed here do not, although there may be a spatial aspect to the social organisation. Membership of a social group asserts a notion of 'us' in opposition and contrast to 'them'. Membership of an 'us' group is of importance to Glengowers, and it is religious identity which is the crucial determinant in defining 'us' and 'them'.

In Northern Ireland, people tend to mix predominantly with their co-religionists and the people of Glengow are no exception to this rule. This arises from a number of interlinking factors, rather than from choice alone. Residential religious segregation exists to a considerable degree across the province (Boal 1971, 1981). Although many towns have a mixed population of Catholics and Protestants, residential segregation along religious lines not uncommonly occurs *within* towns with the result that certain housing estates or certain streets tend to be predominantly populated by people of one religion or another. Education is largely segregated along religious lines (Darby *et al.* 1977; Murray 1983), leisure activities between the two groups differ (Dunn *et al.* 1984; Harris 1972; Leyton 1974 and 1975; Donnan and McFarlane

1983), and Aunger (1975) identified certain differences in occupation and social class position between the two religious communities.

In many places in Northern Ireland, shops and bars are patronised according to the religious affiliation of the owner. This happens to only a limited extent in Glengow. Here, four of the five bars are owned by Catholics, and all but one of these are frequented by Catholics and Protestants alike. Shops in Glengow tend to be patronised by people of both religions, partly because only a few of the shops are duplicated, so the luxury of boycotting a shop 'of the other side' is largely unavailable.

The two communities, Protestant and Catholic, reproduce themselves as largely discrete groups. This is achieved by an endogamous marriage practice whereby the normative behaviour is that Catholics marry Catholics and Protestants marry Protestants. The prohibition on marriage between Catholics and Protestants is one of the more powerful barriers which exist between the two communities and ensures continuity of the two groups as discrete entities. With endogamy the values and customs of each group can be transmitted to the next generation intact. However, some mixed marriages do occur, although they are not common. Mixed marriages are viewed with disapproval by family and the wider kin network as well as by neighbours, for to enter into a mixed marriage is to let the family down.

McFarlane (1979), from his work in 'Ballycuan', suggests three reasons for the negative moral evaluation of mixed marriages, which rest on pragmatic considerations: (i) since all marriages were considered to be important for both the spouses and their families, it was argued that 'mixed' marriages could only add to the strains which might be expected to develop between affines; (ii) the fact that there is an element of choice about the religion in which the children will be brought up is thought to create strain between the spouses; (iii) people involved in mixed marriages may be likely targets for assassination. Certainly these attitudes were expressed in Glengow towards mixed marriages and also towards any relationship between a Catholic and a Protestant that might lead to marriage. For example, when a Protestant man was shot and wounded in Killyullin, it was generally thought to have been because he was going out with a Catholic girl there. In addition, it was said that it was because the girlfriend was thought to be 'turning', that is turning away from her religion towards Protestantism. The Protestant man was not, apparently, 'turning' and this was evident by his attendance, with his girlfriend, at Protestant band parades.

This segregation along religious lines, which is widespread throughout Northern Ireland, is not an outcome of the more recent outbreak of 'the troubles' (i.e. since 1969), but predates it. Harris, whose important study of 'Ballybeg' was undertaken in the early 1950s, stressed 'how separate are the social fields of membership of the two religious groups'. Yet she also pointed to

> the extent to which the people share a common culture ... This similarity extends not merely to their standard of living, to family relationships, ideas about the role of the sexes and attitudes to kin in general, but to ideas about the duties neighbours owe each other, more general values regarding good and bad conduct, what commands and what loses respect. (1972: ix)

It is against this background of similarity and difference that the question of identity needs to be considered.

## Identity: 'Which Foot Does He Dig With?'

There are three aspects to the issue of religious identity in Glengow. Firstly, there is a strongly held view in Glengow and elsewhere in Northern Ireland that the religious identity of a person can be fairly accurately ascertained by using a variety of means. This may take place whether or not a person wishes his or her religious identity to be revealed and may occur in situations in which it is undesirable for it to be so known. Secondly, there are stereotypes which are widely held on both sides as to the character of Protestants and of Catholics. Thirdly, there is the explicit expression of identity which occurs on ritual occasions; for both Protestants and Catholics this takes place mainly during the Marching Season.

To somebody who is not from Northern Ireland and who is unfamiliar with it, the people of Northern Ireland look and sound alike and are not outwardly distinguishable as being 'Catholic' or 'Protestant'. Yet the Northern Irish do make precisely this distinction. They do so by making use of a number of cues, and they do it because they need this knowledge in order to behave appropriately in any ensuing social interaction. A person from Northern Ireland can 'tell', or believes that he or she can 'tell', the religious affiliation of another Northern Irish person after a few minutes' acquaintance.

This concept of 'telling' (first used by Burton (1978) in his study of a community in West Belfast) is 'based on the social significance attached to name, face and dress, area of residence, school attended, linguistic and possibly phonetic use, colour and symbolism' (1978: 37). 'Telling', says Burton, 'is not based on undisputed fact, but, as an ideological representation, is a mixture of myth and reality' (1978: 37). It is a way of identifying and maintaining boundaries and, in a society in which it is generally firmly believed that boundaries need to be maintained, it is of considerable importance.

'Telling' takes place in Glengow, as elsewhere, but so too does a certain amount of direct questioning such as 'What is he?', and, in the classic phrase which is, however, rarely heard these days, 'Which foot does he dig with?', and, to me, when a range of questions failed to elicit the appropriate answers, a blunt 'Well, what religion *are* you?' That I was asked directly about my religion may not be of any great significance for, as an English woman, I did not provide the usual range of cues which enable 'telling' to take place, and secondly, it was not necessary to tread with the same degree of caution as usual, for although there are, of course, English Protestants and English Catholics, they are not expected to share exactly the same values as their counterparts in Northern Ireland. Of greater significance is that there was any direct questioning at all. This I attribute to the specific social, political and geographical situation of Glengow – a small town located away from the major trouble spots of Northern Ireland, with a predominantly Protestant population, yet situated near an area renowned for its support of Republicanism. That is, it is not an area riven by conflict, as the area which Burton studied was and is, but the possibility of conflict exists and awareness of sectarian differences is considerable.

An important aspect of 'telling' is the use of names to identify a person as being a Catholic or a Protestant. In Glengow, as throughout Northern Ireland, there are broad differences between 'Catholic' names and 'Protestant' names. Catholics tend to have Irish names spelt either in the Gaelic way or in an anglicised version: for example, Patrick (Padraig) or Rory (Ruari or Ruadhraigh) or Mary (Maire), and so on. Catholics are commonly named after a member of the Holy Family (Mary, Joseph), or a saint (Theresa, Brendan), or an important holy day (Assumpta, Concepta). In practice, many people tend to be named after a relative. Protestant names tend to indicate an English or Scottish ancestry, and are not infrequently drawn from the Old Testament. Thus names such as Ruth, Leah, Nathaniel and Samuel are found among the more common English and Scottish names of Protestants.

While names indicate religious affiliation and the sectarian divide, this largely arises from the two customs of naming children after family members and from endogamy, rather than from an actual desire to promote and perpetuate sectarian differences (although an element of this certainly exists). Breen (1982: 711) has noted how names can set up relationships of similarity or of difference. In the case of Glengow it appears that the naming of children aims to set up relationships of similarity within the family, yet by doing so also sets up relationships of difference between the two religious communities.

It is not difficult for stereotyped notions about 'the other side' to build up, for while Catholics and Protestants may live within close proximity (although some degree of residential segregation is not uncommon, as already discussed), there may be very little mixing and little chance of getting to know much of each others' life and life-style. Northern Ireland stereotypes have been discussed at length by O'Donnell (1977) and also by Buckley (1982). In general Protestants see themselves as hard-working, thrifty, free thinkers, and clean and tidy. They see Catholics as lazy, priest-ridden, untidy and potentially treacherous. Catholics see themselves as easy-going, friendly, generous, intelligent and educated, and see Protestants as dour, bigoted, mean and lacking in culture. In Glengow, I heard at least some of these stereotypes expressed. A Protestant postman commented on the untidiness of some Catholic houses and how you would see mice running across the furniture. And a Protestant woman, having returned from a visit to the Catholic area of Ballyreagh, expressed great surprise at the cleanliness of an old lady whom they had met there. Resentment was expressed by a Protestant farmer that Catholic hill farmers received subsidies for livestock due to being in designated LFAs (less favoured areas); the implication behind his resentment was that Catholics do not work as hard as Protestants yet receive additional financial remuneration. It was harder to learn directly of the stereotypes held by Catholics about Protestants, for I was generally considered to be a Protestant, and Catholics tended not to speak ill of Protestants in my presence as they would not wish to offend.

### Identity: Flying the Flag

Distinct from the fairly subtle cues of indicating and identifying religious identity discussed so far, are the explicit expressions of religious identity which are inextricably entwined with political ideals and aspirations. These politico-religious displays occur predominantly in the summertime during what is known as the Marching Season, although the graffiti and street painting which is done mainly at this time is seen throughout the rest of the year.

Street and wall murals, graffiti and street painting are widespread in Northern Ireland and are not mainly restricted to urban areas as they are in many places. Even in rural areas and small towns, graffiti and paintings communicate sectarian messages. In Cullydown, a Protestant housing estate three miles from Glengow, a range of sectarian motifs are evident. Early in July the edge of the pavement is painted the red, white and blue of the Union Jack, as are the lampposts. Large paintings on the roadway depict images important to Loyalists, such as the red hand of Ulster, King Billy (William III), and the slogan 'Remember 1690' (the Battle of the Boyne). The communal skip in the centre of the small estate is regularly daubed with sectarian graffiti as well as with the letters NF (the National Front – the right-wing British organisation which has at least informal links with some loyalist organisations). The initials of the local marching band are also emblazoned onto the skip.

Similarly in the Catholic areas, which lie outside the town, there is a certain amount of sectarian graffiti and symbols. The Irish flag is sometimes hung, or its colours painted on the street (although not to the extent of the red, white and blue of Protestant areas), as well as the initials IRA (Irish Republican Army) and INLA (Irish National Liberation Army). In addition, the Starry Plough (originally the flag of the Irish Citizens' Army, and now a symbol of Socialist Republicanism) is frequently seen in Ballyreagh.

This overt expression of sectarianism tends to be seen in areas which are not only homogeneous in terms of religion, but are also predominantly working-class. It is rather disapproved of by the middle-class or the aspiring middle classes. Some people in Cullydown expressed feelings of disquiet over the street painting there, saying that it did not make the place look nice, and that the amount of painting (three large paintings plus the red, white and blue edging) was 'over the top'.

While strong religious and sectarian views are widely held in Glengow and find expression in a number of ways, there also exists a strong sense of the importance of harmonious co-existence and mutual courtesy. There is, in general, a distaste for overt sectarian expression (outside of the traditionally sanctioned occasions) for fear of creating violent situations similar to those found elsewhere in the province. So, although sectarian hostility exists in Glengow, it tends to remain at a low level and is contained and controlled; it manifests itself only in certain parts of the Glengow area and at certain times of the year, in particular during the Marching Season.

Much of the colourful display of politico-religious identity which takes place during the Marching Season owes a large part of its dynamism to the Protestant organisation, The Orange Order, and, to a much lesser extent, the Catholic organisation, The Ancient Order of Hibernians. A brief examination of the background of these organisations is necessary for an understanding of the role which they play in Northern Ireland society today.

## The Orange Order

The Orange Order emerged in the eighteenth century at a time of considerable sectarian friction and after a number of secret societies, both Protestant and Catholic, had been formed. The membership of the early societies was predominantly the rural poor. The Orange Order was formed in 1795 when a need was felt for a federated society, disciplined and respectable enough to attract the patronage of the gentry (Senior: 1973). And as Gray puts it: 'The Orange Order, when it was organised, simply channelled a vast flow of fervent feeling which had already existed into one enormous reservoir of partisan and religious ardour (or bigotry, according to how you view it)' (1972: 57). The Masonic Lodges were taken as a model in terms of much of the ritual and symbolism. The popularity of the Orange Order has waxed and waned over the years with a revival at the end of the nineteenth century at the time of the Home Rule movement.

Since the more recent outbreak of the troubles in 1969, the membership of the Order again increased and in 1972 was estimated to stand at around 100,000 in 2,000 lodges (this includes women's lodges and the junior Orange Lodge which is for boys between the ages of eight and seventeen) (Gray 1972: 198). Exact membership figures are not available as it has never been the practice of the Orange Order to keep a record of membership.

The Order is avowedly a religious organisation. The necessary membership qualifications for candidates are explicitly, and almost totally, religious in content (Roberts 1971). The Laws and Ordinances of the Loyal Orange Institution of Ireland of 1896 (quoted in Roberts 1971) states that the Orangeman must have a 'sincere love and veneration for his heavenly Father, and a humble and steadfast faith in Jesus Christ' and he should 'honour and diligently study the Holy Scriptures'. Much of the meetings of the Orange Order (and the associated Purple Institution) is taken up with prayers and the recitation of the scriptures (Roberts 1971). Despite a love of ritual and symbolism (ibid.) the Order draws its support predominantly from men who are low church members, evangelical and anti-ritualistic. Lack of ritual in the Protestant churches of Northern Ireland is compensated for by the large number of Protestant men who are Orangemen, by the rituals and symbolism of the Orange Order. Women are largely denied the alternative neo-religious expression provided by the Orange Order (although a small number of women's lodges do exist). Interestingly, Harris, writing of 'Ballybeg', noted that 'in those families ... where there was a very strong division between the spheres of the sexes, there was the assumption that the Lodge was to the man what the church was to the woman' (1972: 194). Harris (1972: 193) suggests that 'the Orange Order provided an alternative channel through which an individual could express his loyalty to his Protestant neighbours. He could prove he was a "good" Protestant by attending lodge meetings.'

As well as being a religious organisation, the Orange Order is also an explicitly anti-Catholic one, as can be seen by a study of its rules and by listening to popular Orange songs (see Gray 1972). The rules of the Orange Order, as revealed to Harris in Ballybeg, included such lines as: 'An Orangeman seeks by all lawful means to withstand the spread of Roman Catholicism' and 'An Orangeman is not, never has been, and never will become a Roman Catholic' and 'An Orangeman is not married to and will never marry a Roman Catholic.' Yet they also stated that 'An Orangeman is gentle and courteous, not acting with hostility towards his Roman Catholic neighbours, but seeing by his example and conversation to spread the Protestant faith.'

## The Ancient Order of Hibernians

'The Ancient Order of Hibernians' is an Irish Catholic Society, formed for the defence of Faith and Fatherland' states the Hibernian handbook published in 1936. The Ancient Order of Hibernians, like the Orange Order, claims to have arisen from the agrarian secret societies of the eighteenth and nineteenth centuries such as the 'Defenders' and the 'Ribbonmen'. These organisations were motivated by 'the dual impulses of religious hatred and hostility to landlordism' (Phoenix 1983) and did not set out to overthrow British rule. The Hibernians have always seen their primary role as 'giving protection to both the Roman Catholic faith and the Roman Catholic population in Ireland'. Thus, according to Phoenix, the AOH claims to do for Catholics what the Orange Order claims to do for Protestants.

By the end of the nineteenth century the AOH was flourishing in England, Scotland, Australia, and wherever Irish Catholics as a group felt vulnerable to exploitation. In Ulster the AOH emerged as a counterpart to the Orange Order and to Freemasonry. In 1905 the majority of divisions in the AOH in Scotland and Ireland united under the 'Board of Erin' and drew up a constitution which committed them to the policy of the parliamentary party, i.e. the Home Rule Party (Hepburn 1971). When Home Rule was not obtained without partition the party declined and so too did the Hibernian organisation.

Today in Northern Ireland in general, and certainly in the Glengow area, the AOH is not a thriving organisation. An elderly man who had been a member of the AOH in Killyullin for forty-five years said that there had been a division (i.e. a branch) of the AOH in the parish since 1905, but that interest in it had waned since 1916. During the time that he was a member there had been about forty-five people in the local division, but he thought that there were probably fewer than that in it now for 'the young are not interested in the AOH, they want a faster life'. For his part, he felt that the AOH is 'the only sensible organisation'. For while the AOH wants 'Ireland to be ruled by the Irish, it is a moderate organisation and its members will not take up arms; Sinn Fein and the AOH never saw eye-to-eye.' For, as he explained, the AOH swears allegiance to the government in power, while Sinn Fein does not. While in a number of respects the AOH is the counterpart to the Orange Order, its popularity is not as widespread among Catholics as the Orange Order is amongst Protestants, and this is certainly the case around Glengow, where there is considerable support for Sinn Fein.

## Sectarian Display and Ritual: Two Case Studies

### (i) July

The events of one summer in Glengow will be discussed here in order to illustrate different aspects of the activities which take place during the Marching Season. As Glengow is predominantly a Protestant town and as the Orange Order is such a popular organisation, the greater part of this discussion will be on Loyalist display rather than on Republican display.

There are a number of lodges in the Glengow area, at least four within a three-mile radius. It is not easy to get an Orangeman to speak of his lodge for it is in a number of respects a secret society. It is no particular secret as to who belongs to a lodge; they can, of course, be seen marching in public on certain occasions, notably at the celebrations of 12 July. What is not spoken about is what actually takes place at lodge meetings. The meaning and significance of the many symbols which are displayed by lodges on their banners and on Orange arches are said (by Orangemen) to be understood by all Orangemen and not by outsiders.

It is not always possible to distinguish between general Protestant fervour and Orangeism as the two are inextricably linked. This section sets out chronologically the events which I witnessed, some of which involved Orangemen and some of which did not; the ideology of Loyalism and Orangeism was, however, ever present. A number of the events discussed here took place in Cullydown Park, a working-class Protestant estate outside of the town, where I lived during my period of fieldwork.

The first main event of the Marching Season took place in Glengow on 3 June. This was a band parade organised by a Glengow Orange Lodge, the 'Ancient Heroes LOL (Loyal Orange Lodge) … '. Around ten other bands joined in the parade which was watched by a crowd of people lining the main street; other people watched from their cars. Outside all of the bars, except one, stood small groups of men who had been inside drinking and had come out to see the parade. The only bar where this was not the case was Murphy's, which had the reputation for being frequented by Republican sympathisers and was boycotted by Protestants.

A young Protestant man explained to me around this time that by 12 July, Union Jacks and red, white and blue streamers would be flying outside all of the Protestant bars and shops; if shopkeepers or bar landlords failed to do this there would be protests by many Protestants. About a fortnight before 'the Twelfth', Orange arches would go up, in the main street and on the various housing estates. By July, Orange arches are raised in most towns and villages throughout Northern Ireland where the Protestant population is in the majority, or in Protestant areas of towns where this is not the case. The arch is a wooden structure which stretches across the roadway, normally fastened to a lamppost on either side, which depicts symbols which are of importance to Protestants in general, and to the Orange Order in particular, such as King Billy on a white horse, the Red Hand of Ulster, Jacob's Ladder and the Star of David.

It was not until 23 June that another band parade was held in Glengow, this time organised by the 'Cullydown Young Conquerors'.

However, the Glengow bands were frequently playing at parades in other towns in the area during this period. It should be explained that loyalist bands can be divided into two main groups: first there are the military-style bands which are reasonably sedate and respectable in their style of playing and appearance. These are made up of teenage girls and boys, some younger children, and a few middle-aged men. Then there are the more aggressive style of bands which are variously referred to as 'Blood and Thunder' bands or 'Fuck the Pope' bands or, as the newspapers sometimes euphemistically refer to them, 'Kick the Pope' bands. These bands tend to be composed of young men in their late teens and early twenties. Some teenage girls are also in these bands, often as flag-bearers. The 'Blood and Thunder' bands tend to be rather less musical than the military-style bands and project a threatening image with much heavy use of drums and a swaggering walk. The 'Cullydown Young Conquerors' are a very good example of this type of band. The players dress in blue trousers with a red stripe down the leg, white shirt, and a red jumper with a blue trim and blue epaulettes. They are led by a small boy of around eleven who has a mohican haircut and who plays the cymbals in a very original and energetic way, twirling and twisting while he hits the cymbals above his head, behind his back and between his legs.

On 27 June two teenage boys began repainting the faded red, white and blue stripes that edge all the pavements on the Cullydown estate. They were doing this, they say, 'for the Twelfth'. They finished by painting CYC (Cullydown Young Conquerors) on one side of the communal skip which sits in the middle of the estate, and 'NF' on the other.

That evening a group of teenage boys and a couple of the married men put up Union Jack streamers. They then positioned a large barrel which had previously been painted red, white and blue, inserted into it a long pole, weighted the barrel with stones and hung an Orange arch from the top of the pole across to a nearby telegraph pole. The Orange arch, which had been made by one of the men a few years earlier, was of wood painted orange and consisted of a five-pointed star, King Billy on a white horse, and Jacob's Ladder. The words 'Our faith we shall maintain' and 'God save the Queen' were written across it.

It was noticeable that there was a heightened atmosphere of sectarianism around this time. It was at this time that a young neighbour took to wearing a Union Jack hat and a black bomber jacket which had a large Red Hand of Ulster painted on the back. It was said that for a week or so around 'the Twelfth' no Catholic would drink in the King's Arms, a Protestant-owned bar popular with both Catholics and Protestants, until 'it's all died down'. A Catholic woman, living on a mainly Protestant housing estate, told me that she and her family normally go away for their summer holiday around 12 July, explaining that they do not want their Protestant neighbours to feel inhibited in their celebrations by their presence. A Protestant man told me that on the 'eleventh night' (that is on the night of 11 July), when bands march in the town around midnight, the bands would march to the housing estates considered to be predominantly Catholic, and would stop and play outside the Catholic-owned bars, 'The Grouse' and 'Murphy's', and that he expected that there would be trouble outside Murphy's. He went on to say that the third Catholic bar in the town, 'Donnelly's', would not get any trouble that night as Donnelly 'keeps a good bar', that is an orderly bar where trouble, sectarian or otherwise, is virtually unknown. The actions of the bands were thus expected to be, and turned out to be, deliberately provocative towards Catholics. However, it was also expected that they would discriminate in a very general way between those Catholics who did and did not 'deserve' such provocation.

On the morning of 1 July, two of the twelve houses in Cullydown Park were flying a Union Jack. By that evening another flag had gone up. By the following morning four more flags on a further three houses were flying (two Union Jacks and two Ulster flags) and by 4 July my house was the only one not flying a flag. However, this situation did not last long, for a small Union Jack was attached to my chimney one day whilst I was out. I had previously been told that 'everybody' in Cullydown flies a Union Jack for 'the Twelfth', and this proved to be the case.

While street painting, though not flag flying, tends to be confined to working-class areas, preparation for 'the Twelfth' may take other forms. For instance, around this time a middle-class elderly woman took me out to her garden to show me the Orange Lilies and Sweet William ('for King Billy') that she had been growing 'for the Twelfth'. In some cases the flowers are just left in the garden to stand where they grow, to be seen and admired, but sometimes bunches of Sweet William and Orange Lilies are attached to the drums used in the marches.

On the Sunday before 12 July the Orangemen paraded to church. About 300 Orangemen assembled outside the Church of Ireland and marched up the main street and back down again before going into church. They were led by the Glengow Pipe Band; some wore orange sashes, some wore purple sashes, some had purple cuffs and wore white gloves; these indicate rank within the Order.

On 9 July a new street painting appeared in Cullydown. It was around ten feet in diameter and displayed a number of Orange symbols, such as Jacob's Ladder and a five-pointed star, as well as the words 'Ulster' and 'No Surrender'.

Around 9.00 p.m. on 11 July some members of the Cullydown Young Defenders and of another band from a nearby townland marched into Cullydown Park. They played as they marched and presented rather a straggly sight as they were not in uniform and there were few of them. Some people came out of their houses to watch the band, although it was not an impressive spectacle and did not produce much interest or comment.

Some time after midnight I went into Glengow with a friend to observe the events there. In the main street a motley group of drunk young bandsmen were gathering together. After some time they set off followed by a few drunk teenage girls. They played their instruments (very badly), sang and waved flags. We followed them as they marched into an estate near the centre of the town. They marched into the main square of the estate and stopped and played there for a few minutes. It would have been impossible for anyone to have slept through the noise and all round the square children were peering out of bedroom windows. The band then retraced their steps and set off along the High Street towards another housing estate. As the band members were drunk and slightly belligerent, the atmosphere was of a mildly threatening nature. This was a peaceful year, but on other occasions bottles and stones have been thrown. Only one incident occurred on this night when a window of Donnelly's bar was broken. This was the bar which, I had been told, would receive no bother, despite being Catholic, as Donnelly 'keeps a good bar'. It is not clear what happened and it may well have been an accidental breakage. No trouble occurred at Murphy's bar although it had been anticipated there.

On 12 July I went with a friend and with my next-door neighbour to board the coach which would take us to where the celebrations for 'the Twelfth' were to be held. We were to go to 'the field' at Ballynaclagh, as that was the venue for all the lodges from that part of the county that year. The bus was crowded, and fitted into it somehow were two huge drums. A number of the men were drinking heavily although it was still mid-morning. On arrival at Ballynaclagh we walked through the town to the field and stood and watched the parade march in. As soon as everyone from Cullydown had arrived at the field a large crate of packed lunches appeared and everyone who had been on the coach received a bag of sandwiches and a cup of tea. There were two large tea tents, one run by the women of the First Glengow Presbyterian church, and one run by the women of the Main Street Presbyterian church. There were also a few stalls selling sweets and soft drinks ('minerals') and some Loyalist paraphernalia.

At 2.00 p.m. the speeches from the 'WMs' (the Worshipful Masters of the Lodges) began. They were seated on a stage that had been erected in the middle of the field. Only a handful of people listened to them. It did not seem that for most people the speeches formed an important part of the day's events. Most people were milling around, meeting up with friends and relatives, or drinking tea and eating sandwiches. There was no main activity taking place in the field. The important event had already occurred; the marching of the lodges and the bands into the field. After a while, first one player, then another, then whole bands, began to tune up regardless of one another; this went on for about one hour. Eventually the bands left the field and the marchers retraced their steps and we returned to the coach. On the bus back a good number of the men were very drunk and rowdy and sung a series of anti-Catholic songs, such as (to the tune of 'Clementine'):

> Build a bonfire,
> Build a bonfire,
> Stick a Catholic on the top,
> Put the Pope right in the middle,
> And burn the fucking lot.

The mood on the bus was cheerfully aggressive and belligerent. The men took a far more active role in the events on the bus than the women, as they had taken a far more active role in the events of 'the Twelfth' in general. At one point a group of teenage girls began singing, but they were laughed at and ridiculed until they stopped. The girls giggled and did not attempt to sing again. At this point one of the men who had been leading the singing went across to where they were sitting and said, 'Well girls, what can you sing?' and started to sing a nursery rhyme. In such ways were women made to feel that their role at the Twelfth, the main event in the Protestant calendar, was to watch and to service (provide the tea and sandwiches) and to admire the men, but not to actively participate. Although a small number of teenage girls play in the bands, the events clearly are predominantly masculine affairs.

The passing of 12 July marks the high point of the Protestant calendar. Although a number of band parades continue to take place throughout July and August, they do not produce the same feelings of excitement or have the same political significance as 'the Twelfth'.

### (ii) August

The various activities associated with Protestant celebrations are not only far more prominent than Catholic celebrations in the Glengow area, but were also highly visible to me through my residence in a Protestant housing estate. Of the two Catholic events which are celebrated with parades and marches, St Patrick's Day on 17 March is more widely celebrated, although the Feast of the Assumption or 'Lady Day' on 15 August is the day on which the members of the Ancient Order of Hibernians march and so most closely corresponds to 12 July, and is the event which I describe next.

This event, like that of 'the Twelfth' described above, did not take place in Glengow, but in a nearby town. Such an event could not take place in the predominantly Protestant town of Glengow. A number of Catholics from Glengow, Ballyreagh and Killyullin went to the annual parade of the Ancient Order of Hibernians which was held in a town some twenty-five miles away. I went with two friend-informants from Ballyreagh. One of my companions was a man in his sixties who was a member of the AOH and had always attended the annual event. My other companion was his niece who had, from the age of seven, for a number of years played the tin whistle in the local AOH band. The band no longer played, due to lack of support and lack of funds.

When we arrived at 'the field' we stood at the entrance and watched the bands come down the road and enter the field. There was a great similarity in appearance between these bands and the Protestant bands which I had seen on 12 July. The banners that were carried were decorated in the same style as the Protestant ones, although here they were mainly green and depicted the Pope and Catholic martyrs, rather than King Billy and Queen Victoria.[2] The style of music was also very similar to the Protestant bands although, of course, the actual tunes were different.

After the main body of bands had entered the field we went in to hear the speeches. As on 12 July very few people listened to the

---

2. A Catholic woman told me how, years before, her father, a signwriter, had painted the banners for Protestant bands as well as for Catholic bands. Since the more recent outbreak of 'the Troubles' such a situation is highly unlikely.

speeches, and my two companions were not interested in them. As we left the field, more bands arrived, including some which were not AOH bands but were memorial bands. These were bands from a small town noted for its Republican sympathisers, each of which commemorated a young man who had died in the recent outbreak of the troubles, and which were very different in appearance from the AOH bands. The members of the first of the bands were dressed in khaki and had a strongly military demeanour. They were followed by supporters, mostly young men, who shouted IRA slogans. As they marched, the band and their supporters were surrounded by members of the RUC (the Royal Ulster Constabulary) who kept in step with them and held guns pointed at them the whole time. The next memorial band from the same village was led by a group of teenage girls dressed in black and wearing dark glasses and black berets who marched with military precision.

Some time later, when we were sitting in a bar-restaurant, we heard that there was fighting going on outside and that the police were firing plastic bullets. We went upstairs to look down onto the street from above and could see fighting between the police and other people. A teenage girl, who was also looking out, said that she was rather nervous at doing so in case the police started to fire up at the window, while a young waiter said that he wished that he had a gun so he could shoot at the police; having said this he turned to us and said, 'I hope none of yous are Protestant'.

We stayed in the restaurant for some time in order to avoid the trouble as we had heard that there was fighting on the road where we had left the car. But when we left the restaurant the violence was still continuing. Two men were being hit with batons and dragged by police towards two police vehicles. A man and a woman who ran up to the police to intervene were pushed away. My two companions were very upset by this event and also by other news that we had heard, such as that a pregnant woman had been shot in the stomach.

While there were similarities between the style of the AOH event and that of 12 July, the subsequent events highlighted the fundamental differences between the two occasions and the two groups of participants. For the Protestants 'the Twelfth' is a celebration of an event which took place many years before, namely the victory of William of Orange over James II at the Battle of the Boyne in 1690. In commemorating this event, Protestants assert both their historical and their contemporary political dominance over Catholics. The police who were present on this occasion (as they are on all occasions when a large crowd congregates) are 'their' police, that is they are representatives of the British state to which Protestants profess allegiance. In contrast, the AOH marching and gathering on 15 August are not in celebration. For many of the participants, particularly the marchers and supporters of the memorial bands, the occasion is one of rebellion, defiance and anger. The accompanying police (and the police presence was far heavier on this occasion than on 'the Twelfth') were not 'their' police but are viewed as agents of the British Imperialist regime.

It was apparent from the events which took place, and from comments which were made, that the police were viewed by Catholics on this occasion, at best as a threat, and at worst as an enemy. Although the event of 15 August was primarily an AOH occasion (and as noted earlier, members of the AOH swear allegiance to the government in power), it takes place on an important date in the Catholic calendar and so attracts participation from a wide range of people. Indeed, at the restaurant a number of men were pointed out to me as having been imprisoned or interned for suspected terrorist offences. It is not surprising then that strong Republican anti-RUC and anti-British sentiments were expressed at this event.

The expression of politico-religious identity by Protestants and by Catholics during the Marching Season involve certain similarities in manner and style, and, in the anthropological sense, the events share a similar function. Yet it is important to draw a distinction between the *form* and the *content* of the ritual displays of identity of the two communities. For, as described, the meanings underlying the events are totally different. On the one hand dominance is asserted and, on the other hand, rebellion. In the case of 12 July, for example, not only is an historic event commemorated, but a statement of contemporary political dominance is expressed. Throughout Northern Ireland political ascendancy at a local level is expressed by the activity of marching. As Larsen writes, 'Processions and marches are means of asserting control over territory' (1982b: 289).

Glengow, despite its mixed population, is generally considered to be a Protestant town. Protestant parades regularly take place in the town throughout the summer, while Catholic parades have not been held in the town for a number of years. Protestants ultimately place the greater claim upon Glengow by marching through its streets as part of their annual celebration in a way that Catholics cannot do. The Protestants not only belong to Glengow but implicitly claim that Glengow belongs to them.

## Conclusion

This chapter has attempted to present some of the ways in which identity is expressed by members of a small town in a society divided along politico-religious lines. The everyday expression and acknowledgement of politico-religious identity co-exists with the widely held and expressed belief that political and religious differences should not, in general, be commented upon. The explicit public expression of politico-religious identity is only sanctioned on specific ritual occasions. Its occurrence at other times is considered to be largely due to the hot-headedness of young men or the 'sheer badness' of a few extremists. However, during the ritual celebrations of the Marching Season, the overt expression of politico-religious identity is condoned, encouraged and celebrated by a wide section of the population.

## References

Aunger, E. A. (1975), 'Religion and Occupational Class in Northern Ireland', *Economic and Social Review*, vol. 7, no. 1, pp. 1–18.

Boal, F. W. (1971), 'Territoriality and Class', *Irish Geography*, vol. 4, no. 3.

_____(1981), 'Residential Segregation and Mixing in a Situation of Ethnic and National Conflict: Belfast', in P. A. Compton (ed.), *The Contemporary Population of Northern Ireland and Population-Related Issues of Belfast*. Belfast: Institute of Irish Studies, The Queen's University of Belfast

Breen, R. (1982), 'Naming Practices in Western Ireland' *Man* (N.S.), vol. 17, pp. 701–713.

Buckley, A. (1982), *A Gentle People: A Study of a Peaceful Community in Northern Ireland*. Cultra: Ulster Folk and Transport Museum

Burton, F. (1978), *The Politics of Legitimacy: Struggles in a Belfast Community*. London: Routledge and Kegan Paul

Cecil, R. (1989), 'Sectarianism, Kinship and Gender: A Community Study in Northern Ireland'. Unpublished D.Phil. thesis, University of Ulster

Darby, J., D. Murray, D. Batts, S. Dunn, S. Farren and J. Harris (1977), *Education and Community in Northern Ireland: 'Schools Apart'?* Coleraine: New University of Ulster

Donnan, H. and G. McFarlane (1983), 'Informal Social Organisation' in J. Darby (ed.), *Northern Ireland: The Background to the Conflict*. Belfast: Appletree Press

Dunn, S., J. Darby and K. Mullan (1984), *Schools Together*. Coleraine: University of Ulster

Gray, T. (1972), *The Orange Order*. London: Bodley Head

Harris, R. (1972), *Prejudice and Tolerance in Ulster: A Study of Neighbours and 'Strangers' in a Border Community*. Manchester: Manchester University Press

Hepburn, A. C. (1971), 'The Ancient Order of Hibernians in Irish Politics, 1905–14', *Cithara: Essays in the Judaeo-Christian Tradition*, vol. 10, no. 2, pp. 5–18.

Larsen, S. Saugestad (1982a), 'The Two Sides of the House: Identity and Social Organisation in Kilbroney, Northern Ireland', in A. P. Cohen (ed.), *Belonging: Identity and Social Organisation in British Rural Cultures*. Manchester: Manchester University Press

_____(1982b), 'The Glorious Twelfth: A Ritual Expression of Collective Identity', in A. P. Cohen (ed.), *Belonging: Identity and Social Organisation in British Rural Cultures*. Manchester: Manchester University Press

Leyton, E. (1974), 'Opposition and Integration in Ulster', *Man* vol. 9.

_____(1975), *The One Blood: Kinship and Class in an Irish Village*. St John's, Newfoundland: Institute of Social and Economic Research, Memorial University of Newfoundland

Macafee, W. (1977), 'The Colonisation of the Maghera Region of South Derry during the Seventeenth and Eighteenth Centuries', *Ulster Folklife*, vol. 23, pp. 70–86.

McFarlane, W. G. (1979), '"Mixed" Marriages in Ballycuan, Northern Ireland', *Journal of Comparative Family Studies*, vol. 10, pp. 191–200.

Murray, D. (1983), 'Schools and Conflict', in J. Darby (ed.), *Northern Ireland: The Background to the Conflict*. Belfast: Appletree Press

O'Donnell, E. E. (1977), *Northern Irish Stereotypes*. Dublin: College of Industrial Relations Research Branch

Phoenix, E. (1983a), 'Have Hibs Outlived their Bitter History?', *The Irish News*, 15 August

_____(1983b), 'Growth and Influence of the AOH', *The Irish News*, 16 August

_____(1983c), 'Lloyd George and the Decline of the Hibernians', *The Irish News*, 17 August

Roberts, D. A. (1971), 'The Orange Order in Ireland: A Religious Institution', *British Journal of Sociology*, vol. 22, no. 3, pp. 267–282.

Robinson, P. S. (1984), *The Plantation of Ulster*. Dublin: Gill and MacMillan

Senior, H. (1973), 'The Early Orange Order 1795–1870', in T. D. Williams (ed.), *Secret Societies in Ireland*. Dublin: Gill and MacMillan

# 8

# Wales from Within: Conflicting Interpretations of Welsh Identity

*Fiona Bowie*

## Through the Looking Glass

If one of the chief pleasures of learning a language and living in another culture is the privileged sharing in other people's perceptions of the world, then one of the hazards of ethnography is to see oneself as the object of those perceptions. To look through the glass at others is infinitely more comfortable than to glimpse one's own reflection. I remember my mild embarrassment, during fieldwork in Cameroon, when watching a dance in which performers in white masks mimicked a Western couple with ludicrously exaggerated and obscene gestures. Instead of the benign anthropologist, interested in 'their' culture, I was presented with an image of myself as clumsy outsider and object of ridicule. I had a similar experience more recently while attending a Welsh-language theatre production at Neuadd Ogwen, the village hall in Bethesda, by the North Wales company, Bara Caws. The play, *Os Na Ddaw Bloda*, which could perhaps be translated as 'If the Flowers Don't Grow', dealt with the transformation of public allotments into a private commercial development, based on actual newspaper reports of such incidents. Within this simple structure the play posed much deeper questions as to the nature of community and of commitment to Welsh social and cultural values.

The play relied heavily on easily recognised stereotypes for humour and effect, and these included the Welsh learner, a well-meaning young woman with wellies, rucksack, peace-badges, organic vegetables, a host of good causes and a pronounced English accent.

167

She revelled in what she perceived to be the 'local community spirit' and in the family atmosphere prevailing among the tenants of the allotments, but failed to recognise the Welsh as individuals with very mixed motivations, or to see the all too apparent divisions within the Welsh community. In her desire for acceptance the learner insisted that the others speak to her in Welsh as she had 'crossed the bridge', a frequently used idiom for achieving fluency in the Welsh language. Her mispronunciation and mistakes were played up to the full, although they bore little resemblance to the actual hurdles which trip most learners of Welsh. I could not but feel rather uncomfortable as an English (female) 'learner' in this otherwise Welsh audience, but my discomfort turned to fascination as the values attached to the characters unfolded in unexpected ways. The cohesive 'community', to a large extent the product of the friendly, if naive, concern of the English learner, began to disintegrate as individuals schemed, or were tempted, to buy and then to sell their allotments for personal gain. The learner goes along with this for a while but vacillates and in the end is the only one to stand alongside the single Welshman (the archetype of the Welsh people or *gwerin*), who is willing to defend his allotment (his Welsh heritage) against the forces of greed, indifference and commercialisation. In the Welsh-speaking heartland of Gwynedd the Welsh/English, 'us/them' dichotomy is the very stuff of political satire, but here the normal categories were being inverted. For the writers and actors of Bara Caws, at least, being truly Welsh, or true to Wales, involved a commitment to its land, language and culture. The English learner passed this test whereas the Welsh labourer who allowed himself to be tricked out of his allotment, and was then prepared to collude in its destruction for the sake of a job, and the corrupt local councillor with his scheming, status-conscious woman friend, betrayed Wales out of self-interest and became structurally 'English'.

## The Images Dissolve

If we pursue the looking-glass image for a moment, Wales presents to the rest of the world a coherent picture of cultural self-sufficiency and a firm sense of identity. What outsiders see, however, is not so much Wales as their own reflection, or stereotypes of Welshness, the Wales of the Celticist imagination. As one begins to penetrate beyond this refracted image of Welshness, not least by learning the Welsh language, the unproblematic and monolithic nature of Welsh identity begins to fragment.[1] One is left not so much with a coherent notion of Welshness (*Cymreictod*, a term which carries a much heavier load in Welsh than in English), as with a sense of many conflicting and interlocking definitions of identity which actively compete for symbolic space and public recognition.

The Welsh language has at least three words for 'identity', the most commonly used of which, *hunaniaeth*, has a long pedigree, going back to the eighteenth century. This plurality of terms is no accident. For centuries Wales has been dominated by its more powerful English neighbour, and has been particularly conscious of the need to affirm its identity, whether this be through language, nationalism, culture, religion, or a combination of these factors, in the face of what is perceived to the continual threat of cultural genocide. Isobel Emmett (1982:167), also working in Gwynedd, observed that 'consciousness of national identity saturates life in the area of Wales I know something of and colours or shapes very much observable behaviour.' In this part of north-west Wales, the whole question of identity is framed very much within the politics of the Welsh language. There are strong pressures on incomers, or those brought up English-speaking within Wales but who have learnt Welsh, to identify themselves with a Welsh-speaking culture and its values. To do otherwise can imply that one sides with the forces which seek to destroy Welsh-language culture, either intentionally or by default.

Learning and speaking Welsh can never be a politically neutral act. Welsh speakers sometimes explicitly link learning Welsh to support for nationalist causes or even, as one American 'learner' reported, affiliation with the extremist group Meibion Glyndwr (despite the fact that she had not even heard of them at the time). For the 80 per cent of the population of the principality for whom Welsh is a foreign language any definition of Welshness which gives priority to the Welsh language poses a potential threat to their own sense of identity. The vexed question of the extent to which the Welsh language can be taken as the prime mediator of Welshness and chief criterion of nationhood, reveals deep and unresolved divisions at the heart of Welsh identity.

---

1. Cf. Tonkin, McDonald and Chapman (1989: 17–18): 'It is notorious that minority groups are seen both to have particularly coherent identities, and to find that their real identities are nevertheless curiously threatened and illusive'; and Smith (1988: 2): 'Those whose identities are rarely questioned and who have never known exile or subjection of land or culture, have had little need to trace their "roots" in order to establish a unique and recognizable identity'. A similar theme is taken up by Cohen (1986: 13) when examining symbolic boundaries. He notes that the boundary as the community's public face is symbolically simple, but from within more symbolically complex.

Books with titles such as *When was Wales?* (G. A. Williams 1985) and *Wales: the Imagined Nation* (Curtis 1986) indicates a lack of confidence in the very notion of Wales as an identifiable entity, which afflicts Welsh and non-Welsh speakers alike. Identity is seen as problematic, it needs to be fought for and over, talked about and defended, defined and rejected. It is this unusually self-conscious discourse which I wish to pick up and, where possible, exemplify, from the standpoint of bemused but interested ethnographer. As a participant in this culture I cannot but form part of the discourse, a word, at least, in the sentence of insider identities.

## The Articulation of Identity

People or groups in a structurally weak position are forced, if they are to survive, to make a careful study of their more dominant neighbours. At the same time they need to protect their inner selves from the gaze of outsiders. For the Welsh, the possession of an ancient and distinctive tongue has been for centuries the surface of this two-way mirror through which they view the English. The English, by contrast, see only what the Welsh wish them to see - as often as not their own reflection. The articulation of this process is illustrated by the late Idris Foster, a native of Bethesda in Gwynedd, Professor of Celtic Studies, and Fellow of Jesus College, Oxford. He has been described, affectionately, by someone who knew him well as possessing *deuoliaeth* or 'two-sidedness'. In Oxford Idris Foster appeared as the archetypical English gentleman don. His English was 'accentless', his conversation polished, his religion high church, his taste for port. In Bethesda he was a *Cymro Cymraeg* ('Welsh-speaking Welshman'), a local boy who regularly visited and then retired to the house in which he was brought up, only a few hundred yards from the family grocers shop. No doubt both Foster's Oxford colleagues and the people of Bethesda believed that they knew the 'real Idris', indeed, many would have been surprised by the double life he appeared to lead, despite the fact that Welsh speakers down the ages have adopted the same chameleon-like survival tactics. There is a sense, in Gwynedd in particular, in which if you are not at home and speaking Welsh, you 'become' English.

But what about the incomer who speaks Welsh? Can they really 'become' Welsh, in some sense, as the moral of the Bara Caws play seemed to suggest? There is no simple answer to this question. In Gwynedd, with its largely native Welsh-speaking population, all outsiders, whether they be from anglicised parts of Wales, from east of

Offa's Dyke or from further afield, are liable to be classified by the catch-all category 'English', a term which is frequently used derogatively. Although originally signifying, in communities in which monolingual Welshness was common, someone who was bilingual in Welsh and English, *Sais* ('English') now refers primarily to someone who doesn't speak Welsh. The experience of many of those who learn Welsh is that they can be widely accepted as valued members of the society, particularly if through marriage or other kinship links they can be placed within the tight-knit web of relations which characterise Welsh-speaking Wales. They may still be referred to as 'English' for two generations or more, but to all intents and purposes form part of the same community as their Welsh neighbours. Some incomers, and a few individuals born in Wales with English as their mother-tongue, are determined to 'go native'. They learn Welsh, mix exclusively with other Welsh speakers and where possible find work which allows them to use Welsh. They may change or adapt their names, play down any non-Welsh connections and join some of the more active and radical Welsh language movements.

The experience of Welsh learners varies according to their starting point. Most of those who move to Wales from elsewhere are content to be regarded as 'English', while gaining an increasingly deep awareness of Welsh society and making a niche for themselves within it. The experience of a person who grows up in the Rhondda feeling Welsh, but who is then classified as 'English' in Gwynedd, is altogether more problematic. There are also many Welsh learners, whether brought up in Wales or elsewhere, who regard themselves as 'deficient Welsh' and see the 'recovery' of the language as an essential part of the process of becoming 'true' Welsh men or women. There is a sense in which the Welsh learner remains the 'joker in the pack', fitting neatly into neither the English nor the Welsh category. This can mean belonging nowhere, but can also, on occasions, mean that the learner can play both cards. Observing the shifts that take place as they are categorised as English or Welsh, and the meanings given to these categories, reveals the ways in which identities are negotiated and in which the symbolic boundaries of the community are maintained.[2]

2. Armstrong (1982) discusses the notion of symbolic 'border guards', a concept applicable to the Welsh language in many situations. The differences between the north and south of Wales in this respect are touched upon by Frankenberg (1969).

### English and Welsh in Gwynedd

Everyday interactions in Gwynedd can quickly polarise along Welsh/English lines. By and large the monoglot English incomers and native Welsh lead fairly separate lives. The marina at Port Dinorwic (Y Felinheli), with its modern housing estate, English place names and signs, and its expensive shops and restaurants, is culturally much further from Welsh-speaking Wales than the few miles which separate it from the quarrying towns of Deinolen and Bethesda. In Bangor, a university and cathedral city, there is a choice of both Welsh- and English-medium schools. It is possible for most people to socialise with others in the language of their choice. There are Welsh and English pubs, Welsh and English plays, the student halls of residence are divided according to language, and both staff and students tend to form either Welsh or English language groups in their respective refectories. Welsh and English are handy categories with which to operate. They are used to reaffirm boundaries, but they also disguise other salient factors in a situation.

This process is particularly visible in Bethesda, one of the main centres in what used to be Caernarfonshire, with a population of some 4,000. As a town which grew up around its slate quarries, the largest of which is still one of the main employers in the area, it was never popular with the better-off English immigrants. The university and managerial population prefer the more fashionable coastal resorts on the mainland and on Anglesey to the wind- and rainswept quarry town, with its vast slag heaps, on the edge of the mountains. There is, however, a sizeable incomer population in Bethesda, perhaps as high as 25 or 30 per cent if enrolment in the local primary school is anything to go by. Drawn by the cheap housing and direct bus route to Bangor five miles away, as well as by the instant access to some of the best-known walks and climbs in Snowdonia, Bethesda attracts the married and more independently-minded students, the climbing fraternity, some working-class retirees, chiefly from the metropolitan areas of Lancashire, Cheshire and Merseyside, and a large number of other individuals referred to locally as 'hippies', the children of the 1960s and 1970s who have escaped England's industrial conurbations for a life on the dole in rural Wales. Concentrated in two main areas of Bethesda, the separate 'village' of Gerlan and the part known as Carneddi, many of these incomers, with their more or less alternative life-styles, form a somewhat separate community within a community.

Some animosity on the part of local (Welsh) residents is directed towards this latter group. They are seen as being lazy, feckless and immoral. Stories of drug-taking and wife-swapping abound. While the Welsh go off to do an honest day's manual or professional work, the hippies play their guitars and fly their kites on a grassed-over quarry. To some of these incomers the Welsh, and especially the local council, typify all that they consider to be backward-looking and parochial in Welsh life. The language is often cited, now as so often in the past, as a sign of this reactionary tendency in the Welsh. The latent tensions are normally kept under the surface of a polite outward courtesy, but on occasions find a definite focus. The long-running dispute over the fate of the old Pant Dreiniog quarry is one such point of conflict. The council, who now own the land, partially levelled and grassed-over much of the quarry, and then decided to let part of it to a local man to graze some sheep. There were a series of hostile encounters as the farmer apparently attempted to take more of the land than he was entitled to and some of the incomers decided that this was unacceptable. In retaliation they removed his fence-posts. The boundary of the field was redrawn but the public were still denied access to almost half the total area of the quarry. An association was formed, the Friends of Pant Dreiniog, and public meetings called. The Friends put forward alternative suggestions for the use of the quarry, such as an adventure playground or nature reserve, but were shocked at the anti-English sentiments which surfaced at these meetings, uncovering a depth of hostility towards them as 'English' people, which they hadn't realised existed. The sheep won the day, and what is left of this open space is given over to the kite-flyers and to the roaming packs of dogs, turned out of the little rows of terraced houses adjacent to the quarry.

Another place in which tensions between the local Welsh and the 'English' incomers becomes apparent is on the local bus. Despite large and prominently displayed notices, in both Welsh and English, asking members of the public not to smoke downstairs (on a double-decker) or at the front of the bus, some passengers invariably do, and so too do some of the drivers. Although anywhere else in the country I usually pluck up enough courage to ask smokers to put out their cigarettes or to move to a smoking section, somehow in Bethesda I never do. In the community in which I live I do not want to go out of my way to make enemies and an intuitive sense of self-preservation tells me that this would be an easy way to do it. My initial suspicions on this score were soon confirmed. In an incident not long after my arrival in Bethesda a young woman asked a man, in English, not to smoke. When he refused she asked more pointedly and appealed to the driver. The other passengers rallied to the man's defence and some became extremely aggressive, telling the English woman in no uncertain terms that 'it is not for you English to tell us Welsh what to do in our own country'. When I expressed my sympathy with her complaint the angry and distraught woman responded with the words 'it is only because I am English that I can say it', perhaps implying that the Welsh wouldn't dare, or perhaps would not wish to interfere? Whatever her precise meaning, the English/Welsh categories were evident, although in another part of the country the categories local/incomer or middle/working-class might have surfaced instead.

On another occasion a visiting friend caught the bus from Bangor and arrived at our house rather shaken, having been rash enough to ask a smoker to observe the no-smoking signs; and one night I thought that I was in danger of being assaulted by an inebriated passenger who had correctly interpreted my opening the window next to me as a sign of disapproval of his smoking. As a final example of this territoriality, expressed in racial and linguistic categories, my husband (a South Walian and a Welsh speaker) gave a pointed look to a delinquent bus-smoker who retaliated by repeating under his breath, but quite audibly, 'English go home, English go home'. I do not believe that these are random incidents, not that the users of the local buses are either particularly addicted smokers or inherently racist. What we see is a clash of values between different communities, languages and life-styles. The categories 'Welsh' and 'English' are merely a telegrammatic means of expressing these tensions.

## Wanting To Be Welsh

The need to claim or to forge a Welsh identity is apparent among many of those I have encountered in Gwynedd who have chosen to learn Welsh. In one case a friend from Llandudno, a Victorian sea-side resort which is one of the most anglicised towns in Gwynedd, changed her first and second names to their Welsh forms, bought a cottage in Bethesda and set about improving her school Welsh to something approaching native standards. She avoids learners' organisations such as CYD (*Cyngor y Dysgwyr*/'Council for Learners') and takes part in as many local Welsh activities as possible, including successfully competing in the Dyffryn Ogwen *eisteddfod* (Welsh cultural festival). Although her mother-tongue is English,

Anwen [3] has a Welsh-speaking father and was born and brought up in Gwynedd. She has countered implicit suggestions that she is not 'really Welsh' by immersing herself in the language and culture of Welsh-speaking Gwynedd, and has no difficulty in being accepted as Welsh by other native speakers, even though they are aware that she has learnt the language. To have remained monoglot English would have meant that she remained as distanced from the Welsh-speaking world around her as the latest immigrant from the Wirral, with no real claim to a Welsh identity, or only at one remove through Welsh-speaking relatives she seldom saw or hardly knew.

For Welsh learners from other parts of Wales the same acceptance can be more difficult to achieve. Helen, born in Newport in Gwent, always thought of herself as Welsh until she moved to Gwynedd and found herself reclassifed as 'English'. She lives in a Welsh-speaking village on Anglesey and is regarded as English by her neighbours. Although the villagers were pleased when she started to learn Welsh, which she now uses professionally, they used to take advantage of her limited knowledge of the language by teaching her unsuitable phrases to which they would supply false translations. The extent to which Helen has also come to see herself as English is illustrated by the following remark. When faced with the virulent anti-Welsh sentiments of some of her bed and breakfast guests she stated that: 'I sometimes say I'm Welsh, even if I'm not, I'm so ashamed of them.' Although born, educated and working in Wales, Helen has internalised the categories of her Welsh-speaking neighbours who regard all those who do not speak Welsh as a first language as English. Caroline, also from South Wales, arrived in Bethesda in the mid-1970s and immediately resuscitated some of her school Welsh in order to speak to her new neighbours. Like Helen, she was stung by finding herself referred to as English, although while speaking to me she continually used the categories English and Welsh, identifying herself with the former, when describing her relationships within the community. Both Helen and Caroline have English-speaking husbands, but their children are bilingual, thanks to their schooling. Caroline has worked hard in and for the community but finds that her inadequate knowledge of Welsh debars her from paid employment as a community worker. This fact, together with the rigidity of the Welsh/English divide, has made her somewhat cynical about the possibility of real integration. She gets on well on a personal level with many of her neighbours, but she is

3. The names given here are all pseudonyms.

equally aware of a powerful, if seldom articulated, view of the non-Welsh speaker as a permanent outsider. One seemingly simple solution would appear to be to learn Welsh. Many incomers do so to a high level of competence and fill top jobs in local government, education, business, and so on, in which they use Welsh professionally. More common among English speakers, however, is a psychological block towards the Welsh language. As everyone (almost) can speak English, why, they ask, is it necessary to learn Welsh? English is a major international language, Welsh a minority and dying tongue. They lack the confidence and motivation necessary to achieve fluency in what is a relatively difficult language, and thereby proclaim, albeit unintentionally, that Welsh, and all it stands for, is not worth this degree of effort or deserving of that much respect.

There are many people who come to Gwynedd from outside Wales who already think of themselves as Welsh. One such was an Anglican priest, Gregory, born in Surrey to a Welsh father, with a parish on the south coast of England, who managed to take a few weeks' sabbatical to attend a Welsh course in Bangor. Back in England he would celebrate St David's Day on 1 March and he knew the words of the Welsh National Anthem, *Hen wlad fu nghadau*, long before he could utter a simple greeting in the language. When asked why he was learning Welsh Gregory replied, 'to become a more complete Welsh person'. This motivation is not uncommon among learners with tenuous Welsh connections. Such efforts do not mean that the Welsh-identified learner can find easy acceptance as Welsh within Gwynedd. Gregory had previously offered his services to the Diocese of Bangor, with an undertaking to learn Welsh on the job. Despite a shortage of priests and many vacant parishes, the parish councils could not agree to accept a non-Welsh speaking priest. (Ordinands who are not Welsh-speaking are asked to leave the diocese if they are not willing, or able, to learn Welsh).

James, a linguist who worked for the University of Wales as a Welsh translator, also had a Welsh father and, like Gregory, was brought up in Surrey. He learnt Welsh as an adult and achieved native fluency and accuracy in the language. When working in Dyfed he felt fully accepted as a Welshman. He was not aware of any barriers between himself and native Welsh speakers and was able to feel part of a Welsh-speaking culture. In Gwynedd, however, he found that he was never fully accepted as a Welshman and had to defend his Welsh credentials. At work his colleagues would identify themselves as 'the Welsh group', excluding James, although there was no difference in their linguistic competence. It is evident that in these circumstances the terms 'Welsh' and 'English' are used as ciphers for 'insider' and 'outsider', and serve to distance incomers from locals and learners from first language Welsh speakers.

To qualify as Welsh, in the eyes of many native Welsh speakers, a person should satisfy a number of closely related criteria. These include speaking Welsh as a first language, being born in Wales, preferably in a Welsh-speaking area, having relatives who are well known within the small Welsh-speaking world and, among those who have 'lost' the language, a fluency in Welsh as a second language. No one of these factors will alone suffice, and some combinations are more likely to win acceptance than others. Those who fall short according to these indicators of Welshness can find themselves classified as English, or as 'not quite Welsh'. This process was illustrated during a television interview in which I took part, along with David, another Anglican priest, this time from an anglicised part of mid-Wales. There was no difficulty in placing me as an English incomer who had learnt Welsh (although with a Scottish name and forebears I had always thought of myself as British rather than English). When, however, the North Walian interviewer asked David (in Welsh) where he was from and the latter replied 'Brecon', the interviewer responded (also in Welsh) with, 'So you're a sort of Welshman then'. This earned the quick riposte, 'Not a sort of Welshman, a proper Welshman'. The interviewer conceded the point, although he did not look entirely convinced that anything Welsh could come out of Brecon!

For those brought up English-speaking in Gwynedd the sense of incompleteness associated with not speaking Welsh can be keenly felt. A woman born locally whose Welsh-speaking parents used English with their children described how she used to seethe with frustration when returning to Gwynedd from her home in England. When she heard people on the train speaking Welsh to one another she felt that this was her language and heritage, but that she was shut out of it. She learnt Welsh in later life and went on to win the 'Welsh learner of the year' competition for her efforts. Another Bangor-born man, who has never learnt Welsh, is sometimes teased by his Welsh-speaking wife, 'you're Welsh, but you don't speak Welsh'. This sense of anomaly is concomitant with a conceptual world which operates with the clumsy but long-established pair of categories, Welsh and English.[4] It is

---

4. Ardener (1989) has noted that while the content of a message may change over time the form may remain constant. In the present context it would appear that the Welsh/English categories, defined in opposition to one another, are a long-standing feature of life in Gwynedd, although the precise meanings given to these terms has varied.

difficult for someone to think of themselves as Welsh and to sustain this form of self-ascription if those around them, with apparently more valid credentials to Welshness, refuse to acknowledge the Welsh identity of the individual concerned.

## Becoming 'One of Us'

Various studies of Welsh identity have indicated that Welsh speakers respond more positively to requests for help if they are made in Welsh rather than in English (Giles and Taylor 1978). This attitude is not confined to those who speak Welsh as a first language. I have heard Welsh learners, both English and Welsh, confirm that at their places of work they deal more quickly and willingly with members of the public who address them in Welsh. There is a feeling among many learners of having joined an élite club, and using Welsh reinforces the sense of solidarity which belonging to a small supportive group can engender. A problem facing all English speakers trying to learn another language, that of the respondent turning to English, is often outweighed in Gwynedd by the preference of the other party to use Welsh. I have often tried to conduct professional conversations in English, but as soon as my inadequate knowledge of Welsh is established, I am invariably congratulated and encouraged to complete my business in Welsh. This is more likely to happen among the educated and professional classes, who are confident of their own standard of Welsh and who are linguistically aware, than among people with less education who either feel embarrassed about their colloquial Welsh when talking to outsiders, or who are just unused to speaking Welsh to learners.

There are also many occasions in an area such as Bethesda, where the majority of people speak Welsh as a first language, when speaking Welsh is just taken for granted, such as when someone comes to the door (with the post, to collect the milk money, canvassing, and so on). In these circumstances not speaking Welsh would be to label oneself as an outsider. In areas which are less Welsh, using the Welsh language is a political statement in itself. One man described how he had to pluck up courage each time he wanted to ask for stamps in Welsh in the post office in Aberystwyth, a town with a sizeable non-Welsh-speaking population. He knew that there was a good chance he would not be understood, but persisted as he wished to use his own language in his own country. My Welsh-speaking father-in-law in Cardiff, where Welsh speakers are a small minority, had a network of shops and businesses which he would patronise because he knew that there he could use Welsh. Public servants in Gwynedd, among others, will usually answer the telephone in Welsh, although switching to English if need be, giving the caller the opportunity to continue the conversation in Welsh if they wish to do so. This ability to assume a knowledge of Welsh and to use it in all the areas of public life is fairly recent and had been fought hard for. Welsh, even in Gwynedd, does not as yet have the status of, say, Catalan in Catalonia, and the notion that Welsh is an optional extra to be applied for rather than automatic right has an irritant and undermining effect on native Welsh speakers and serious learners alike. Using Welsh is a way of affirming that Wales exists.

The notion that by learning and, of course, by speaking Welsh, one becomes a fuller member of the community is axiomatic in much of Gwynedd. The usual question to a learner is not 'Are you Welsh?' (*Cymro/Cymraes 'dach chi*?), but 'Are you Welsh-speaking? (*Cymraeg 'dach chi*?), the latter, until recently, automatically implying the former. When in the local supermarket I started using Welsh rather than English I provoked the apology (in Welsh), 'I'm sorry, I didn't realise that you were Welsh [-speaking]', and not 'that you can speak Welsh'. My accent was obviously not Welsh, but my efforts to speak the language were acknowledged and accepted. On another occasion I was walking our dog along the old quarry railway track beside the river in Bethesda and trespassed onto private land. A farmer emerged and asked, in English, whether he could help me (put me back on the footpath and off his land). I responded in Welsh and we had an amicable conversation in which he complained about tourists, and their dogs, tramping across his fields. I listened sympathetically and when we parted his parting shot was, 'well at least it's in Welsh', which could only have referred to the medium of our conversation. Although obviously not local, my speaking Welsh made me more acceptable and differentiated me from the (English) tourists. Many learners, myself included, have the frequent experience of hearing friends and acquaintances express anti-English sentiments in Welsh without any sense of embarrassment that they might be offending the present company. It is as if by taking part in a Welsh-medium conversation the Englishness of the learner becomes invisible. If challenged, the speaker will often look surprised and add 'off course I didn't mean you', i.e. 'by "the English" I mean those who do not speak Welsh'. The corollary of this is that the English learner is subsumed into the same category as the Welsh speaker.

The final accolade in terms of crossing this invisible insider/outsider, Welsh/English boundary was when after a few weeks' attendance at a bilingual Church in Wales Sunday service in the neighbouring parish the lay reader drew me aside and said in a stage whisper (in Welsh): 'we said the service in Welsh this morning to show that you are one of us now, because your Welsh is good enough for you to understand.' In point of fact the mixture of Welsh and English in the service has been the same as usual. Many monolingual English speakers who are on good terms with their Welsh-speaking neighbours are unaware of the constraints that exist in their relationship, not realising that English and the world that it represents remains 'foreign' and that without the Welsh language the outsider cannot hope to cross the invisible barrier that separates them from Welsh-speaking communities. Speaking Welsh does not necessarily enable the learner to 'become Welsh' but, as both the Bara Caws play and the above examples illustrate, it can, in some circumstances at least, invest the individual with an 'honorary Welsh' status.

## Maintaining Boundaries

Attitudes towards Welsh learners in Gwynedd can also be hostile. One does meet the attitude among native Welsh speakers, 'how silly wanting to learn Welsh, after all, they can never be Welsh'. By learning the language the incomer has claimed the most salient marker of Welsh identity, but may at the same time reject other aspects of Welshness. It is not uncommon to come across English people who have learnt Welsh whilst maintaining strongly 'anti-Welsh' positions. They may fight against Gwynedd County Council's bilingual education policy, the profile of the Welsh language in public life, and the notion that there is anything of cultural value in the Welsh language or in Welsh literary and cultural traditions. Although these attitudes are most common among non-Welsh speakers, they are also expressed on occasions by the native Welsh speakers as well as by learners. It may not be regarded as acceptable in many circles to express distrust of Welsh learners, but any anomalous group will provoke some antagonism and negative stereotypes of the learner express this. The Bara Caws *dysgwraig* was interesting precisely because she transcended the usual learner stereotype. The more familiar stock figure is the awkward convert nationalist who is desperately keen but who fits into neither Welsh nor English society, thereby condemned to live in a shadow world of other Welsh learners.[5] Here stereotyping is used as a tool to distance and control the incomer, who has the potential to breach the protective screen of language, the safeguard of a private Welsh identity. Some of the most 'anti-English' are in fact, as one might expect, other learners who, having invested considerable emotional effort in gaining access to Welsh society and forging for themselves a new Welsh identity, feel threatened by the intrusion of other learners who might expose their own position.[6]

The strength of feeling surrounding the maintenance of a local identity which is based so markedly on the Welsh language has its roots in Gwynedd's past. The economic and political history of this corner of Wales have served to perpetuate the divisions between the English, non-Welsh speakers and the local Welsh-speaking Welsh. When Edward I defeated the last of the semi-independent Princes of Gwynedd in the thirteenth century he established a network of castles and English settlements in order to keep the Welsh down. The Edwardian castle towns of Beaumaris, Conwy, Harlech and Criccieth, so popular with tourists, remain to this day centres of anglicisation and are studiously ignored by many Welsh speakers. (Of the Edwardian castle settlements only Caernarfon, which has become the administrative centre of Gwynedd, has the feel of a Welsh town). It is the castles of the Welsh princes in Deganwy and Dolwyddelan, the graves of legendary heroes and the places associated with eminent Welsh men and women – places seldom on the tourist itineraries – rather than the symbols of English domination, which fill the landscape for the Welsh.

In the eighteenth and nineteenth centuries a few large landowners carved up the county between them. With the immense wealth they accumulated from the West Indian slave trade, agricultural rents and slate quarrying, they 'bought their way into the aristocracy' (Lovering 1983: 12). The landowners were English or anglicised Welsh who had little in common with the mass of the Welsh people. After initially

5. A derogatory view of both Welsh learners and monoglot English speakers is well illustrated by a recent article in the magazine *Safiad* (no.3, May 1989, p.13).

6. This vulnerability among learners who have painfully constructed a new Welsh/Welsh-speaking identity for themselves is neatly illustrated by Tony Bianchi in his short story 'The Last Laugh' (in Bowie and Davies 1992). Two old 'friends' from London meet accidentally; one of them has tried to create a new Welsh identity for himself but the other is happy to acknowledge his non-Welsh origins, thereby posing a threat to the cover of his former acquaintance.

seeking to repress the use of Welsh they realised that the vigorous Welsh-language culture which was fostered by the concentration of manual workers could be used to serve their own interests in creating an 'acceptable docile Welshness' (ibid). The real threat to their power was unionisation, which was savagely resisted, and not the Welsh language. As the quarry and estate managers were usually brought in from outside, often from Scotland, the economic structures which divided the working class from the landowners and industrialists were masked by linguistic and ethnic divisions. The experience of the people of Gwynedd was of the cruel dependence of local Welsh speakers on outside English power.[7]

At the beginning of the nineteenth century the landed aristocracy transferred 'their' capital out of Wales,[8] dealing a crippling blow to the local economy and sucking many Welsh speakers along with it, the majority of them skilled workers. New industries tended to bring their senior management with them, using the Welsh as a cheap source of disposable semi-skilled labour. As Lovering (1983:24) observed, by 1939 the economic patterns of the 1980s were already visible, including rural depopulation, high levels of unemployment, weak local authorities and working-class organisations, poor public services, widespread poverty alongside pockets of affluence and unequal opportunities for Welsh and English speakers.

The increased pace of immigration, mainly from the industrial areas of mid and northern England,[9] poses a problem for Welsh communities and for organisations which are trying to strengthen the official status of the Welsh language. There can be a polarisation of feeling along language lines which sometimes leads to civil action or criminal violence. In 1986 the Race Relations Act was used against Gwynedd County Council who refused a permanent job working with old people to a monolingual English speaker, and in 1988 the Chief Constable of

7. As well as Lovering's (1983) account of Gwynedd's economy, the nineteenth-century industrial history of Gwynedd, and some of Bethesda in particular, is dealt with in Merfyn-Jones (1983) and Lindsay (1987). Hubback (1987) also gives a useful account of the Bethesda area from an archaeological and historical perspective.

8. In 1896 only one Welsh landlord peer was also a company director. By 1920 this figure had risen to 26 (Lovering 1983: 19).

9. See Carter (1988), Day (undated) and the 1981 Census figures for Wales for accounts of immigration into the principality. For Gwynedd in particular see *Strategaeth Llŷn, 1990–2000*, Antur Llŷn, 1989; *Gwynedd Structure Plan*, Gwynedd County Planning Department, Jan. 1989; and *Language, Planning and Housing in Gwynedd: A Memorandum to the Secretary of State for Wales*, July 1988.

North Wales tried to prohibit the use of Welsh among members of his force. As recently as December 1989, a headline story on the Welsh television news and in the national papers concerned an English businessman with a firm in Porthmadog (Gwynedd), who forbade the use of Welsh among his workers. This was, he claimed, a condition of employment, understood by his staff, who were told when appointed that they were to use English only, even with one another or when dealing with Welsh-speaking clients. The case attracted the attention of the media when a secretary walked out after repeated tellings-off for speaking Welsh in office hours. The Welsh language civil rights group, CEFN, agreed to take up her case but, in the absence of an effective Welsh Language Act, the only body to which representation can be made is the Race Relations Board. This is unsatisfactory to most language campaigners as the Welsh make no claim to separate racial status, and in the past the Race Relations Act has been used to support the rights of English rather than Welsh speakers, arguably in contravention of the spirit of the Act, which was designed to protect minority rights.

Even those who had been brought up in and managed to live their lives largely through Welsh, and who had never considered the possibility of their language and culture being under serious threat, are now confronted with the possibility of becoming a minority within Gwynedd. Improved road links and the subsequent rise in property values anticipated in the 1990s, can only serve to open Gwynedd to further English immigration, while pricing local Welsh people, among the lowest paid workers in Britain, out of the housing market. County planning policy, which tries to limit the growth of commercial developments which could have a devastating effect on Welsh-speaking communities, such as the proposed holiday village near Llanberis and marina at Pwllheli, is powerless against the appeals of the developers to Cardiff and Westminster. The experience of Capel Celyn, the Welsh village drowned by the Tryweryn Reservoir in the 1950s to provide Liverpool with water, in the face of massive local and national (Welsh) opposition, is being re-enacted throughout Gwynedd. The underlying socio-economic structure of the area, exacerbated by the weakness of local democratic institutions, continues to emphasise a division along outsider/English, insider/Welsh lines.

In this atmosphere of threat from uncontrollable outside forces, there is a crisis of confidence within Welsh-speaking communities in their ability to maintain their own identity. It is not only the Gwynedd poet R. S. Thomas and the occasional school teacher who have spoken out in defence of the ten-year arson campaign of the extremist group calling themselves '*Meibion Glyndwr*'.[10] One poll estimated that as many as 85 per cent of the population of Dwyfor (a county council division within Gwynedd) supported the aims, if not the methods of the fire-bombers. Despite the pacifist and Christian (Non-Conformist) traditions with which many Welsh people identify, the violent actions of an extremist group seem to act as a kind of safety valve, giving vent to feelings which have been suppressed, but which under the surface have reached boiling point.

## Conflicting Claims to Welshness

It is almost unimaginable in Scotland, or in the Republic of Ireland, for those born and brought up in their native country to feel the need to establish their claim to Scottish or Irish identity *vis-à-vis* their fellow country men or women. The outsider who imagines that the Welsh are all the same, either romantic Celts or dishonest scoundrels, is perplexed to discover that there are at least three different Wales,[11] divided by geography, language and history.

The native Welsh speakers living in the heartland areas of the language in Gwynedd and in parts of Dyfed are apt to consider themselves to be the only true Welsh.[12] This is a claim that is hotly denied by many non-Welsh speakers. A south Walian friend from the Rhondda Valley, who learnt Welsh in his teens as a second language, still remembers with anger hearing the owners of a farm in Dyfed, on which he was working one summer, explaining his non-native Welsh to neighbours by saying (in Welsh) 'his parents are English you see'. To come from the heart of industrial south Wales with its proud and distinctive cultural history, and to hear one's people described as 'English', is a source of much bitterness to many south Walians, although the slight is usually unintentional on the part of first language Welsh speakers.

---

10. *Meibion Glyndwr* ('the Sons of Glendower') take their name from Owain Glyndŵr, a Norman/Welsh nobleman who, in the early years of the fifteenth century, succeeded briefly in uniting Wales as an independent country before being defeated by Henry IV.

11. Balsom (1985) developed what he called the 'Three Wales Model', which divided Wales into (1) the Welsh-speaking, Welsh-identified areas, *Y Fro Gymraeg*, (2) the non-Welsh-speaking, Welsh-identified areas, 'Welsh Wales', and (3) the non-Welsh-speaking, non-Welsh-identified areas, or 'British Wales' (see map, p. 188).

12. Similarly, it is claimed that only works written in Welsh can be called 'Welsh literature': cf. Wyn Griffiths (1950: 66) and Conran (1989).

A political dimension to this attitude is expressed by *Adfer*, an organisation which campaigns for a separate Welsh-speaking area of Wales as the only way to preserve Welsh as a living language. A few years ago proponents of this group were particularly dominant in the Welsh-speaking students hall of residence in Bangor. One friend, then living in the hall, innocently invited an English student friend back for a cup of coffee. She was told afterwards by some of the other students that 'in this hall we have a policy not to socialise with English speakers'. Like so many other Welsh-speaking students, she soon found that her social world at college was entirely confined to other Welsh speakers. Although from an impeccably Welsh background with a Welsh-medium secondary education behind her, she felt that coming from Cardiff already marked her out as a semi-outsider in the highly charged atmosphere of Welsh language politics which prevailed in Gwynedd at that time (the early/mid-1980s).

The majority of Welsh speakers, however, do not come from the rural areas in which the Welsh language is still strong, but from the more densely populated south of the country. Although there are small pockets in which Welsh is still widely spoken, such as Llanelli and the Swansea Valley, the majority of the population of the industrial Valleys are English-speaking. Nevertheless, the people of the Valleys retain a strong sense of Welsh identity and their English bears the imprint of the Welsh language ('Wenglish'). It is difficult, if not impossible, for the Welsh speakers of these areas to regard their non-Welsh-speaking neighbours as 'non Welsh'. One or more of the parents or grandparents of these *Cymry di-Gymraeg*, today's 'English-speaking Welsh', may well have known Welsh, either as a first or adopted language, and have attended a Welsh-language chapel. Mixed marriages resulted in many monolingual English children, and Welsh-speaking parents often chose not to pass on the language to their children in the belief that it would hold them back. This attitude, similar in its motivation to that of first generation German immigrants to the USA who spoke broken English to their children, is movingly described by Gwyn Thomas who wrote that: 'My father and mother were Welsh-speaking, yet I did not exchange a word in that language with them. The death of Welsh ran through our family like a geological fault. Places like the Rhondda were parts of America that never managed to get to the boat' (quoted in Osmond 1988: 149).

It is not uncommon for parents to speak Welsh to some children and English to others, reflecting their changing perceptions of the language and of its pragmatic value at different stages of their lives. The demand for Welsh evening classes and for Welsh-medium education, particularly among the middle classes, has further blurred the distinctions in the south between Welsh and non-Welsh speakers.

While the Welsh/English division that pertains in Gwynedd is hardly pertinent in the Rhondda, an English-language Welsh identity is not entirely unproblematic. This is poignantly, and perhaps emblematically, expressed in the two collective names for the people and their country. To the outsider or to the native English speaker the people are 'Welsh', derived from the Anglo-Saxon word *wealh*, 'foreigner'. To the Welsh speaker they are the *Cymry*, the 'kinsfolk' who inhabit not the 'land of strangers' (Wales), but the 'land of fellow countrymen/women' (*Cymru*). English speakers can only describe themselves as 'foreigners'. The collective name of the people is thereby inverted and nullified.

The non-Welsh-speaking Welsh identity appears, to the outsider at least, to be on the defensive. Whereas in Gwynedd and Dyfed the perceived crisis is that of English immigration accompanied by Welsh emigration and the consequent loss of the language, in the industrial south the Welsh language has long departed from most areas as a community tongue. It is not self-evident that identity depends upon speaking Welsh, but there is an awareness that with the loss of the Welsh language there is the loss of a heritage. Welsh is the medium of the literature, history and mythology of the country, of so much that has formed the Welsh as a separate people down the ages and which makes them different from the English. The meanings of names, the rhythms of Welsh poetry and the multifarious associations of spoken and literary Welsh are incapable of translation.

Here is a complex issue with feelings of guilt, resentment and nostalgia associated with the disappearance and, to some extent, reappearance, of the Welsh language. Welsh speakers sometimes reject the language, either out of solidarity with the non-Welsh-speaking working population, who they fear might suffer discrimination in a new linguistically conscious Wales, or out of a more old-fashioned anglicised snobbery. Some monoglot English speakers who have tried and failed, or who resent the suggestion that they should attempt to learn Welsh, are vociferous in their rejection of its claims. Others in this position respond by supporting the cause of the Welsh language, while regretting their own inability to communicate in Welsh. Whatever the individual response, there are few who would not admit that if a fluent knowledge of Welsh could be acquired instantly and painlessly they would welcome the opportunity to speak the language, and would feel more Welsh because of it. This is borne out by one study in south Wales in which non-Welsh-speaking people evaluated Welsh speakers more highly than those who could not speak the language, although they found it difficult to identify with them. They were therefore placed in the position of feeling socially distanced from the group to which they felt most attracted (Giles and Taylor 1978; cf. Khleif 1978).

There is a third Wales, neither the Welsh-speaking north and west, nor the culturally distinctive Valleys. This is the British Wales of south Pembrokeshire, parts of South, West and Mid Glamorgan, and the eastern border counties. The majority of residents in these areas prefer to identify themselves as British or English, rather than Welsh. As may be expected, efforts to spread the use of the Welsh language in these localities often faces heavy opposition. In 1988 Ogwr Council in Mid Glamorgan passed a resolution that 'Council's business, including contact with the public, will not be in Welsh or bilingual.[13] Financial considerations probably aggravate an already existing indifference or antipathy to the Welsh language. Bilingualism requires a firm commitment and does not come cheap. Councils argue that the Welsh Office and Central Government support fails to cover the cost of implementing a bilingual county policy. Despite the interest which can be generated by holding an *eisteddfod*, or by opening a new Welsh school in these areas, the predominant attitude appears to be a rejection of a specifically Welsh identity, associated with the Welsh language, and an adherence to an alternative British identity. There is not here the strong feeling of the southern Valley communities that they possess a separate but equally valid form of Welshness.

There is a complex interaction of class, politics and national or ethnic identity in south Wales. The Labour politician, Neil Kinnock, an English monoglot south Walian married to a Welsh speaker, stresses socialist unity at the expense of a separate Welsh identity. In speeches he sometimes used the terms 'British' and 'English' interchangeably when referring to England and Wales. In this he was expressing the common English attitude to national identity, which sees 'England' as

13. See Suzanne Greenslade, 'Here in England' (in Bowie and Davies 1992). There are hints here of the attitude promoted by the education inspectors of 1847 and their infamous 'Blue Books', reports which castigated the Welsh for their backwardness, blamed upon the Welsh language, and which recommended that all education be in English.

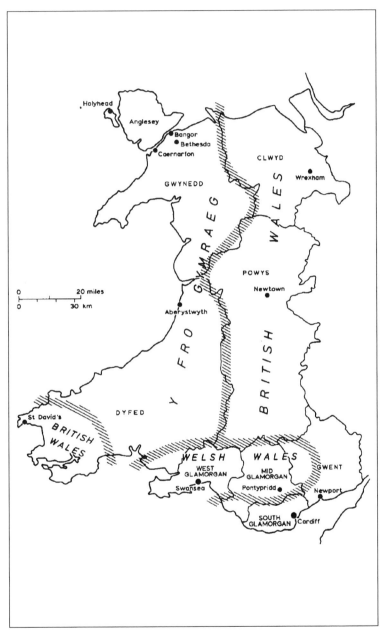

**Language and Identity in Wales. Based on 'The Three Wales Model' (Balsom, 1985).**

**Percentage of Population Speaking Welsh (aged 3 and over)**

| County | % |
| --- | --- |
| Clwyd | 18.7 |
| Dyfed | 46.3 |
| Gwent | 2.5 |
| Gwynedd | 61.2 |
| Mid Glamorgan | 8.4 |
| Powys | 20.2 |
| South Glamorgan | 5.8 |
| West Glamorgan | 16.4 |
| Total Wales | 19.0 |

*Source*: 1981 Census Returns, OPCS, 1983

synonymous with 'Britain' and which regards Wales as an English region. Patriotism is separated from nationalism and the latter loaded with purely negative connotations. Politicians like Neil Kinnock, Leo Abse and George Thomas have played upon the fears of the English-speaking population in Wales, claiming that a Welsh-speaking élite would attempt to impose a false sense of Welshness upon the country as a whole (how this might be achieved is never explained). Instead of asserting an English-speaking Welsh identity they appeal to a British/English identity which will totally marginalise the Welsh-speaking minority and which denies the distinctive Welshness inherent in the history and cultural traditions of the Valleys. Pressure for Welsh national institutions and a stronger, separate, Welsh identity, as opposed to mere regionalism, is now coming from bodies such as the Welsh Trades Union Congress and from the British Labour Party as a whole, overriding the aversion to nationalist politics which has characterised so many south Walian Labour MPs (but not Welsh-speaking Labour politicians from the north).

## Picking Up the Pieces

The Welsh learner can be a determined and committed creature. I have attended many meetings, and spent many sociable evenings with friends, in which the proceedings and conversation are entirely in Welsh. Not unusual in Wales, you might think, but it is not uncommon for everyone in the room to have learnt Welsh as a second or foreign language. Some families and individuals who have learnt the language as adults adopt Welsh as their chief medium of communication, and many others use Welsh regularly when in the company of other Welsh speakers. Welsh classes feed the learner with a diet of Welsh folk-heroes and legends, describing nationalist achievements and giving the uninitiated an education in the struggles that have been fought for the Welsh language.[14] Some learners continue their Welsh education by joining Plaid Cymru, *Cymdeithas yr Iaith Gymraeg* (The Welsh Language Society) or one of the many other Welsh social and political organisations. It can be something of a disappointment for the learner, therefore, to reach towards a new Welsh identity, or understanding of Welshness, only to discover that there is not one but many ways of being Welsh.

The difficulty of finding common concerns and of bridging the gap between the Welsh and non-Welsh speakers, between north, east, south and west, between the industrial and rural areas, native-born Welsh and incomers, has been *the* great problem facing any party or group attempting to promote a Welsh cause or to forge a national Welsh identity. Within Wales the search for coherence, meaning and cultural roots is an age-old national concern. The English have the psychological advantages of a dominant people. Their language, values and identity are seldom threatened or even questioned. The Welsh, like other minority peoples, are expected to have a distinctive identity, but at the same time are seen as quasi-English, and Wales as an English administrative unit. When faced with this lack of recognition from without, the Welsh have turned to the creation and recreation of a Welsh people, using historical myths, literature, religion and above all, language, the medium through which all these other facets of national identity were, and are, expressed. The English are an essential ingredient in Welsh identity, not in making the people what they are, but in providing a symbol of what they are not. It is in opposition to Englishness that Welshness is defined. From the perspective of Gwynedd, where to be Welsh means to speak the Welsh language, the English-speaking Welsh can fall into the same category as the English in England and as incomers who may have learnt the language. To the Welsh-identified southerner this is unacceptable, and new definitions of Welshness which can embrace all those who consider themselves to be Welsh need to be found if any sense of a wider national identity is to be sustained.

---

14. Popular stereotypes of the drunken, womanising Welshman are predominant in the books of Heini Gruffydd, author of some of the most popular and widely available material for adult learners of Welsh. See Noragh Jones (1989) for a critique of sexism in Welsh course material.

This exigency has particularly preoccupied Plaid Cymru in their attempts to define Welsh identity in ways which can support separate nation status. Economic and moral arguments are often presented in favour of separation from Westminster, but the strongest appeal is to the emotions and to what are perceived as cultural and spiritual values. The prospect of a federal or confederal Europe is seen by nationalists in Wales as an opportunity (though not without potential dangers) for independence and the assertion of a Welsh identity. This contrasts with the centralist politics of the Conservative Party, who fear any diminution of power in Westminster, and until very recently of the Labour Party, who have rightly seen Scottish and Welsh devolution (or independence) as undermining their own power base in Westminster. Questions of national sovereignty can appear rather differently according to which side of Offa's Dyke one is standing. The former President of Plaid Cymru and Member of Parliament for Meirionydd Nant Conwy in Gwynedd, Dafydd Elis Thomas, wrote in his 1989 European Election Communication (in Welsh only): 'There is the opportunity to pull Wales out of a British way of thinking. We are no longer obliged to think of ourselves as a minority within Britain, but as part of the varied pattern of Europe.'

Ten years after a devolution referendum, which apparently rejected the prospect of a separate Welsh identity, the mood within Wales has changed dramatically. The economic and social benefits associated with rule from Westminster no longer seem as real or as necessary as they did before, and the changes in Eastern Europe have allowed people to think in terms of smaller independent nations linked by co-operative economic ties, rather than in terms of larger power blocks deciding the fate of the smaller nations within their sphere of interest. Wales is increasingly looking out, towards Europe, as well as within, at its own mixed population, its bilingualism and its cultural roots. I perceive a new confidence and determination by Welsh-speakers, incomers and English-speaking Welsh people alike, to forge a Welsh identity which builds on all these disparate groups and experiences. It will be different from the Wales of the imagination and from the Wales of the past, but it will also be distinctively and assertively Welsh.

## References

Aitchison, J. and H. Carter (1985), *The Welsh Language 1961–1981: An Interpretive Atlas*. Cardiff: University of Wales Press

Ardener, E. (1989), 'The Construction of History', in E. Tonkin, M. McDonald and M. Chapman (eds), *History and Ethnicity*. ASA Monographs 27. London: Routledge

Armstrong, J. (1982), *Nations before Nationalism*. Chapel Hill: University of North Carolina Press

Balsom, D. (1985), 'The Three-Wales Model', in J. Osmond (ed.), *The National Question Again: Welsh Political Identity in the 1980s*. Llandysul: Gomer

Bowie, F. and O. Davies (eds) (1992), *Discovering Welshness*. Llandysul: Gomer

Carter, H. (1988), *Immigration and the Welsh Language*. Published by the Court of the National Eisteddford

Cohen, A. P. (1986), *Symbolising Boundaries: Identity and Diversity in British Cultures*. Manchester: Manchester University Press

Conran, T. (1989), ' Anglo-Welsh Manqué?', in *Planet*, vol. 76, Aug/Sept.

Curtis, T. (ed.) (1986), *Wales: The Imagined Nation: Studies in Cultural and National Identity*. Bridgend: Poetry Wales Press

Day, G. (undated), '*A Million on the Move*'? *Population Change and Rural Wales*. Aberystwyth Economic Papers, Occasional Paper no. 27, University College Wages, Aberystwyth

Emmett, I. (1964), *A North Wales Village*: *A Social Anthropological Study*. Dartington Hall Studies in Rural Sociology. London: Routledge and Keegan Paul

———(1982), '*Fe godwn ni eto*: Stasis and Change in a Welsh Industrial Town', in A. P. Cohen (ed.) *Belonging: Identity and Social Organisation in British Rural Cultures*. Manchester: Manchester University Press

Frankenberg, R. (1969), 'British Community Studies: Problems of Synthesis', in M. Banton (ed.), *The Social Anthropology of Complex Societies*. ASA Monographs 4. London: Tavistock

Giles, H. and D.M. Taylor (1978), National Identity in South Wales: Some Preliminary Data', in G. Williams (ed.), *Social and Cultural Change in Contemporary Wales*. London: Routledge and Kegan Paul

Greenslade, S. (1992), "Here in England"', in F. Bowie and O. Davies (eds), *Discovering Welshness*. Llandysul: Gomer

Griffiths, W. (1950), *The Welsh*. Harmondsworth: Penguin

Hubback, D. (1987), *Time and the Valley*: *The Past, Present and Future of the Upper Ogwen Valley*. Llanrwst: Gwasg Carreg Gwalch

Jones, G. E. (1988), *Modern Wales: A Concise History, c. 1485–1979*, Cambridge: Cambridge University Press

Jones, N. (1989), 'Blod and the Brush Salesman', *Planet*, vol.76, Aug./Sept.

Khleif, B. (1978), 'Ethnic Awakening in the First World: The Case of Wales', in G. Williams (ed.), *Social and Cultural Change in Contemporary Wales*. London: Routledge and Kegan Paul

Lindsay, J. (1987), *The Great Strike: A History of the Penrhyn Quarry Dispute of 1900–1903*. Newton Abbot and London: David and Charles

Lovering, J. (1983), *Gwynedd – A County in Crisis*. Coleg Harlech Occasional

Papers in Welsh Studies, no. 2, July

Merfyn-Jones, R. (1983), *The North Wales Quarrymen 1874–1922*. Cardiff: University of Wales Press

Osmond, J. (1988), *The Divided Kingdom*. London: Constable

Smith, A. D. (1988), *The Ethnic Origins of Nations*. Oxford: Blackwell

Tonkin, E. M. McDonald and M. Chapman (eds) (1989), *History and Ethnicity*. ASA Monographs 27. London: Routledge

Wenger, C. G. (1978), 'Ethnicity and Social Organisation in North-East Wales', in G. Williams (ed.), *Social and Cultural Change in Contemporary Wales*. London: Routledge and Kegan Paul

Williams, G. A. (1979), *When Was Wales?* BBC Radio Lecture

Williams, G. A. (1985), *When Was Wales?* Harmondsworth: Penguin

# 9

# Copeland: Cumbria's Best-Kept Secret

## *Malcolm Chapman*

**M**y title is taken from a Cumbrian tourist board publicity campaign, the aim of which was to encourage people to visit Copeland.[1] The slogan was quickly abandoned, because various Copeland authorities objected to it. It was felt to be too true – too painful a subject, as it were, for frivolity: as if it were really saying 'Copeland – don't worry if you haven't heard of it; nobody else has' (see *Whitehaven News* [henceforth abbreviated to WN], 3/9/87, p. 1).

Copeland is an ancient name for a relatively new unit of local and national government, Copeland, which contains most of the old area of Allerdale above Derwent. It comprises a large part of West Cumbria, and it is West Cumbria in a rather general sense that I wish to discuss. The title, with its secrecy, serves as a useful motif.

The new county of Cumbria takes in the old counties of Cumberland and Westmorland, and parts of northern Lancashire and north-western Yorkshire. It covers, in effect, the mountain massif of Lakeland, and the areas surrounding it on all sides. Cumbria takes its name from the same British 'Cymry' that inhabit Wales (the name, in both these forms, means, in effect, 'of the same country', or 'ourselves'). It has, throughout recorded history, been a place of refuge and passage, outside the obvious run of political events (for general background see Housman 1800; Britton and Brayley 1802; Hughes 1965). Throughout the post-Roman period, when most of England was

---

1. The first version of this paper was prepared for a rather general audience, containing nevertheless a good proportion of social anthropologists. It was delivered in January 1988, reporting the situation in early 1987. The occasion of this delivery was a one-day conference on 'ethnography and ethnicity', and I have not included, in this paper, discussion of the anthropological background to such issues, since much of this could be taken for granted in the immediate context of the conference. My concern was, rather, to present a particular example in a lively manner. I have since twice presented the paper to a lay audience, containing a good proportion of Cumbrians, and was pleased to find that my analysis was for the most part approved.

undergoing the progressive consolidation of the Anglo-Saxon kingdoms, Cumbria was home to a bewildering variety of peoples and powers. It was peripheral to the landed power of the Anglo-Saxon world, but it was a natural landing place to those that sailed the Celtic sea. British from Strathclyde and Rheged, Saxons of Bernicia, Gaelicised Norwegians of Ireland, Gaels of Dal Riata and the Isle of Man, all made their homes here. The Gaelic power of early mediaeval Scotland once ruled here, until the Normans extended their power to Cumbria during the reign of William Rufus. The place names of West Cumbria are, in consequence, a rather pleasing and unlikely combination of almost every possibility that the British Isles offer – p-Celtic, q-Celtic, Norse, Anglo-Saxon, and French; names from each of these linguistic traditions sit side by side on the map, curiously to an ear accustomed to more homogeneous regions of England or Scotland. When a bill permitting the formation of a new railway company in the Whitehaven area was going through Parliament in the late nineteenth century, some amusement was caused when a member asked it if could be true that they were seriously debating a railway line that was going to link up Corkickle, Rowrah, and Keekle (McGowan Gradon 1952). My own sentiments were much the same, when I first went to live in West Cumbria – many of the names sounded as if somebody had just rather capriciously made them up, ancient though they are – Lamplugh, Mockerkin, Frizington, Lowca, St Bees, Egremont, Aspatria.

It is not simply that West Cumbria has been *isolated* from the rest of the world, although this is certainly how its problem is often perceived. Rather, its 'remoteness' has taken the form of a peculiar vulnerability to external interventions, and to the often alien rhythms governing these. It has had in it a great variety of ill-recorded peoples, and a constant exposure to external economic rhythms of coming and going, booming, busting and leaving (see Davies-Shiel and Marshall 1969). It is, in this respect, rather like the West Highlands of Scotland (where, as Ardener has it, 'canonical levels of "remoteness" are to be found', 1987: 43).

When the population of England thinks of Cumberland and Westmorland, or Cumbria, or the Lake District, it is the mountains, lakes and valleys which come to mind. The area has great symbolic importance in the intellectual and moral history of England. It was here, in the late eighteenth and early nineteenth centuries, that new attitudes to wild and untamed rural places found their exemplar. Lakeland is not just a wild and beautiful landscape; it is, rather, in the history of the English and European intellect, one of *the* wild and beautiful landscapes. Many of our metaphors for understanding landscape and beauty, and for the relative appreciation of rurality and urbanity, grew to strength here. Wordsworth was born here, and lived here with his sister Dorothy, receiving more or less lengthy visits from Coleridge, Lamb, Scott, Shelley, Byron and so on. During the period of the growth and development of urban and industrial England, 'the Lake District' grew alongside, as a symbol of all that urban and industrial England was lacking, or needed for its completion. The tourist industry in the Lake District is as old as pastoral tourism itself.

Fell walking, mountain climbing and rock climbing (and particularly the last of these) can all be argued to have their origins in the Lake District. They have become Europe-wide, even worldwide, sports; millions of people indulge in them, and great amounts of money are spent on them: but they have their origins in Langdale and Wasdale, and on the cliffs of Scafell, Great Gable and Pillar (see Hankinson 1972).

As the Lake District began, so it has continued. A large part of the area is now a National Park. It receives great numbers of tourists. It is home to many retired people. The demands and requirements of outside interests have to a great extent come to determine what the place is, and what is allowed to happen in it. This interest in the Lake District comes to it, however, from the South and East. Its termini are Kendal, Windermere, Ambleside, Penrith and Keswick.

Along the narrow coastal plain to the west of the Lake District, however, lies the area commonly known now as West Cumbria, stretching from the Solway Firth to the Barrow Peninsula. This area is emphatically not part of the Lake District. It is, by contrast, an area of small towns based upon traditional heavy industry, upon coal-mining, iron and steel production, mineral extraction, and chemical industries (see Bouch and Jones 1961). The great majority of the British population knows little or nothing about this area. From the outside, it is commonly unrecognised, in that people, if asked about the location of Whitehaven, Workington, Maryport, Cockermouth, or Millom (for example), will either guess wrongly, or admit ignorance.[2] The existence of the area is, most importantly, scarcely acknowledged by most people who frequent 'The Lakes', even by those who imagine

---

2. I could illustrate this from many conversations and experiences, but a family note will convey the point well. My father, as a teenager in the 1930s, occasionally went by train from Bradford, in West Yorkshire, to Workington in West Cumbria, to watch football matches. Even *after* this experience, as an adult he still did not know where Workington *was*.

themselves to know the area well. It is an area which few people visit, and of whose location many are uncertain. Hundreds of thousands look out over it, from the summits of Lakeland peaks, but their eyes are on the horizon.

The presence of rich coal and haematite reserves in West Cumbria has meant that the area has attracted small-scale industrial interest for as long as men have been interested in iron and coal (see Fletcher 1881). The modern industrial history of the area begins, however, with the growth of coal-mining in and around Whitehaven in the seventeenth century. By the end of the eighteenth century, Whitehaven had become a major port, with a virtual monopoly of the coal trade to Ireland, and a thriving import industry in the commodities of North America, especially tobacco. In the period immediately preceding the American War of Independence, Whitehaven had passing through it every year a tonnage of goods exceeded in Britain only by the port of London, and far in excess of that going through Liverpool, Newcastle or Bristol. Most of this was coal, and most of it was on short haul to Ireland. Nevertheless, to anybody that has seen the small-scale dereliction of Whitehaven today, the comparative figures are chastening (see Hay 1966; Hughes 1965). Whitehaven grew up as an elegant and well-planned Georgian town, and the structure of this period has largely remained, although the elegance is now difficult to perceive, so overlain is it with the effects and perceptions of poverty and decline. The coal industry in West Cumbria in the twentieth century has been in relentless contraction, and the last Whitehaven deep-mined pit closed in 1986. There has been no alternative prosperity, no wealth, and no burgeoning population clamouring for housing, which required or allowed that a great deal of change be made to old Whitehaven. It is today, in consequence, a combination rare in Britain – a largely unspoilt Georgian town, whose fabric is in a state of serious and long-term decay.[3]

Whitehaven in the nineteenth century, unlike Liverpool, had no great hinterland of industrial towns to serve, which accounts in the

3. Since the 1980s British Nuclear Fuels has put a great deal of well-spent money into various renovation schemes in Whitehaven, in a spirit of what might be called 'enlightened public relations'. Parts of the town are transformed as a result, although evidences of the general downward trend to which I refer are still ubiquitous. There are, in the British Isles, few small coastal towns with picturesque fishing harbours where no pretence is made at being a 'seaside town'; Whitehaven is one of them. One might, at least, be permitted to hope that the downward trend of Whitehaven has been arrested, if not definitively turned around.

main for its relative decline. There were, however, iron deposits in the coastal plain, and throughout the nineteenth century these were increasingly exploited. The ore was very high-grade haematite, and as such capable of producing high-quality iron even in the absence of sophisticated techniques. The area became pocked with iron workings, and small towns and villages grew up to house those who worked in the industry – Frizington, Cleator Moor, Kirkland, Lowca, Workington and so on (see Brown and Hayton 1986; Caine 1916; Sugden n.d.).

As long as unsophisticated iron-working techniques required high-grade haematite of the kind that the area supplied, the local iron industry boomed. From the end of the nineteenth century, however, and particularly since the end of the 1914–18 war, lower-grade deposits elsewhere in Britain and the world became easily workable, and the local iron industry virtually disappeared. The settlements that it provoked, however, have remained. Whitehaven, through the coal industry, already had long-standing links with Ireland, and many people emigrated from Ireland to work in coal-mining, and later in iron-mining. The small mining town of Cleator Moor, of which more later, was particularly known for the high density of Irish Catholics that lived there.

A chaotic network of railway lines and railway companies was established to serve the area in the mid-nineteenth century (McGowan Gradon 1952). The lakeland mountains, however, cut the region off from any easy communications with the rest of England, other than north through Carlisle, or south down the coastal plain to Barrow and Lancaster. Local lobbies attempted to have the main north-south London-Glasgow railway line routed around the coastal plain, but without success. The main line was forced over Shap Fell, to the east of the mountains, in 1846 (see Davies-Shiel and Marshall 1969: 188), linking Lancaster with Carlisle, and by-passing West Cumbria altogether. Similarly, campaign was made in the middle twentieth century to have the main north-south road built along the coastal plain from Lancashire to Carlisle, and similarly the new motorway was built following the railway, over Shap Fell (see Barber 1976: 55). West Cumbria is now, and foreseeably, about as far off the main transport network of England as it is possible to be. Whitehaven, as the crow flies, is under fifty miles from Lancaster (and thus the route to the south). The journey, however, takes about six hours on a train, and about two and a half hours on the fastest roads – in both cases, one is obliged to travel around the north of the Lakeland massif.

The small towns of West Cumbria were hastily built, to house poor workers in dirty industries whose expectations of domestic comfort were not, in the first place, high. Since the virtual collapse of the main local industries of iron and coal, there has been, as in Whitehaven, little impetus to new development. As a result, the small towns, while still inhabited, look much as they did several decades ago, except that much of their energy and prosperity have left them. They are typically of small terraced houses, built of stone reddened with the presence of iron, and giving straight onto the road in front. As one writer on Cumbrian villages has remarked, 'in this part of the Whitehaven hinterland the villages seem doomed to ugliness' (Smith 1973: 113). Cleator Moor is 'a drab mining village' (ibid.: 113). Rowrah is 'a long village of uninteresting houses stretched along the A5086' (ibid.: 112). Lowca is a 'grim, dingy village' (ibid.). Everywhere around them are traces of the industry which once gave them life – disused railway lines, sites of industrial dereliction, spoil-heaps and mine workings.

Given this unappealing appearance, and the uncompromisingly industrial atmosphere of West Cumbrian towns, coupled with the isolation of the area from the transport network of England by the Lakeland fells, it is perhaps not surprising that the area attracts so little attention from the millions of visitors to Lakeland, so close by. It is worth dwelling on this. My wife and I spent three years living on what might be regarded as the 'frontier' between West Cumbria and Lakeland, where Ennerdale opens out to the coastal plain. The village where we lived is on the extreme edge of the area of the Lakeland National Park, but with many of its social and moral links to the west, into West Cumbria. Our weekend walks took us east, into the hills, while our social life and work took us west, into the coastal plain. The frontier was a fascinating place, for it was a meeting of two very different worlds.

Ennerdale is a valley leading out of the heart of the Lakeland mountains down to the coastal plain. It is the only one of the major lakeland valleys and lakes which has no public road running its length. The only road to it comes from the west, from West Cumbria, and goes no further than the near, western end of the lake. We have seen that the great bulk of the traffic to the Lake District comes from the south and east. Few cars make it right round to the west side, to come up

Ennerdale, and few walkers, starting from the major centres, come as far west as the lower Ennerdale valley.[4] Ennerdale is, in consequence, by a long way the least visited and most quiet of the major Lakeland valleys, and it has had this position ever since tourism to the Lake District began. It is commonly described in general tourist literature as 'the most remote' of the valleys of Lakeland, and this is true in an important sense. The description gives us a good clue to the dominant patterns of moral geography in the area, however, for of course Ennerdale is, for the towns of Whitehaven, Cleator Moor and Egremont, and for the people of this part of West Cumbria, by some way the nearest and most accessible of the valleys. The western end of the lake has long had a place in the symbolic geography of local West Cumbria as somewhere a boy might take his girl out on a fine evening, or somewhere the family might go with the dog after Sunday dinner (see, for example, Watson 1868: 20–1; 29–30). The company on the lakeside track on a Sunday afternoon is, in consequence, interestingly

---

4. I do not know of any official statistics on these matters; my comments are about relative proportions, and are based on personal experience. I could, however, try and quantify the matter thus (assuming for comparison a knowledge of the crowds and traffic jams of Eastern Lakeland): there is one principal car-park giving access to Ennerdale Valley; it holds about sixty cars; on weekdays in the winter months it is usually empty, while at weekends there may be a handful of cars – four or five, say; at a weekend in the height of summer, I have never experienced a parking problem. The nearest village of a size to offer services to pleasure-seekers has one shop – a post-office and general store which also offers maps, local guides, postcards and the like. The village contains only two establishments which offer accommodation to tourists or walkers (compare and contrast, say, the much larger Ambleside, where almost every house is a 'bed and breakfast' or hotel).

The presence of walkers in the area has recently been changed somewhat by a characteristically 'Lakeland' phenomenon. The late A. R. Wainwright codified the experience of walking in the Lake District in a series of justly popular books, published between 1955 and 1966 (see, for example, Wainwright 1966). Having covered the entire Lakeland fells, and achieved great publishing success, he turned his attention to the creation of a 'coast-to-coast walk'. This walk runs from St Bees, on the West Cumbrian coast a few miles south of Whitehaven, to Robin Hood's Bay on the east coast of Yorkshire. The fame of Wainwright's other works has rubbed off onto the 'coast-to-coast walk', and increasing numbers of walkers are attempting this passage, which brings them from St Bees, across the coastal plain, and up Ennerdale Valley. Wainwright's route seeks rurality, but he is obliged to bring it through Cleator, a small town which is effectively part of the now larger Cleator Moor. Elsewhere in this paper, I discuss the moral divide between the Lake District (where the walkers are heading, or from which they have come) and urban West Cumbria; Wainwright's comment on the matter is short and telling: he advises Coast-to-Coast walkers passing through Cleator that 'the primary concern of the inhabitants is to earn a living for themselves, not to cater for the leisure of others' (Wainwright 1973: 8). The affinity of St Bees with the Lake District, tied together now by Wainwright's walk, and the dissonance provided by West Cumbria more generally, is shown also through many other structures and associations (see below, pp. 201–6).

mixed. Some are purposefully dressed in out-of-doors clothes – walking boots, thick red socks, breeches, check-patterned shirts and waterproofs, carrying sticks and rucksacks. They are in the Lake District, and perilously close, if only they knew, to falling off its edge. Others are dressed in Sunday best, having left the car a few hundred yards away. They are wearing fashion-shoes and smart casual clothes, even suits; some are smoking, perhaps. They are in West Cumbria. The two groups display characteristic, and very different, patterns of verbal and non-verbal communication, and there is only infrequent ambiguity as to which category a family or individual belongs.

I could write at length about the divide between the two, for it is a rich theme, so different are the two worlds. I will limit myself, however, to two descriptions. The first is of my own introduction to the area. In 1978, I went walking in what I then knew as 'The Lakes' with my brother. He was 31, I was 27, we were both Oxford graduates, and had been born and brought up in a large industrial town in West Yorkshire. We both considered ourselves, not without reason, to be rather 'outdoor' types, who had walked and climbed in most of the mountainous areas of the British Isles. We had, as children, made regular family visits from our home town of Bradford to the Yorkshire Dales. We felt, I think, that the Yorkshire Dales were, in important respects, 'ours' (and this is a common West Yorkshire urban perception, I suspect). I also felt, even though I had rarely visited the area, that the Lake District was mine as well. I was an outdoor type, and the Lakes were an outdoor-type's sort of place. I had assumed knowledge of the Lakes, and a kind of proprietorship, even before I had visited them (and this sentiment about the Lakes dates right back to local primary school experience in Bradford). It sometimes came as a surprise to me, on meeting people that did know about the Lakes and had been there, that I did in fact know almost nothing about them – that I could not, for example, when asked, express an empirically based preference for, say, Buttermere over Thirlmere, or for Great Gable over Helvellyn. The names belonged, so to speak, in a moral geography which I had occupied in advance of my arrival. Wordsworth said more or less the same thing – he gave the Lakes to all Englishmen, and I had received the gift.

I met my brother in Penrith railway station, and we walked, over the course of the next few days, up Ullswater, over to Ambleside, up Langdale, over Great Gable to Honister and Borrowdale, and back over Scafell into Wasdale. On the last day of our holiday, we proposed to walk up out of the head of Wasdale, over Pillar into Ennerdale, and down Ennerdale to the sea. For those who know the area, the resonance of these names will be quite sufficient to indicate the nature of our enterprise. We had not paid much attention to the final part of the journey, beyond making Whitehaven the place where we would get bed and breakfast, or perhaps find a little hotel. Doubtless we had looked at the map, but the reality had not registered. I imagined, and still can do so in the dimmer corners of my mind, that the Lakeland fells simply cascaded into the sea, with rocky inlets and beaches, clear waters, and the smell of seaweed; perhaps, here and there, a small fishing village of whitewashed houses, with bed and breakfast signs in the windows. I was, no doubt, thinking of the West Highlands of Scotland.

We climbed up out of Wasdale, and went over Pillar, the presiding mountain of Ennerdale. We went down past Pillar Rock, and into Ennerdale valley; as the afternoon wore on into evening, we walked down the forestry paths that lead to the lowlands. We came to the village of Ennerdale Bridge near the foot of the lake, by this time rather tired. Ennerdale Bridge was not much different from what we might have expected, except that it was strangely quiet and small. There were no gift shops, climbing shops, or fellow outdoor types. There were no bed and breakfast signs either.

We were obliged, then, to carry on walking to what we doubtless thought of, to ourselves, as 'the next village'. This was Cleator Moor. It is difficult for me to do justice to the experience of walking to Cleator Moor, and arriving there, for it remains in my memory as one of the most vivid, surprising and unexpected experiences of my life. By the time we got within sight of Cleator Moor, we were tired, and the light was failing. Instead of a coherent little village of slate-built houses, welcoming pubs and hotels, shops catering to our interests, and a population indulgent towards, tolerant of, or even sharing, our lively fell-walking activities, we had arrived at twilight in another world. We found ourselves walking down a street with terraced houses on either side – small, closely built houses whose frontdoors opened directly onto the pavement, and whose domestic space spilled out onto the road. People lingered in the evening air in the doorways or on the pavements, watching us with unfriendly curiosity as we passed. The clothes that we were wearing, so appropriate in the streets of Ambleside or on the summit of Scafell, began to feel like ludicrous fancy-dress – the bare shins, the breeches, the boots and brightly coloured socks, the orange waterproofs, the rucksacks. Instead of feeling intrepid, as one is permitted to feel on descending from a modest Lakeland mountain into the streets of Ambleside, Keswick or

Penrith, we began to feel acutely out of place. We had both been brought up in industrial West Yorkshire, and we knew the signs – this was a tough place.

In the centre of Cleator Moor, we discovered that there was a bus to Whitehaven in twenty minutes, and we decided to wait. The bus shelter stood alone in the centre of the market square, in the centre of Cleator Moor. The local youth, perceiving us as objects of interest, moved in. The effect, and I think also the intent, was threatening. They were not quite as big as we were, but there were many more of them, perhaps a couple of dozen. There was no escape either. There was no elegant teashop to which we could retire, and the pubs, from external appearance, and from the look of those hanging around their doorways, were not for us. So we stayed where we were, by now surrounded. Our bags were picked up and examined, and we were subjected to cross-questioning in an unfamiliar accent – where had we been?, had we been in the Lake District?, were we married?, did we like sex?, what jobs did we do?, how much did we earn?, were those things waterproof?, how much did they cost?, did we like walking?, why?, had we got any cigarettes? We answered, among other things, that we had been up Pillar. 'Where was that?', came the response, 'was it in the Lake District?' 'I went to the Lake District once', one volunteered; 'I went up Pillar', said another, 'too much like hard work.'

This sounds tame enough, but it felt like fire and deep water at the time. The questioning was persistent, and there was no doubt of its latent hostility, nor of its determination to put the strangers out of countenance. We had stepped unwittingly out of our prepared ground, and laid ourselves open to the very justifiable resentment of urban poverty for the self-regarding privileges of 'Lakeland'. Every non-linguistic message that our dress and pastime gave out was, in the immediate context, provocative and alien. Eventually the bus arrived, and we were carried from Cleator Moor to Whitehaven. From frying pan, so it seemed, to fire. As I have said, we knew a bit about northern industrial towns, and we could see at a glance that this also was a tough one, not the kind that you wandered round in at night in knee breeches, speaking the wrong accent. Instead of the seaside town of our imagination, this was a larger version of Cleator Moor. Nevertheless, we tried to get bed and breakfast in the only town-centre hotel. Both of us felt that here, at least, we would be welcome, bringing custom to a hotel in so unappealing an area. 'Sorry', they said at reception, 'we're full up.' 'Full up?', we queried; 'Yes, we're usually full of commercial travellers during the week.' We were told that there was nowhere else in Whitehaven, and that we had better go to St Bees. Hungry, weary and desolate, we caved in, and got a taxi to this strange-sounding location – a small seaside village, as it turned out, with a modest tradition of catering for pleasure-seeking visitors – the Morecambe of the West Cumbrian plain.

I filed this chaotic experience of social anomaly away in my mind, as something an anthropologist might perhaps go back to look at. I did not know, of course, as I walked through Ennerdale Bridge those years ago, that my wife and I would come to live there for an extended period, nor that Cleator Moor was to become the town to which, ten years hence, we would go to do the daily shopping. Having lived in the area now for three years, and been closely associated with it for longer still, I am able to tell the personal tale of my first meeting with Cleator Moor with a conviction that the problem it expresses is genuine and concrete – the Lake District and West Cumbria are close together, with a great gulf between them. More walkers come down the same route than did, perhaps, ten or fifteen years previously, and Cleator Moor is not without signs of revival. I know, however, that for many walkers who cover the route something like the same footsore moral Odyssey is in progress. I have occasionally used my car to rescue stray walkers from the consequences of their ignorance, but in general I leave them to their activities – watching them, perhaps, with the characteristic local mixture of pity, disdain and incredulity.

My second description of the moral divide between the Lake District and West Cumbria is morally and geographically analogous to the first, and comes from a travellers' guide to the Lakes published in 1864. The writer says that 'until Ennerdale has the benefit of carriage ways along its banks, it will remain comparatively a terra incognita to the tourist world' (Lynn Linton 1864: 228), and so it has proved. The writer goes on to describe a journey from Ennerdale to the coast, almost exactly like that upon which my brother and I were channelled over a hundred years later:

> Those who want variety in scenery would do well to pass from Ennerdale to St Bees. A more thorough diversity could scarcely be found, from the lonely mountain lake imprisoned within its iron barriers, through flowery country lanes, and by dirty and ugly mining villages, down to the mighty sea – the term and bound of all things. The character and spirit of the way change strangely as you go on. When you leave Ennerdale you pass first through the dear old country roads, narrow, tortuous, bordered with hedges full of flowers – in this early autumn time silvered with great bindweed,

azured with hairbells passing into the deeper purple of the tufted vetch, and gilded with hawkweed, bright yellow vetchling, and heavy ragwort – country roads diversified by stretches of copse wood and the sudden windings of the Ehen – by pretty bridges such as that of Wath Bridge, with the fine span of arch so customary to this country – by picturesque cottages, and healthy, honest faces; but gradually losing all these features as the way leads you into the mining district. And then you come to a new order of things; to a village like Cleator, formal and ugly, with evil faces and squalid looks haunting every door and window; with ragged children; girls and women unkempt, flaring, and untidy; men lounging and vicious, sometimes brutal-looking for a change; in a word, with the outward signs, so fatal and so easily recognised, of a trade that excludes healthy physical influences, and where bodily waste is supplied by sensual excess. They all look sodden and hard-worked, and in the whole of the two villages you will pass through you will not perhaps see one well-looking woman – meaning by that, modest and cleanly – nor one really cared for child. The very colour of the earth, too, is altered from that of the lake-land proper. The rich browns and pure greys of the mountains have given place to a coarse hard red, which ruddles everything to the same ochreous tint alike. The roads are red and the houses are red, the carts and the horses and the slouching canvas-clothed men and the bare-footed children – they are all daubed and saturated with red. About the Big Rigg works, where the landslip took place on the high road one day, the redness is singularly offensive; but by-and-by the mining district yields to the clean, close-shorn uplands of the sea-side; and when you mount the last hill, leading to St Bees, you are in another world (ibid.: 228ff.).

Making due allowance for the literary flourishes, and for the general changes in social and economic conditions since 1864, Linton's piece expresses a moral divide which is still tangible and relevant.[5] For those who know Lakeland, the journey from Ennerdale to St Bees, via Cleator Moor, is still a bumpy, surprising, alarming, and even offensive ride. The Lake District is the *locus classicus* of high-minded and privileged leisure, wealthy, rural and beautiful, a national playground for the healthy and the thoughtful, with stone-built hotels in parks of

5. It will be obvious, I hope, that I do not cite Lynn Linton to agree with her, any more than I cite my own first experience of Cleator Moor as evidence of what Cleator Moor is really like. I have, I might now say, a great deal more respect for Cleator Moor's first reaction to me, than I have for my own first reaction to Cleator Moor. I cite these evidences, of literature and experience, not as objective accounts, but in order to characterise a persistent and common perception of one area by another.

rhododendron. West Cumbria, and Cleator Moor particularly, represents a desolate and unregarded landscape of industry declining, industry departed, and high unemployment.

Those who live in West Cumbria know, of course, that the Lake District exists, for they can see the lakeland mountains every day on their horizon. They also know what the Lake District represents, and what to expect of those visiting it. Those visiting the Lake District, however, typically know very little about West Cumbria, even, as we have seen, to the extent of being ignorant of its existence. I have spoken to many people about this subject, and many are either very hazy in their knowledge of what happens west of the hills, or, having discovered the nature of West Cumbria, deeply offended that their pastoral idyll should have been spoilt by its proximity. The basic structure of this experience and perception is widely shared among those who visit the area, or stay in it for a little while.

Those who live in West Cumbria are not, typically, rich or powerful, and they tend not to be at the hub of British economic, political, and literary activity. Visitors to Lakeland, by contrast, contain among them an unusually high proportion of well-educated and middle-class people from urban southern England. They have come in order to indulge in the worship of the countryside, open spaces and mountains which is so striking a feature of the leisured thought and practice of privileged English people. One aspect of this worship of the countryside, of course, is a tendency to regard urban industrial life as inherently unpleasant and undesirable, and best avoided. The Lake District is, as it were, a highly controlled 'natural' environment, within which thoughts such as these can be enjoyed without obstruction. Those thinking along these lines do not know about industrial West Cumbria, and do not want to know.

There is an imbalance, therefore, in the way in which knowledge of the area is fed into the general British consciousness. The Lake District, and its pastoral charms, are known to virtually everybody. The Lake District is widely celebrated and visited. If you were, say, an Oxford-educated member of the educated middle classes, and you stayed on top of Scafell or Helvellyn, or in the main street of Ambleside or Keswick, for ten years, you would probably meet, at least once during the period, a surprisingly high percentage of the people you had been at Oxford with, and most of your colleagues, past, present and future. You would undoubtedly meet, even unbeknown, many of the powerful and influential people in the land. The top of Helvellyn is like Piccadilly Circus, in that eventually you meet everybody you have ever known, only a much better class of them. By contrast, you could sit in the Commercial Arms in Cleator Moor for a decade without meeting anybody connected with anything you had previously experienced. You would make some very good and worthy friends, but you would not meet the opinion-formers of the land. West Cumbria's story is, therefore, little told, and the area is, as Barber has it, 'Lakeland's poor relation' (Barber 1976).[6]

Much has been written about the tension between the urban pastoral idyll and the realities of country life, and I claim no great novelty for what I have so far said, other than, perhaps, locating a particularly high-voltage junction at the boundary between the Lake District and West Cumbria (and specifically at Wath Brow Bridge). The area has a particular place in contemporary debate, however, because it is home to Sellafield. Sellafield, rather like the Lake District, is something every thinking person in Britain has an opinion about, without necessarily feeling the need to go there. It is, characteristically, mocked and reviled, just as the Lake District is admired and revered.

The Windscale/Calder Hall complex (henceforth, and popularly, called 'Sellafield') is a nuclear installation including both power generation and nuclear fuel reprocessing. It is a major industrial installation, and as such has had a profound effect on the economy of West Cumbria. It would not be an exaggeration to say that the economy of West Cumbria, particularly of the area surrounding Whitehaven, has come to depend on it.

In characterising the tension between the industrial and the pastoral in West Cumbria, it must be remembered that most people from outside the area have heard of the Lake District, and feel, at least, as though they know something about it. Very few, by contrast, have heard much about, or know much about, the coal mines, iron foundries, steel works and chemical plants of the coastal plain. A correspondent to the *Whitehaven News* said: 'I went to live in London in 1975. No one had heard of Whitehaven. The nearest "landmark" I could think of, was "Windscale"' (WN, 27/2/86, p. 14). When, therefore, Sellafield is discussed in the national media, the simplest way of locating it is 'on

---

6. I am specifically indebted to Barber's book on Cleator Moor, for drawing my attention to the work of E. Lynn Linton, cited above. I would also like to express a very broad appreciation of Barber's work; his politics are not mine, but his study of Cleator Moor is insightful and erudite, making fruitful use of historical and modern material, oral testimony and formal records, and so on. The inspiration of his work is not social anthropological; nevertheless, his book is a good ethnography of a British community, all the more valuable for drawing attention to so little-documented and disregarded an area.

the edge of the Lake District'. It is often contrasted, in its massive industrial dirtiness, with the rural peace of Lakeland. Less often is reference made to the small industrial towns of the area, for these towns, and the population which lives in and around them, are not social entities into which Sellafield has difficulty fitting.

On the contrary. West Cumbria has a history of more or less short-lived dirty industry, with boom and bust following one another. The local population has had long experience of working in jobs that more fastidious corners of the country could afford to refuse (in mining, mineral extraction, chemicals, iron and steel), and has had long experience of facing insecurity of employment. The British media, when they look at Sellafield, might see a dangerously polluting industry despoiling a uniquely beautiful pastoral landscape; the local population, however, rather tends to see an expanding and hopeful industry to replace all the other dirty industries that have already come and gone.

A great deal has, of course, been written about the nuclear industry, both nationally and internationally. To characterise this work fully would be a major work in itself. A few broad comments can be made here, however. On one side is the enormous corpus of technical literature. This contains within it work on the social and medical consequences of technical failure and of radiation exposure, but it does not deal with opinions of nuclear power; as is perhaps proper to its positivist charter, it deals only in empirically measurable detail: values, opinions, perceptions and politics are (ostensibly, at least) outside its concern. Accompanying this is work on the social and political advantages and disadvantages of nuclear power. This is again very varied, but it tends to be of two kinds – one, produced by industry and government sources, and the second, produced by self-avowedly 'anti-nuclear' opinion. Most popular journalism on the subject is about the antagonistic meeting of these two positions. 'Pro'-nuclear opinion characterises itself, often in the form of statements emanating from national bodies, as in the national interest. This position is commonly challenged by the 'anti'-nuclear lobby, which commonly makes two claims: first, that the 'pro'-nuclear position is not in the national interest, and second, that the 'anti'-nuclear position is a championing of local opinion (at, say, a nuclear site), in defiance of national power interests. This second claim is often taken at face value by journalists.

The view that national industrial requirements and local social requirements must inherently be in conflict is not without some justification. Nor, indeed, is it without precedent. SSRC (Social

Science Research Council) commitment to research on the social effects of North Sea oil development in Scotland in the 1970s, for example, was based upon the assumption that the interests of incoming industry, and the interests of the local population, were almost bound to clash. In the case of an industry with an increasingly bad reputation, such as the nuclear industry has developed over recent years, this assumption of antagonism between the local population and the requirements of the industry seems to follow without need for further consideration. This is not only true within the world of journalism and popular educated opinion, but sometimes within the academic sphere.

In the context of West Cumbria, however, the equations do not work. The Sellafield complex is perceived by the majority of the local inhabitants as a positive advantage to the region. It is an industrial employer, in an area accustomed to industrial employment (and unemployment). It is a relatively munificent employer, in an area used to hardship. It is, to all appearances, a clean industry, in an area used to dangerous and dirty industry (see WN, 27/2/86, editorial, p. 14; WN, 3/4/86, editorial, p. 12). The national media, however, have been reluctant to abandon the rhetoric of confrontation of local and national interests, with which they have commonly made sense of nuclear installations and nuclear protests. This has led, at a national level, to systematic and long-term misrepresentation and under-representation of local opinion, and considerable local ill-will towards outside interference in such matters.

Some of the dimensions of local and national opinion and disagreement can be gained from a brief survey of relevant newspaper articles and published letters. Many different themes are played and elaborated, but there might be said to be two main trends. One, in the national press, is a tendency to regard the Sellafield plant as a national and governmental imposition upon the helpless people of West Cumbria; from this viewpoint, it is an act of virtue to stress the radioactive leaks, health risks, secrecy, dirt and pollution, which the local population is made to suffer, and to advocate the closure of Sellafield. The second, prominent in the local press, is a pronounced scorn for national media opinion on the subject, and a resentment of the media's long, southern, sanctimonious nose.

In the *Whitehaven News*, the local paper which covers the Sellafield area, letters commonly refer to national media misrepresentation of local affairs. One referred to '... recent hysterical outpourings from the anti-nuclear campaigners, most of whom are not even local inhabitants' (WN, 27/2/86, p. 14). Another referred to 'The alarmist outcry against

Sellafield', and 'the repetition of misleading and wrong information ...
What is hardest to bear is that the emotions are being stirred by people
whose motives are highly suspect. The media – well, sensational
outpourings are the essentials of their industry' (WN, 27/2/86, p. 14).
'Too many mountains are being made out of the pimples on a molehill'
(WN, 20/2/86, p. 12). 'The local community continues to suffer at the
hands of self-appointed guardians of public safety' (WN, 13/3/86, p. 11).
'Gosforth Parish Council member ... has accused the media of mounting
a "sinister" campaign aimed at "destroying" Sellafield'; '... the views of
ordinary people should be represented' (WN, 20/3/86, p. 14).

> I am driven to write this letter by my total disgust in an article on Sellafield,
> which appeared in the Daily Mirror on February 21. It was entitled 'Our
> Life in the Shadow of Fear' ... In my view, and in that of everyone I have
> spoken to, this article was sensationalist journalism at its worst, deliberately
> playing on the fact that there are many people in this country who know
> very little about Sellafield, reprocessing, the surrounding area, the local
> people or how they really feel. They are therefore starved of facts and
> susceptible to this emotive drivel (WN, 20/3/86, p. 14).

'Like a lot of other people living in Cumbria, I'm sick of the constant
adverse publicity about BNFL at Sellafield' (WN, 26/3/86, p. 12). 'The
thing that annoys me most is that the majority of people who support
Greenpeace's latest efforts are from down south. We aren't causing the
fuss here, it's the southerners. Perhaps they can't find anything better
to do' (WN, 17/4/86, p. 11).

Local fishing interests complained, not about radioactive discharges,
but about adverse and detrimental publicity relating to these: 'Cumbrian
Sea Fisheries Committee wants to see the media giving better coverage
to reports of cuts in the radioactive discharges from the Sellafield plant';
'Cumbria is being damaged by "warped" comment' (WN, 13/3/86,, p.
15). Local trades union officials complained, not about the Sellafield
plant, but about criticism of it (see WN, 20/3/86, p. 3). Those involved
in the tourist industry complained not about polluted beaches; instead
they 'attacked the bad publicity which has kept tourists away from
Cumbria' (WN, 3/4/86, p.11; also p. 13). 'The media is killing Cumbria
– in 1984 we nearly went out of business because of the bad publicity'
(WN, 10/4/86, p. 1); 'many visitors on our small camp site ... express
concern about radiation levels in Cumbria, believing the lashings of guff
poured out by Press and Television' (WN, 24/4/86, p. 12). Fishermen,
trades unionists, hoteliers, camp-site owners, and finally landowners as
well: 'Bad publicity about Sellafield is causing drastic reductions in

land price, it is claimed by the Country Landowners Association' (WN, 17/4/86, p. 14).

The national media had, as I have described above, a rather rigid view of what was happening, of what kinds of events were newsworthy, and of the benefits that their fearless investigations were bringing to the local population. '… the media have their opinions and they are sticking to them … all that is wanted is a sensational story and not the truth' (WN, 17/4/86, p. 12). This security of media opinion is pronounced, both in national coverage, and in the local experience that some national media representatives contrive to have. Some journalists were clearly willing to create the events that they wished to find. *The Sunday Times*, 23/2/86, and *The Times*, 13/3/86, both published a photograph of the Sellafield plant, in which the foreground was conspicuously filled by a cemetery and its gravestones. In relation to this, a correspondent to the *Whitehaven News* wrote:

> I have written to the Editor of that paper [*The Sunday Times*] to congratulate whoever took the accompanying photograph. It was taken from St John's Cemetery, Beckermet, and whilst the end wall looking towards Sellafield looks correct, the headstones in the foreground are 'all wrong' and have, no doubt, been superimposed.
>
> The photograph certainly gave the desired sensational impression that the plant was surrounded by one huge cemetery full, no doubt, of radioactive corpses, and our friends from down South rang us last Sunday to say just that.
>
> In fact, the choice of this particular cemetery to try to create this impression was rather unfortunate, as it contains the remains of quite a large number of iron ore miners – my late father-in-law included – who died of a very real industrial disease – silicosis.
>
> … The *Sunday Times* article did, in some measure, try to present a reasonable approach, but the underlying trend was still the usual scaremongering, which I feel the great majority of local people deeply resent.
>
> When will the well-intentioned cranky environmental groups, the media and even foreign governments realise that, having lived all or most of their lives in this area (some through the Depression), local people are far more likely to be haunted by the spectre of 10,000 people being put out of work than by hysterical pressure groups or 'contrived' spooky newspaper photographs? (WN, 6/3/86, Mr E. I. Edwards)

In response to the local experience of national media distortion, local organisations for the defence and support of Sellafield appeared:

'We love Sellafield' was the message from a packed meeting in Ravenglass on Friday night ... angry criticism of the way the media had 'totally distorted reality and spread unnecessary alarm and concern about Sellafield' ... 'the impact has been very damaging to the community and businesses in Copeland'; ... residents had complained about the way a TV film crew chased people off the beach to enable them to film the deserted beach as an indictment of the Sellafield effect; ... 'When asked if they cared what effect their publicity might have on the area, they [said] they didn't care about local people. This sort of thing, along with the lies being printed, got a lot of people angry'. (WN, 26/3/86, p. 13)

Another correspondent confirmed:

I also feel that the TV and Press are badly advised in continually consulting the same people while ignoring the opposing opinion of other villagers who, when protesting to a visiting media team were told to 'clear the beach', and 'get inside and shut up' (WN, 3/4/86, p. 14). People here are absolutely pig sick about what has been happening with the media; ... they only ever speak to two or three individuals who are known to be violently opposed to the place. (WN, 10/4/86, p. 3)

And again:

'the same people were being interviewed on behalf of the village [of Ravenglass] and Seascale and Gosforth and the ordinary folk were not being consulted'; a 'group, calling themselves Cumbrians opposed to Media Misrepresentation, were formed' (WN, 3/4/86, p. 2)

Similarly, the inaugural meeting of the 'Friends of Sellafield' was advertised for 'anyone willing to (1) publicly support Sellafield; (2) counter the misleading propaganda in the media' (WN, 3/4/86, p. 12). The inaugural meeting of this society, on 2 April 1986, was packed to the doors (see WN, 10/4/86, p. 1).

The combination of media appetite, and repeatedly upgraded safety standards, led to a curious definitional inversion of events: the more closely monitored and controlled the plant was, the greater the frequency of detectable radiation escapes, and the more the media interpreted these as sensational failures of monitoring and control. 'On safety, he [Christopher Harding, Chairman, British Nuclear Fuels] said that BNFL's record was actually very good, but he recognised that was not the way it was generally perceived. There had been too many incidents which, while mainly non-events in real terms, nevertheless added up to a total picture which people found unacceptable' (WN, 3/4/86, p. 2). A local newspaper editorial struggled with the problem:

> In the eyes of a majority of people in the British Isles and Northern Europe – outside West Cumbria that is – the Sellafield nuclear establishment is becoming a big and dangerously untidy mess, threatening the health and safety of its workers and the public at large.
>
> Those 'unfortunates' who live in the vicinity are pitied, and well-meaning sympathisers everywhere take up cudgels on their behalf, insisting that residents should not be subjected to serious risks from the effects of radioactive contamination.
>
> [ ... ]
>
> But this 'outside' concern is not shared by the vast majority of Sellafield's 10,000 employees, and most of their families in the anti-nuclear firing line. They see nuclear energy as the safest and cleanest industry Man has yet devised.
>
> [ ... ]
>
> Of course, the media are blamed by Sellafield's staunch supporters for the sensational reporting of events that do not appear to warrant such treatment. Yet the media merely reflect the very emphasis that is repeatedly placed by scientists, governments and the industry itself on the monitoring of, and protection from, that mysterious physical phenomenon called radiation!
>
> It is a chicken and egg situation in that media also reflect the public opinion they have helped to create by actually reflecting it! (WN, 27/2/86, p. 14)

The above quotations are mostly from early 1986. Since this time, the situation has not changed in essentials, although there have been interesting developments. A note on these must suffice.

The Sellafield issue became important, locally, in the 1987 General Election. The constituency might be regarded as a natural Labour seat, and the incumbent, Jack Cunningham, was locally highly regarded. Labour Party policy, however, inconsistently expressed as it was, favoured the run-down of the nuclear industry. In West Cumbria, that sounded like 'closing down Sellafield'. Any such overt policy would be electoral suicide, in an area which knows how much it benefits from the employment that Sellafield provides. Mr Cunningham was more or less allowed to say that whatever a Labour government might do at a national level, Sellafield would remain. The argument did not entirely carry conviction, however, and the Conservative candidate seized on the issue. It went a long way, during the campaign, to turning the constituency from a safe Labour seat into a marginal. In the event, Jack Cunningham came home with a much reduced majority.

BNFL, British Nuclear Fuels, has recognised the folly of being seen to try to keep its operations at Sellafield shrouded in secrecy. It has, therefore, made a conspicuous public virtue out of a kind of nuclear *glasnost*. This policy is relatively recent, and it has had a remarkable effect upon styles of reporting and perception of events. The visitor centre at Sellafield was one of the national tourist successes of the late 1980s. The great influx of visitors to Sellafield does not, it might be noted, much change the great rift in experience and perception between those who visit the Lake District and those who live in West Cumbria, for the visit to Sellafield (for Lake District visitors) is an experience largely insulated from West Cumbrian urban and industrial life.

When the nuclear reactor exploded at Chernobyl in 1986, a large cloud of radioactive debris passed over Great Britain. In favourable weather conditions, this would have continued on over the Atlantic, and dissipated itself more or less harmlessly. By chance, however, as the cloud of radioactive dust was over England and Scotland, these areas suffered particularly heavy rain – conditions ideal for washing the radioactive dust out of the sky, depositing it on vegetation, and setting the radioactive particles on their way through the ecosystem. The heaviest rain at the time was, predictably, in upland areas like the mountains of Wales, Yorkshire and Cumbria. The heaviest rain of all was recorded within fifteen miles of Sellafield. In consequence, many upland farms found that their sheep carcasses contained an unacceptably high level of radiation, and restrictions were placed on the sale of meat from these areas. Cumbria, as the area worst affected, had restrictions the longest. The entirely fortuitous association of radioactive meat with the proximity of Sellafield was not lost on the imagination of anybody who thought about the matter, although there was no doubt, from a scientific point of view, that the radioactivity in question came from Chernobyl and not from Sellafield. Even if this was conceded, however, the question posed itself – if Chernobyl today, why not Sellafield tomorrow? The importance of sheep-farming to the rural economy of the Lake District, and to the image of the area in the popular imagination, gave the meat restrictions a peculiar poignancy, with Sellafield just down the road.

The discussions on a long-term store for the country's nuclear waste are looking more and more to Sellafield and West Cumbria to provide the answer. The temperature of local and national debate is once again beginning to rise.[7]

Global warming, arguably the result of the burning of fossil fuels, is making many, even among the environmentally conscious, look with a new and fonder eye on the nuclear industry.

There are many areas of discussion which the West Cumbrian example leads into. It well illustrates what I tend to call 'moral geography' – how the social imagination invests qualities in different places, and sees or disregards these places according to rules which are only loosely related to objective reality (as it might be recorded by geologist, cartographer or demographer). Judgement of distance between places, their relative location and relative qualities, and even their apparent existence, are determined within selective perceptual constraints that are both social and arbitrary. This is familiar enough within symbolic or phonemic analysis, but not everybody would be prepared to see thousands of square miles of soil and rock thrown around in the same capricious manner. The problems, however, are of the same order – the semiotic system in question, however loosely articulated it might be, has a profound and real effect upon what people see, know and experience. I am of the opinion that 'moral geographies' of this kind, from the most local level to the transcontinental, exert profound influence (often low-key and long-term, though sometimes dramatic) upon the social world, and would always repay study. They have a surprising capacity for self-perpetuation, and they seem to be only slowly and fitfully subject to revision from experience. I suspect that social anthropologists might be particularly well-equipped to deal with these, although other disciplines have declared an interest.[8]

7. The question of the relationship between the nuclear industry and leukaemia, which has been often raised in connection with Sellafield, is considered too complex and delicate for summary discussion. Even the concentration of attention upon the problem, however, which has led to studies of the possible linkage, is itself a manifestation of the conventions of the discourse that I have tried to describe.

8. The interest of the social geographers in 'conceptual maps', while useful, seems to want for an awareness of the multi-dimensionality of conceptual spaces of this kind. Such spaces are subject to potential investment from any of the areas of human experience, with fluid exchange across the dimensions (the interlinking of spatial co-ordinates with structures of morality, philosophy and politics, for example, for visitors to the Lake District, is almost always evident, although it takes many different forms). 'Conceptual maps' would also benefit, I think, from a full awareness of the potent reality-defining power of conceptual systems. This is an insight which social anthropologists, again, should find relatively easy to provide and apply. For further related work, in sociology and social history respectively, see Collison and Kennedy 1981 and Chartier 1988: ch. 6.

My main aim, however, in introducing the Copeland material, is to draw attention to a moral and political problem raised within it. It has been my intention to show that there are different ways of looking at Sellafield – different 'realities' if you like – according to the moral and geographical framework of inspection. I have wished to imply that no one view is necessarily correct; I have also wished, however, to make the point that one important indigenous view – that of many people who live near, and work in, Sellafield – is more or less censored or distorted in national debate.

The various receptions given to this paper, in the several forms in which it has been delivered, are testimony to this. People with experience of West Cumbria have tended to be sympathetic to the main thrust of the paper, whatever their personal views about Sellafield. This is not surprising, since it is from conversation with them that I came to see the nature of the problem. There are, of course, West Cumbrians who form part of the national 'thinking' consensus in the matter, and their views are an important part of the local scene as well; they have no need of allies, however.

There is no doubt, of course, that the reason why Windscale, and subsequently Sellafield, are where they are, is because of the nature of the place – obscure, disregarded, and 'remote' from the lives of the decision-makers of the land. To that extent, Sellafield might be regarded as yet another burden forced upon an underprivileged community. I have stressed, however, that Sellafield fits rather well into the political economy of the area, and that it has been in many ways domesticated into local activity. It is not, for the most part, perceived as an oppression.

Within the national discourse of those whom we shall call, for want of a better term, the 'thinking class',[9] both the Lake District and Sellafield are highly emotive symbols. The 'Lake District' invites unthinking conceits of affinity and approval, just as 'Sellafield' invites unthinking conceits of rejection and disdain. I do not mean to suggest that thought is never applied in these areas – only that it is not necessary for the acquisition of a ready portfolio of opinions. Within these symbolic conceits, there is, for reasons that I have tried to outline, a ready place for a local population that needs to be helped in its struggle against the dark forces of the nuclear industry; the idea of a

---

9. I derive the term from Edwin Ardener. Some journalists use the equally pejorative 'chattering classes'. Conventional sociological class analysis provides no term for this grouping – perhaps for the same reasons that fish do not talk of water.

local population that needs to be helped in its struggle against anti-nuclear misrepresentation can, by contrast, be formulated only with difficulty – it sounds like a category error, or a joke (I have given, above, a local attempt at expression of this problem; see p. 213). I have, on two occasions, suggested to a general intellectual audience in Oxford that there is a local West Cumbrian view, in favour of Sellafield, which is under-represented in national discourse. I have suggested that the local view has a powerful fund of reality and experience built into it; I have suggested also that the national 'thinking class' view, by contrast, is swathed in shadow and ignorance.

In spite of this, however, my presentation has tended to be taken as an invitation to discuss how and why the local people get things so wrong. If I may refer back to the 'unthinking conceits' of the previous paragraph, it seemed that it was more difficult to abandon these conceits, than it was to abandon the people of West Cumbria – abandon them, for example, to 'false consciousness', 'oppression', desperate compromise in difficult circumstances, even ignorance. Nobody, outside West Cumbria, has taken the opportunity, offered though it was, to conclude that the people of West Cumbria were simply right, and that the moralities and discursive conventions of intellectual social-scientific academia were indeed their own form of 'false consciousness'. In the circumstances, the question of who is oppressing whom becomes rather delicate.

## References

Ardener, E. (1987), '"Remote Areas" – Some Theoretical Considerations', in A. Jackson (ed.), *Anthropology at Home*. London: Tavistock

Barber, Ross (1976), *Iron Ore and After (Boom Time, Depression and Survival in a West Cumbrian Town, Cleator Moor 1840–1960)*. York University, with Cleator Moor Local Studies Group

Bouch, C. and G. Jones (1961), *The Lake Counties–1500 – 1830*, A *Social and Economic History*. Manchester: Manchester University Press

Britton and Brayley (1802), *A Topographical and Historical Description of the County of Cumberland ... etc.* (printed for Sherwood, Neely and Jones)

Brown, G. and D. Hayton (1986), *Kelton Iron – The Making of Kirkland*. Published by G. Brown, Simon Kell, Cold Fell, near Haile, Egremont, Cumbria

Caine, Caesar (rev.) (1916), *Cleator and Cleator Moor: Past and Present*. Kendal: Titus Wilson

Chartier, R. (1988), *Cultural History*. Oxford: Blackwell

Collison, P. and J. Kennedy (1981), 'The Social Pattern of Personal

Geographies', *Regional Studies*, vol. 15, no. 4, pp. 247-62

Davies-Shiel, M. and J. Marshall (1969), *Industrial Archaeology of the Lake Counties*. Newton Abbot: David and Charles

Fletcher, H. (1881), 'The Archaeology of the West Cumberland Iron Trade', *Transactions of the Cumberland and Westmorland Antiquarian and Archaeological Society*, vol. 5, pp. 5–21

Hankinson, A. (1972), *The First Tigers*. Dent; revised ed 1984, Keswick: Melbeck Books

Hay, D. (1966), *Whitehaven*. Whitehaven: Whitehaven News

Housman, J. (1800), *A Topographical Description of Cumberland, Westmorland, Lancashire, and a Part of the West Riding of Yorkshire*. Carlisle: printed by Francis Jollie

Hughes, E. (1965), *North Country Life in the Eighteenth Century, Vol. II: Cumberland and Westmorland 1700–1830*. Oxford: Oxford University Press

Lynn Linton, E. (1864), *The Lake Country*. London: Smith, Elder and Co.

McGowan Gradon, W. (1952), *The Track of the Ironmasters (A History of the Cleator and Workington Junction Railway)*. Whitehaven: *Whitehaven News* for the author

Smith, K. (1973), *Cumbrian Villages*. London: Robert Hale

Sugden, E. (rev.) (no date, but probably 1897 or soon thereafter), *A History of the Parish of Arlecdon and Frizington*. Published for the author by R. Burlington, Whitehaven

Wainwright, A. (1966), *A Pictorial Guide to the Lakeland Fells, Book 7: The Western Fells*. Kendal: Westmorland Gazette

    (1973), *A Coast to Coast Walk (St Bees to Robin Hood's Bay) – a Pictorial Guide*. Kendal: Westmorland Gazette

Watson, R. (1868), *Egremont Castle and Miscellaneous Poems*. Whitehaven: John Welsh and Co.

# The Construction
# of Difference:
# An Anthropological
# Approach to
# Stereotypes

## *Maryon McDonald*

### 'Europe': A World Without Stereotypes?

The building of a post-imperial and, for some, post-nationalist 'European Community' has put stereotypes on the agenda. In recent decades, debates in self-consciously 'European' institutions have frequently urged the banishment of stereotypes. Stereotypes are deemed to be deeply implicated in the 'xenophobia' and 'racism' from which so many evils, past and present, have stemmed and which the whole construction of the Community is often said to have been designed to transcend.

Europe's symbolic '1992' injected, from the early days of its formulation, further urgency into such discussions. This was partly because a common policy seemed necessary on 'third country' immigrants, and partly because the internal movement of labour which 1992 was said to herald seemed to mean that greater mutual tolerance and understanding would be required. Nowhere in these discussions has there been explicit awareness that the construction of any common policy could well involve, at the level of the policy-makers themselves, the articulation of perceptions, whether mutual or shared, which could be termed stereotypes. However, the 'Ridley Affair' in Britain in 1990 (to which I shall return in later paragraphs) briefly underlined the point that stereotypes, and an inability to deal with them, permeate all levels of discussion and debate.

Liberal denunciations of prejudice, or the dismissal of stereotypes as either pathological or simply untrue, have been common in European debate; this is obviously not enough. For even as such denunciations and dismissals are made, the Europe being constructed, at the boundaries of itself and in the bounding of its own constituent units, would seem to be engaged in modes of defining and understanding difference which could be said to be, in many respects, stereotypical. The following paragraphs do not attempt to give extensive details of the imagery of 'us' and 'them' through which 'Europe' (or, indeed, 'Western Europe') and the 'Europeans' are themselves defined; nor am I attempting to set out the details of the mutual perceptions of both nation and minority within and between European States.[1] Some of these details are contained here, but what I want to offer above all is a general, anthropological handle on the question of stereotypes in both its conceptual and empirical aspects. In one way or another, social anthropology has long been concerned with the critical examination of stereotypes. Contemporary anthropological insights now enable us to take stereotypes apart, and to understand how they are constructed conceptually and also – importantly – how they seem to achieve empirical confirmation.

## Some Social Science Views of Stereotypes

The term 'stereotypes' seems to derive from the printing industry – where it designated a metal plate which could be used again and again for thousands of impressions, without needing to be replaced (see Harding 1968). The origin of its current social science usage is generally attributed to the American journalist Walter Lippmann, in his book entitled *Public Opinion* (1922). Lippmann noted that, in a modern democracy, political leaders and ordinary citizens alike made decisions about a variety of matters which they did not really understand, and which concerned persons or peoples of whom they had no direct knowledge. They believed that their views of these people were accurate. For Lippmann, they were not. They were, rather, 'stereotypes', by which he meant inaccurate representations.

1. All the points mentioned here form part of a larger project, funded by the Economic and Social Research Council, involving historiographical research on 'Europe' and an ethnographic study of the European Parliament. Some of the European Parliament's concerns about 'racism and xenophobia' can be found in Doc B 2-1379/85; Doc A 2-12/86; Doc A 0261/88; and Doc A 3-195/90.

Stereotypes seemed to betray a lack of 'direct experience' of the people so represented. The major features of stereotypes which Lippmann introduced with the term itself – that they were erroneous representations acquired other than through direct experience of the reality they claimed to represent – have generally persisted in social science writings on the topic.

Lippmann's term and ideas were already in social science use in the 1930s, but the Second World War gave new impetus to the subject. In psychology, analyses of prejudice (notably Allport 1954) encouraged stereotypes to be seen as perceptions linked to pre-existing cognitive categories, but ultimately to be the unfortunate by-products, or the maladaptive end, of an information-processing continuum. In other words, stereotypes became the products of more generally posited cognitive mechanisms of information-processing, storage and retrieval but were in themselves the pathological outcome of these processes at an individual level. At the same time, it was felt that there was perhaps a 'kernel of truth' in stereotypes (see especially Klineberg 1950), with this truth seen to reside in a more than random correspondence between the characteristics of a social group and the beliefs which others held of them. Psychology has continued to pose this issue, and to pose it in scientistic terms (see, for example, Peabody 1985), resulting in many naive attempts to 'test' a stereotype's 'accuracy' against the 'reality' it purports to describe. Psychology has been stuck not only in its own scientism, with notions of innocent scientific observation, but also in an individual/social dichotomy. Old models persist, therefore, in which it is either the 'stimulus' who produces the stereotype bearing the characteristics it describes, or it is the perceiver who autonomously generates the stereotype through some kind of autistic information-processing or because of individual ego-defensive functions; where the social world enters these models at all, it tends to do so through a whole series of tautologies, teleologies and reifications, with social groups generating stereotypes for the satisfaction of imputed needs.[2]

Since the 1930s (and especially the work of Katz and Braly 1933), much social science research has concentrated on ethnic stereotypes. In some sociology and anthropology, the combined influence of the Second World War and decolonisation, and the local presence of 'ethnic groups' and 'minorities', have given the question of stereotypes a moral and political life in which analyses have taken the form of little more

2. For a critical review of some of the psychology literature, see Condor and Henwood 1989.

than catalogues of nasty things which a majority has said about a minority.[3] The social context in such schemes has often been a politico-economic reductionism of some kind, with a social system reproducing itself through stereotypes which 'function' in the majority's favour. The majority/minority categories, and their modern political dress, have also been read back into the past and become a structure for its interpretation. As a result, the history in these same schemes tends towards a story of the majority's wilful historical malice, of its unrelenting foul play. Since the 1960s especially a very persuasive sociological edifice has been constructed, and it has been very difficult, morally and politically, to think and to write outside it. Said's well-known study of Orientalism (1978) seemed, in some respects, to encourage anthropologists and sociologists to think rather differently about a well-worn topic. Nevertheless, it was itself very much an active party to the moral construction of two central categories – 'Europe' and 'the West' – which are still largely unexamined but which seem, for many social and political scientists worldwide, to have become important metaphors of blame or of self-castigation.

## Continuity and Discontinuity

Some of the imagery in stereotypes can appear to be very similar, no matter what group of people they might claim to represent. An important aspect of this apparent similarity or continuity resides in the experience of categorical mismatch. Putting this point very crudely, we might say that the cultural worlds in which we live are all in some sense category-based and that when different category systems meet, they do not match up; the resultant experience is one of indeterminacy, or unpredictability perhaps, of wavering and uncertainty, and of riot or splendour, at the boundaries of our categories which do not match those we encounter. Edwin Ardener first outlined this point, and some of its implications, in lectures in Oxford and in some of his published work (see especially Ardener 1982). From his research in south-eastern Nigeria, he offers us a simple example of a lack of fit between category systems which could easily give rise to misinterpretation, and which is the very stuff of which stereotypes are made.

Amongst the Ibo of south-eastern Nigeria, the term *aka* covers from just below the shoulder to the tips of the fingers. There is no linguistic

---

3. An ethnographic examination of this approach can be found in McDonald 1989.

equivalent of 'hand'. The English division of 'hand' from 'arm' does not, for the Ibo, find backing in language. The placing of a conceptual boundary in English allows the possibility of a different classification of greetings – shaking hands is not the same as an arm-grip. The British mode of shaking hands, therefore, can appear to the Ibo to be a peculiarly abrupt and stand-offish mode of salutation, with an odd restriction of movement, whilst an Ibo shaking the *aka* in greeting can appear to the English speaker to be over-familiar, with little sense of good manners (for details, see Ardener 1982).

When we turn to other anthropological accounts of stereotypes in action, the conceptual, categorical mismatches involved are not always quite so clearly drawn, but we can see them at work. Susan Benson's study of multi-ethnic Brixton in London notes how 'differences in conversational convention, linguistic usage, and non-verbal devices such as gesture, movement and eye contact' often served to generate and reinforce 'suspicion and hostility' between different sectors of the population:

> For example, one reason given by English boys for their reluctance to share club premises with West Indians was their fear of violence; English boys found it difficult to distinguish between West Indian teasing and testing behaviour and intimations of real trouble. Similarly, adult English people tended to interpret the much higher levels of interpersonal aggression, both verbal and physical, tolerated in interaction by West Indian males as evidence of the 'excitability' and propensity to violence that their stereotyped view of the 'uncontrolled savage' led them to expect. (Benson 1981: 42 – 43)

Chapman (1982) draws directly on Ardener's insights to note a not dissimilar possibility of serious misunderstanding between Irish and English. He takes the anecdotal example of an Irishman at home in his village in western Ireland and someone from the same village who has come to England. In the Irish village, a few drinks are being drunk in a bar when:

> … a simmering resentment between two adult men erupts into crisis. Protagonist 1 leaps to his feet, and says something like 'I'll kill him! Hold me back, someone, for I'll not be responsible for what I do to him if I get my hands on him'. Protagonist 2 voices similar sentiments, expressing his eager desire to fight, and his hope that somebody will hold him back, and thus prevent him from killing Protagonist 1. The two will threaten to square up to one another, at the same time maintaining their pleas to the world in

general that somebody hold them back. In normal circumstances, and according to the local patterns of kinship, friendship and obligation, people will appear from the background to hold the two men apart. Once the two men are safely held back, they can then make eager attempts to get away from those that are holding them back, in demonstration of their burning desire to get at one another's throats, and fight it out. Eventually the holders-back will manage to persuade the two that they should not fight, and the protagonists will reluctantly agree, out of respect for the judgement and feelings of their holders-back, that they will put off their quarrel to another day. Honour is satisfied on all sides, and no blood spilt. (Chapman 1982: 136-7)

In this context, such 'fights' regularly run their course in this way and are a 'means for the expression, resolution and determination of local conflicts, personal prestige, alliance of kin and friends, and so on' (ibid.). Transposed to an English context, however, in which such key elements of the Irish context either do not exist or are ordered differently, the 'fight' – with all its attendant ritual boasting and bravado – suddenly takes on a very different reality, imploding into the physical violence that was lacking in Ireland. In the two contexts, the complex of category systems in which 'fight' takes its meaning do not match up. The Irish villager may come to England, go to a pub and take a few drinks. Somebody may cause him offence, an insult that is heard and cannot be ignored without loss of face. The Irishman leaps to his feet, as he would in the home context, and similarly shouts to bystanders to hold him back. The other drinkers in the pub stare at the ceiling, or carry on drinking:

> Henceforth, everything is upside down. The Irishman, in order to persuade somebody to hold him back, emphasizes at length the truly appalling consequences that will follow if he is not contained, such a fighter and hot-tempered man he is. The audience remains unmoved. The more he boasts in order to persuade somebody to stop the fight, the more inevitable does it become that he will be honour-bound to force a fight in order to make good his boast. Nobody holds him back. There is a fight. (ibid.: 137)

The English bystanders in the bar might well feel they were seeing for themselves here 'the hot-tempered, impetuous, over-emotional, belligerent, red-haired Paddy'. The Irishman, for his part, could easily feel 'appalled by the cynical lovelessness of a people prepared to sit by and let a perfectly peaceable, self-respecting Irishman get his head broken' (ibid.: 137-8). Each party to such misunderstanding can place itself on the side of order, finding disorder in the other. The more powerful centres of self-definition, however, have inevitably generated the more powerful and persuasive images of order for themselves, locating disorder on their margins.

There is much in these examples – ideas of excitability and impending violence, for example – which seems common to many stereotypes. Given the mismatches involved, these ideas are perhaps not surprising. The common and summarising image of the 'uncontrolled savage' has itself a long, although not unbroken, history. In a 1788 issue, the influential *Gentleman's Magazine* described the 'Negro' as 'possessed of passions not only strong but ungovernable; a mind dauntless, warlike and unmerciful; a temper extremely irascible; a disposition indolent, selfish and deceitful; fond of joyous sociality, riotous mirth and extravagant shew' (cited in Walvin 1982: 60). Unbridled sexuality, warlikeness, untrustworthiness and general extravagance: such traits and many similar were earlier attributed by writers in Elizabethan England to Africa, and by medieval Europe, in the process of self-definition, to Africa, the Orient, America, and everywhere else on its conceptual frontiers (see Mason 1990). Scholarly confirmation of the veracity of such imagery was then found, as was the vogue, by looking back to classical texts. The 'Celts' are perhaps the best-known invention of the classical imagination, and the imagery through which they were constructed gathers up many of the elements which civilisation, in its own self-definition, found apt to locate more generally in the 'barbarian' hovering at its frontiers.[4] Celts were boastful, extravagant, drank too much, were quick-tempered and high-spirited, and generally manifested – and are still required to manifest – all the aspects of surfeit and disorder which categorical mismatch generates.

It is tempting here to see many simple continuities in the 'stereotypes' held, say, by classical writers of the barbarian, by Christians of heathens, by Europe of both Africa and America, by the English of the Negro, by whites of blacks, and so on. Certainly, there are continuities, many of which have been effected through various modes of repetition, studious copying and reference, but all of which are part of the encounter of different category systems. Observers have often seen a ruleless unpredictability, anarchy or reversal, disorder and

---

4. A sample of this imagery can be found in Chapman 1982, and a scholarly appreciation of the imagery set in its own time is given in Woolf 1990.

inversion, at their borders, and could use some aspects of others' writings and observations to give their own further conviction and credence. For instance, where gender constructs and kinship systems did not match, then wild promiscuity, matriarchy and incest regularly filled both the record of the classical authors writing about the barbarian – and the record of others who looked back to these writers and who, centuries later, in the context of different imperial preoccupations, turned the apparently innocent observations of antiquity into the substance of new, nineteenth-century debate about the essential nature of primitives or about origins.[5] Through esteem and continual re-readings of the 'classics', so much has been made common between, say, the classical writers' sense of what lay beyond order and knowledge, and the views of nineteenth-century learned men of the Empire, that some aspects of discontinuity seem important to stress. The classical writers made sense of their Celts and other barbarians through a metaphoric of *feritas*, for example (Daugè 1981; Woolf 1990), which, in the self-definition of Roman *humanitas*, gathered up priorities and preoccupations which were already alien to the travellers and writers of medieval Europe who found their own Wild Man, unclothed, on the borders of their Christian world (Mason 1990); and this figure, again, could not make sense wholesale to the eighteenth- and nineteenth-century primitivists and romantics who were both able and keen to celebrate the naturality and irrationality dancing on the fringes of rationality and nations alike. In each case, the dominant preoccupations of the self-defining centre determined where and how the relevant difference was seen, sought or understood. The centres of definition in each case were quite disparate social and political worlds. Each offered its own means, its own socially credible discourses, for both locating and making sense of difference.

It is the differences sought and constructed in the context of nineteenth-century nationalisms, in the development of both national units and 'science', which still tend now to construct the most common mode and means by which differences are drawn and understood. With the definition of national units came the definition of what the nation was not, and the construction of national origins and national peripheries alike. 'Cultural difference', in both popular and academic understandings of it, still tends to be located, in priority, at national and at majority/minority (or 'ethnic') boundaries. Language (along with 'race')

---

5. For an indication of how anthropological kinship studies were launched in this way, with some help from a classical education, see Kuper 1988; Trautmann 1987.

has been an especially important marker of difference, and linguistic difference itself actively pursued, since nineteenth-century nations found part of their repertoire of self-definition in comparative philology and in national education systems. Moreover, difference is often understood still in terms evocative of the dualities of what we might term Enlightenment rationality and its moral alterities, summarised in the dichotomy of positivist rationality and romanticism. I have briefly suggested that the dominant rationalities of Europe had, in contemplation of themselves, and in definition of their own characteristics, long sought and constructed on their boundaries their own moral contraries. To this definition of self and other, however, positivism and romanticism gave enduring and systematised expression in which nation could define itself against nation, and majority against minority, in a mutual dependence which increased in momentum and conviction as it began also to organise everything from sex differences to ethnology to politics to cognition to the human brain. These twin discourses also prepared the space in which, in the second half of the twentieth century, moral advantage could turn from majority to minority identities, in protest or dissent or 'alternative' ideals. The national minorities had appeared conceptually with the majorities, and a loss of identity, whether to be regretted or celebrated, was always a feature of the identities which the minorities were later to assume. Perception was laden with theories dividing civilised and uncivilised, rational and irrational, reason and emotions, modern and traditional, knowledge and folklore, science and belief, logic and intuition, and other dichotomies making up the context and rhetoric of national self-definition and progress within which majority and minority were born together, and the minority born as disappearing. Experience of mismatch, and the observations of earlier observers and scholars, could easily be made sense of within, and give substance to, the metaphors of opposition which positivism and romanticism supplied, and these conceptual oppositions have rolled on to elide with more recent political moralities in which minority identities have become morally and politically compelling. The constructs of romanticism once danced helplessly on the boundaries of positivism, with the priorities of rationality and the resources of identity firmly at the centre, but since the 1960s everyone seems to know where true identity is located, what it is made of, that they are alienated without one, and educated members of the majority are seen racing, in self-redefinition, to the social margins (see McDonald 1989). At the same time, continuities have been constructed, and those nasty things which majorities have said about minorities can be read right back into the Dark Ages and beyond.

## The Construction of Difference

I have suggested that it might be helpful to distinguish between categorical mismatch and the current mode of systematising this – between categorical mismatch and the current discourse or *genre* in which difference is understood and discussed. We could go further and distinguish not just two but three points about the way in which difference is constructed.

Firstly, any question of identity is clearly dependent on the social and political maps of the time, on the categories available for the marking of self/other or us/them boundaries, and on the particular salience of any one set of these categories. Secondly, difference does not exist simply and solely between supposedly homogeneous wholes called 'cultures' coincident with these categories (in the way that nationalism and various scientisms have encouraged us to believe). It is not simply that national education systems now produce common repertoires, or that village gossips induce an ideally uniform set of values: the important point here is that it is also at the boundaries available to us, whatever and wherever they may be, that we are *more likely to notice difference*. It seems likely that we might term category mismatch, or cultural mismatch, or a lack of fit between category systems, will be picked up particularly at that boundary of self/other or us/them, evoking it and giving it expression, and – importantly – empirical confirmation. Thirdly, the apprehension of mismatch, or lack of fit, will usually have a dominant discourse (or *genre*, or systematised way of talking about it) in which to find ready expression. These points are not meant to describe stages, conscious or otherwise, of thought, but a simultaneity of definition, image and experience, a unity of theory and observation.

One further example might help to illustrate these points. The categories 'France' and 'England' are a salient part of our contemporary social and political maps, and 'French' and 'English' may well be the categories of identity which some readers of this volume might themselves occasionally assume. Now the self-consciously rational Englishman 'knows', within a now very common discourse of representation, that Frenchmen are emotional and passionate, and differences of verbal and body language – in which the French can appear to get very excited with their words and tone, and wave their arms about and, good heavens, kiss each other – readily confirm the imagery and its distribution between the two halves of the English/French pair (the us/them boundary operative in this instance).

In this brief example, the first point about having to have the categories available is perhaps obvious enough, and the second point, concerning the mismatch of category systems mentioned earlier, is one to which anthropologists are now becoming accustomed. We can see from examples earlier in this chapter that one set of cultural practices, when observed or heard through the structures of another, can make its practitioners seem volatile, unpredictable, irrational, inconsistent, capricious, or even dangerous. My third point is merely to do with the socio-historical contextualisation of this apprehension. The lack of fit between category systems, an apprehension of indeterminacy, easily becomes confirmation of a rational/irrational dichotomy, and of the various systematised versions of this (in notions of reason/emotions, logic/intuition, facts/values, intellect/passion, and so on) which 'positive' reasoning and romanticism, accompanying the construction of nations and their peripheries, have left us in legacy. The common image of the excitable, fun-loving, soulful, and sexy or passionate French held by the self-consciously rational English should come as no surprise.

This is an image which France, in relation to other nations, has readily assumed for itself and turned to virtue. In the early nineteenth century, and many times thereafter, France dressed itself occasionally as the sensitive and emotional soul against the rational Anglo-Saxon, Teuton, German, and others who were required thereby to be, as the context required, the ethnological face of positivism. In its own nationalist claims, however, Germany's own production and appropriation of romantic priorities were generally, with outside help, the more powerful; for much of the nineteenth century, both Britain and France freely allowed Germans a musicality, spirituality, mysticism, and emotionality which their own pursuits of rational progress seemed sometimes to be threatening to eclipse, or which – in the case of Britain – claims of racial kinship enabled the Teutonic cousins to share. However, this was not to be the side of the dichotomy that the Germans were generally to be left to inhabit. The Franco-Prussian war in 1870 was the first major event in literally turning the tables in this imagery. The nation of 'poets and thinkers' became a mob of barbarous and brutish Huns. The First World War then moved any lingering British 'cousins' of the Germans to cut off ties, and join the French. French historians (for example, Foustel de Coulanges) had already written the Germans out of their own national histories. In general, the Germans now gathered an imagery in which they were 'superhuman in efficiency and subhuman in indelicacy of feeling'

(Firchow 1986: 41). The metaphors in which they were constructed, for the British especially but also, in varying recensions, for the French and for others, drew on an increasingly common complex of symbolic oppositions out of which masculinity and femininity were also constructed, but whereas the Germans had once been aligned with what were otherwise deemed 'feminine' qualities, they were now firmly attributed the 'masculine' capacities of Europe's humankind. They were, for example, rigid where the British were spontaneous; supporters of duty rather than given to love; prone to display force rather than sensitivity; brutal rather than gentle and civil; ruthlessly logical rather than intuitively able; meticulously professional rather than muddlingly amateur; boastful rather than modest; and so on. The reign of the efficient, German bully had begun.[6]

Confirmation of these qualities in the Germans has not been difficult to find, even if only in armchair contemplation of the German language. More than one modern scholar, when comparing German and English, has found evidence of one or all of the above qualities, and even the proclivities and traces of Hitler's Reich, in the seemingly 'ruthless shape of the German sentence' (W. Muir 1966, cited in Firchow 1986: 20).

Events ranging from apparently trivial daily encounters to the Prussian invasion and victory of 1870, the First and Second World Wars, and on to the strong Mark in the European Monetary System, have generally placed Germany and the Germans, from a British point of view, on what has been morally coloured as the 'wrong' side of the dualities involved. This was evident during the 'Ridley Affair' in Britain in July 1990. In a magazine interview (see Lawson 1990), Nicholas Ridley, a British Cabinet minister, collapsed the German position and aspirations in the European Community into the German aspirations of the Second World War, and not only likened the German Chancellor Kohl to Hitler but also seemed to say that where the Germans had previously failed in military terms, they were now intent on winning through economically dominating displays of their insensitive rationality. It then transpired that this view might be but one brief glimpse of more general British government feelings and fears. An apparently confidential memo was 'leaked' to the press which

---

6. A fuller contextualisation of these changes in imagery and historiography can be found in Ewen 1948 (especially pp. 723 – Firchow 1986 (especially ch.4), James 1989, Schulze 1991, and Thom 1990. I am grateful to Anna Bramwell, formerly of Trinity College, Oxford and to Catherine Sutherland Walker of the German Department, Goldsmiths' College, London, for their helpful discussion of these points.

summarised discussions that had taken place that March between eminent academics and government politicians on the question of Germany and the Germans. The 'Europe' within which Britain now found itself was very different from, say, the Europe of the mid-nineteenth century; the distribution of confidence and perceived power had changed. With German re-unification on the horizon, it had apparently seemed imperative to discuss 'German characteristics' and to try to assess the 'accuracy' of 'stereotypes' about the Germans (see the *Independent*, 16/7/90, and for a full version of the memo, the *Independent on Sunday*, 15/7/90, p.19). The general view which emerged seemed to be that, if the Germans had any of the 'sentimentality' sometimes attributed to them, then it was mixed with a 'capacity for excess, to overdo things', and this capacity was also more evident in their 'aggressiveness' and 'assertiveness' and their tendency to 'throw their weight about' in the European Community. In such statements, many common images have been essentialised, as they usually are, and deemed to be what the Germans are 'really' like. It is very difficult to de-essentialise any stereotypes, given the great weight of empirical 'proof' that the most trivial encounter might offer, but especially difficult when the weight of historical association seems to draw up simple continuities which help to confirm old ideas of some innate 'national character'. The common nineteenth-century idea of 'national character', which had once been seen as something that would evolve with the construction of a nation-state, had become entangled early on its in life with notions of race such that each nation was seen to have, at its foundation, a natural set of capacities and proclivities. In the British media discussion in which the 'Ridley Affair' was constructed, ideas of a natural and inalienable 'national character' re-emerged, evidently with some force. Even the most optimistic who tried, with a post-Second World War or new 'European' self-consciousness, to talk of possibilities of change in Germany, found themselves tied up in rhetorical dialogues about whether or not a 'national character' was changeable (see, for example, Geoffrey Wheatcroft in the *Daily Telegraph*, 17/7/1990, p. 16).

Anthropology has moved relatively easily from nineteenth-century, essentialist understandings of 'national character' to 1970s and 1980s deconstructionist analyses of the 'Other'.[7] This means that just as in

---

7. A brief summary of some of the literature, and examples of its implications, can be found in Fabian 1983, Mason 1990. On the development of the notion of the 'Other', as a critique of post-war Freudian ego-psychology (notably by Lacan, in France), see Mitchell 1982, Lash 1991.

matters of gender and ethnicity (where the biologistic understandings of sex difference and race have been displaced) so, too, in understandings of imagery more generally, it has become commonplace to assert that our understandings of what people are 'really' like are inevitably constructs forged in particular social and historical contexts; and that constructs of 'others' or of 'them' are conceptually, and morally and politically, intertwined with constructs of self or 'us'. This, at least, would seem to be the main argument of the English-language analytical literature on the 'Other', which can otherwise appear dense, obfuscatory or curiously rhetorical. This literature is derived in large measure from French sources, and often seems itself, quite unwittingly, to say a good deal about Anglo-French relations; a mysterious Frenglish and the uncritical aggrandisement of a now conventional capital 'O', usually wholly divorced from the context of French discussion in which that capital took its significance, might itself suggest the status of France and the French as the titillating 'Other' of England and the English. There has inevitably been some suspicion amongst the more empirically minded that critical self-awareness is missing in writing of this kind, or a suspicion that much of it emanates from philosophical and literary traditions which do not always have to take the sometimes messy trivia of daily events into account. Nevertheless, it is an important approach which has helped many to stop trying to assess the 'accuracy' of images or stereotypes by 'testing' them in some way against traits or characteristics deemed to inhere in any persons or groups. It has helped to emphasise the relative autonomy of discourses of representation, placing them within the world of those claiming to do the representing. To understand persons, places or groups, it has become important to find the meaning or reality of the persons or groups – of the 'Negro', of the 'Celt', of 'American', of the 'Germans', and so on – not, in priority, in the persons or places represented, but in the worlds of the representers.

This approach (which tends to deal only with my third point, above) is only part of the story. One of the several things missing is the important question of empirical confirmation. It is not difficult to imagine how images of the Germans are confirmed in daily encounters, whether these be encounters by tourists, say, or those of government ministers. We have already seen how English views of the French, for example, can appear to find 'proof' in the mismatches involved. Or similarly, how West Indians can seem, to English youths, to be truly threatening. And so on. A lack of fit between category systems regularly provides a real, observational, experiential basis for judgements. Anthropologists can talk of misunderstanding or misinterpretation, therefore, whilst at the same time acknowledging the authenticity, persuasiveness and autonomy of the discourse of representation for those claiming to do the representing, and of the experiential or empirical reality it can have for them.

## Acquiring Identity

On several occasions in the past, I have carried out research in Brittany. This was done among several disparate social groups, including militants of the Breton movement on the one hand, and native Breton-speaking peasants on the other. The Breton movement, which seeks official status for the Breton language in France, is largely made up of people well-educated in French, who have learnt Breton. Within a left-wing rhetoric which demands a 'right to difference', these militants also claim to represent 'the people' of Brittany at large. They are part of the very widespread tendency in France and elsewhere to seek true identity in the social margins, and they use and produce, live and reproduce, in opposition and dissent, the post-1960s imagery of centre/periphery relations which I have already mentioned. They know what identity is, where it is located, and they obey its compulsions.

As part of my research with the Breton movement, I regularly attended Breton-language courses organised by the members of the various language-promoting groups. At the very beginning of my fieldwork, I attended one of these in a village in western Brittany, in a private school closed for the holidays. The atmosphere was definitely one of a holiday, and the use of Breton encouraged the conviction that normal rules no longer applied. At meal-times, some delighted in throwing bread. On one occasion, an enthusiast put his feet up on the dinner table. Through 'Breton' came a flurry of releases that ranged from a scorn of 'structure' and 'grammar' in the classes to a flouting of conventional manners. On one occasion, when food was thrown and snatched at meal-time, it was explained to me that 'peasants do not say "thank-you", you see'. In the class, we were told that 'Breton does not have a word for *merci*', because politeness was all part of a 'bourgeois, French world'.

The question of *merci* (or 'thank you') and its related politenesses is interesting. As we have just seen, the militants sometimes live their image of the popular peasant world by flouting normal manners. Food is not usually thrown or snatched by peasants in their own daily world, however, and such behaviour would be considered rude. The popular

Breton-speaking world has, on the contrary, its own often strict politenesses (see Hélias 1975, 1977). My own experience with Breton-speaking peasantry suggests, however, how this misinterpretation might arise, and give substance to its metaphorical convenience and moral and political aptness in the world of the militants themselves. Social eating in the peasant world, beyond the immediate family, is commonly part of a system of giving and repaying, with its own obligations and courtesies. It is usually only when something is given (food or otherwise) that is not part of the local system of reciprocation that 'thank you' is said, as *merci*. There is often reluctance to say *merci* because it can imply acceptance of a debt to the giver, which the receiver has neither the means nor the intention of repaying appropriately: *merci* would, in this sense, close reciprocation. *Merci* is also used in the same routine sense that it has in the French-speaking world; as such, however, it is more commonly used by the women at village level, and also on special occasions, or with outsiders who are ambiguously placed in the local system of reciprocation.

The *merci* of local Breton speakers is, therefore, rarer than the *merci* of the wider French world. The non-linguistic courtesies and obligations of peasant reciprocation do not find linguistic expression, and cannot be translated either linguistically or socially into the militant world, where no comparable system of reciprocation exists. The impression is readily formed, therefore, that 'peasants do not say "thank you"' and that, on this evidence, they live in a world of healthy rudeness and naturality. This exploitation of mismatch by militants brings feet on to the table, bread flying though the air, and makes a playful holiday world seem like peasant authenticity (McDonald 1989: 164-7).

We would seem to be a long way now from those histories of wilful malice, or from views of stereotypes as simply erroneous, maladaptive or lacking direct experience. Or, indeed, from simple denunciations of 'prejudice'. We are, instead, very much within the domain of common cross-cultural experience, where different category systems, linguistic or otherwise, meet. One problem, we know, is that the power and persuasiveness of so much 'identity' rhetoric in what passes for Western Europe often means that those who are thereby deemed to be represented are powerless to contest the image created of them. In the allegories of mental health which 'identity' is now required to bear, protest brings instant moral and political diagnosis, in which 'alienation' is still perhaps the best-known, but not the only, pathology (for details of this in the Breton case, see McDonald 1989). This is perhaps an important aspect of what some anthropologists have seen as a 'crisis of representation' within the discipline itself (see Nencel and Pels (eds) 1991). Much anthropology in the past has been flatly lacking in contextuality, with assertions about what 'the X say', 'the X do', 'the X believe', 'the X are' , and so on, and it has itself been steeped in – rather than examined – the romanticisms and post-1960s dissents and radicalisms (with active pursuits of difference) to which I have alluded at various points. The belated problematisation of these areas, encouraged now by an increasing interest in anthropologies of Europe, seems speedily to have generated a sense of 'crisis'. How can we ever claim to 'represent' anyone or any people again? Well, we can do so if we realise that, in an important sense, our representations are on the same level as people's own perceptions of themselves, and may directly feed into them. We can also do so if we attempt, perhaps through the simple and sometimes laboured points of this brief chapter, to examine critically where and how we perceive difference. This is the self-aware empiricism which, amid some flurry and crisis, much anthropology now actively seeks and which political common sense of both right and left, within Europe and beyond, often seems to lack.

# References

Allport, G. (1954), *The Nature of Prejudice*. Reading, MA: Addison Wesley

Ardener, E. (1982), 'Social Anthropology, Language and Reality', in D. Parkin (ed.), *Semantic Anthropology*. London and New York: Academic Press

Benson, S. (1981), *Ambiguous Ethnicity*. Cambridge: Cambridge University Press

Chapman, M (1982), '"Semantics" and the "Celt"', in D. Parkin (ed.), *Semantic Anthropology*. London and New York: Academic Press

Condor, S and K. Henwood (1989), 'Stereotypes, Social Cognition and Social Context'. Unpublished typescript, Department of Psychology, Lancaster University

Daugé, Y. (1981), *Le Barbare. Recherches sur la conception romaine de la barbarie et de la civilisation*. Brussels: Collection Latomus 176

Ewen, F. (ed.) (1948), *The Poetry and Prose of Heinrich Heine*. New York: The Citadel Press

Fabian, J. (1983), *Time and the Other: How Anthropology Makes its Object*. New York: Columbia University Press

Firchow, P. (1986), *The Death of the German Cousin: Variations on a Literary Stereotype, 1890 – 1920*. London: Associated University Presses.

Harding, J. (1968), '*Stereotypes*' in *The International Encyclopaedia of the Social Sciences*, vol. 15. Basingstoke: MacMillan

Hélias, P.-J. (1975), *Le Cheval d'Orgueil*. Paris: Plon

_____ (1977), *Le Savoir-Vivre en Bretagne*. Chateaulin: Jos Le Doare

James, H. (1989), *A German Identity, 1770–1990*. London: Weidenfeld and Nicolson

Katz, D. and K. Braly (1933), 'Racial Stereotypes of One Hundred College Students', *Journal of Abnormal and Social Psychology*, vol. 28, pp. 280–90

Klineberg, O. (1950), *Tensions Affecting International Understanding: A Survey of Research*. New York: Social Science Research Council Bulletin, no.62

Kuper, A. (1988), *The Invention of Primitive Society*. London and New York: Routledge

Lash, S. (ed.) (1991), *Post-Structuralist and Post-Modernist Sociology*. Aldershot: Edward Elgar

Lawson, D. (1990), 'Saying the Unsayable About the Germans', *The Spectator*, 14 July, pp. 8–10

Lippmann, W. (1922, 1944), *Public Opinion*. New York: Macmillan

McDonald, M. (1989), *'We Are Not French!' Language, Culture and Identity in Brittany*. London and New York: Routledge

Mason, P. (1990), *Deconstructing America. Representations of the Other*. London and New York: Routledge

Mitchell, J. (1982), 'Introduction', in J. Mitchell and J. Rose (eds), *Feminine Sexuality, Jacques Lacan and the Ecole Freudienne*. London: Macmillan

Nencel, L. and P. Pels (eds) (1991), *Constructing Knowledge*. London: Sage

Peabody, D. (1985), *National Characteristics*. Cambridge: Cambridge University Press

Said, E. (1978), *Orientalism*. Harmondsworth: Penguin

Schulze, H. (1991), *The Course of German Nationalism. From Frederick the Great to Bismarck, 1763–1867*. Cambridge: Cambridge University Press

Thom, M. (1990), 'Tribes Within Nations: The Ancient Germans and the History of Modern France', in H. K. Bhabha (ed.), *Nations and Narration*. London and New York: Routledge

Trautmann, T. (1987), *Lewis Henry Morgan and the Invention of Kinship*. London and Berkeley: University of California Press

Walvin, J. (1982), 'Black Caricature: The Roots of Racialism', in C. Husband (ed.), *'Race' in Britain: Continuity and Change*. London: Hutchinson

Woolf, G. D. (1990), 'Cultural Change in Central France under Roman Rule'. Unpublished Ph.D. thesis, University of Cambridge (Classics)

# Notes on Contributors

**Fiona Bowie** has carried out fieldwork in Cameroon for a D.Phil. (1985) in social anthropology at Oxford University. More recently, she has been living, observing and writing in Wales. She is co-editor (with Oliver Davies) of *Logos: The Welsh Theological Review/ Cylchqrawn Diwinddol Cymru* and *Discovering Welshness* (Gomer, Llandysul, 1992); and (with Deborah Kirkwood and Shirley Ardener) of *Women and Missions* (Berg, 1993). She is also a part-time lecturer in the Department of Theology at the University College of North Wales and an Open University tutor.

**Rosanne Cecil** is a Research Fellow in the Health and Health Care Research Unit, Queen's University of Belfast. She studied at Goldsmiths' and Queen Elizabeth Colleges, London, and Edinburgh University before carrying out fieldwork in Northern Ireland, leading to her D.Phil. (University of Ulster) in 1989. She is co-author (with John Offer and Fred St Leger) of *Informal Welfare: A Sociological Study of Care in Northern Ireland* (Gower, 1987).

**Malcolm Chapman** has conducted ethnographic research focused on Scotland and Brittany (D.Phil., Oxford, 1986). He was a Junior Research Fellow at Balliol College, Oxford, and is presently a Research Fellow at Bradford School of Management. His current reseach is focused on Eastern Europe. He is author of *The Gaelic Vision in Scottish Culture* (Croom Helm, 1978) and *The Celts – The Construction of a Myth* (Macmillan, 1992), editor of Edwin Ardener's *The Voice of Prophecy and Other Essays* (Blackwell, 1989), and co-editor (with Elizabeth Tonkin and Maryon McDonald) of *History and Ethnicity* (Routledge, 1989).

**Ronald Frankenberg** is Professorial Research Fellow at Keele University. He has carried out fieldwork in Africa, Wales and, more recently, in Italy. He is the author of the classic studies *Village on the Border* (Waveland Press, Illinois, 1989; orig. 1957) and *Communities in Britain* (Penguin, 1966), and editor of *Custom and Conflict in British Society* (Manchester University Press, 1982), among other works. He has most recently edited *Time, Health and Medicine* (Sage, 1992).

237

**Jeremy MacClancy** is Research Associate at the Institute of Social and Cultural Anthropology, Oxford University. He has carried out fieldwork in Nigeria, Melanesia (D.Phil., Oxford, 1983), London auction rooms and Northern Spain. Author of *Consuming Culture* (Chapmans, 1992), he is at present completing a book on political ritual in post-war Spain.

**Maryon McDonald** is Senior Lecturer in Social Anthropology at Brunel University, London. She has been Research Fellow (CNRS) at the Université de Haute Bretagne, Rennes, and Research Fellow at Girton College, Cambridge. She has conducted fieldwork in Brittany (D.Phil., Oxford, 1983), and is now carrying out an ethnography of the European Parliament. She is author of '*We Are Not French!' Language, Culture and Identity in Brittany* (Routledge, 1989), co-editor (with Elizabeth Tonkin and Malcolm Chapman) of *History and Ethnicity* (Routledge, 1989), and editor of *Gender, Drink and Drugs* (Berg, 1993).

**Sharon Macdonald** is a Lecturer in Social Anthropology at Keele University. She has carried out ethnographic research on language, history and identity in the Scottish Highlands (D.Phil., Oxford, 1987). More recently, as Research Fellow in the Centre for Research into Innovation, Culture and Technology, Brunel University, she has conducted fieldwork in the Science Museum, London. She is at present completing two books on identity and knowledge construction – one on Scotland and the other on museums.

**Rosemary McKechnie** has conducted fieldwork in Corsica and the Isle of Man. A former Research Fellow in the Centre for Science Studies and Science Policy, Lancaster University, she is currently completing a D.Phil. at Oxford University, and working as a researcher in the Department of Public Health and Primary Care Medicine, Oxford University.

**Oonagh O'Brien** is completing a Ph.D. at University College, London, based on fieldwork carried out in North Catalonia, France. She has been a lecturer at the Universitat Autonoma de Barcelona and at Hammersmith and West London College. She is currently working on a European Community funded research project on HIV and AIDS in relation to the Irish in the United Kingdom and the Republic of Ireland.

**Cris Shore** is Lecturer in Social Anthropology at Goldsmiths' College, London. He studied social anthropology at Sussex University and conducted fieldwork in Italy leading to his Ph.D. (1985). His publications include *Italian Communism: The Escape from Leninism* (Pluto Press, 1990).

# Index

*Ian Fowler*